CITY OF CONSTANTINE
324–1453

By the same author

THE TOWER

BRIDGE, CHURCH AND PALACE
IN OLD LONDON

St Saviour in Chora (Kahriye Mosque)

City of Constantine
324–1453

JOHN E. N. HEARSEY

John Murray

FIFTY ALBEMARLE STREET LONDON

Made and printed in Great Britain by
William Clowes and Sons, Limited, London and Beccles
and published by John Murray (Publishers), Ltd.

TO MARY

Contents

Illustrations

** reproduced by courtesy of the Byzantine Institute, Washington, D.C.*
† reproduced by courtesy of the Turkish Tourist Association, Ankara
All other photographs were taken by the author

Plans and Sections

All plans and sections by the author

Acknowledgements

I should like to express my thanks to the staff of the Hove Public Library, especially to J. Dove, Esq., Librarian and Curator, and Miss L. Green, Reference Room, for assistance in obtaining books, both from their own and other libraries.

To the Byzantine Institute, Washington, U.S.A., and to the Turkish Tourist Agency, Ankara, I should like to offer my thanks for photographs of the interiors and mosaics of Santa Sophia and St Saviour in Chora. Also, my warmest thanks to Miss K. Pickford, in London, and in Istanbul to Mr and Mrs Peter Gregor Macgregor for their help and kindness whilst in that city.

Lastly, my thanks to all those who have helped bring the book itself into being.

J.E.N.H.

Chapter 1

324–330

The origins of Byzantium. Its growth as a Greek trading city. Two-year siege by Septimus Severus. Constantine chooses it as the new capital of the East Roman Empire. Byzantium enlarged. Column of Constantine. Its buildings. The Hippodrome. Obelisk of Constantine Porphyrogenitus. The Serpentine Column. Chariot races. The Blue and the Green factions. The Emperor. The senate. The consuls. The people. The inauguration of Constantinople.

In nearly three thousand years of history the triangle of land jutting out from the European shore towards the entrance to the Bosphorus has known three civilizations and four names. Even before the Greek colonizer, Byzas, and his sailors founded their city of Byzantium in either 658 or 657 B.C., there was a small fishing village near the tip of the peninsula, called Lygos. They were not the first from Megara, on the road from Athens to Corinth, to come so far afield. In 674 B.C. Greeks had settled on the opposite shore, in Asia, where they built the town of Chalcedon (Kadiköy). Before setting out Byzas consulted the Oracle at Delphi, asking where he should bring his city into being. 'Opposite the blind', was the enigmatic reply. From Eleusis they sailed north-east, between the islands of Euboea and Andros, across the Aegean, past the site of Troy itself, into the Dardanelles, across the Sea of Marmara, until they came to the town of Chalcedon and the entrance to the Bosphorus. There Byzas realized what the Oracle had meant: 'Opposite the blind.'

The founders of Chalcedon must have been blind not to realize what an infinitely better site it was for a city on the point of land on the European side, with a land-locked harbour almost without rival: the future Golden Horn.

Byzas crossed the half-mile or so of water, and founded the city that would one day become the capital of the largest empire the world had seen.

As a trading city Byzantium grew, its wall encircling the whole of the First Hill; its citadel on the site now occupied by the Seraglio of the Sultans. In the fifth century it saw the Persians in its streets, when Greece itself was overrun. Then in 340 B.C. Philip of Macedon besieged the city, but the moon gave away his plans for an intended attack by night, and Byzantium adopted the crescent, associated with the goddess Hecate, as its emblem. Nearly eighteen hundred years later the crescent would return, and there it remains to this day, glittering over Santa Sophia, a score of one-time churches and countless mosques.

Alexander knew the place. He captured it, and it was from there that he set off on his campaign that would take him as far as India. The greatest treasure in the Archaeological Museum in Istanbul is his reputed sarcophagus, brought from Sidon in Lebanon, when it was still part of the Ottoman Empire.

In the first century Byzantium sided with Pescennius Niger in his war against Septimus Severus, and paid dearly when in A.D. 196 it was captured by the latter after a two-year siege. The defences about the citadel were dismantled and the soldiers of the garrison and their leaders put to death. But soon the walls were rebuilt, and in A.D. 203 Septimus Severus added the Hippodrome, baths, and palaces. Now it was a typical Roman provincial city of considerable importance.

Then as the old pagan Roman Empire died violently and convulsively, with four emperors fighting for the right to rule, the centre of attention and also of geographical importance shifted from Italy to the meeting place of Europe and Asia. At Adrianople in A.D. 324 Constantine the Great defeated his last rival, Licinius, who made his way to Byzantium and across the Bosphorus to Chrysopolis (Scutari, now Üsküdar) where on

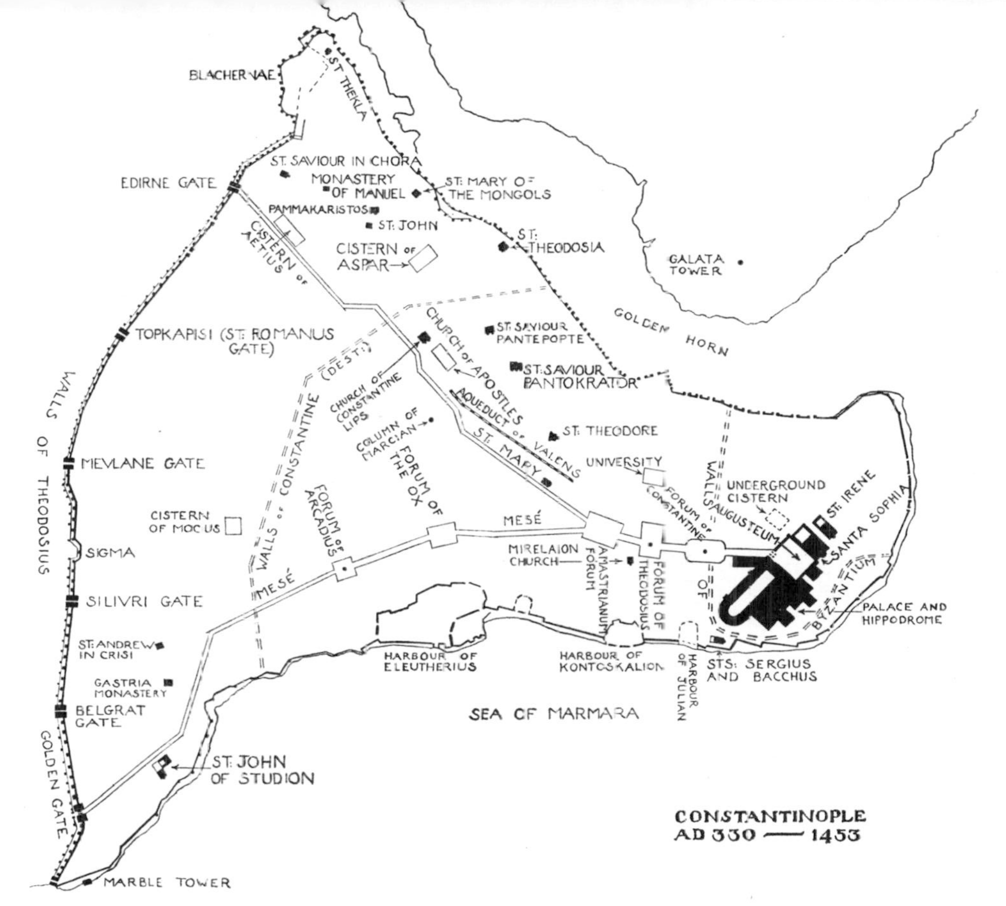

CONSTANTINOPLE
AD 330 — 1453

the 18th or 20th of September, 324, his hopes were completely smashed in another and decisive battle.

The next day the victorious Constantine recrossed the Bosphorus, and without a fight Byzantium fell to him.

Although it was not until death was only a matter of weeks away, in 337, that Constantine was baptized a Christian, he had regarded them sympathetically for most of his adult life. Now, in 325, Christianity was to become the religion of the state. The long years of persecution were over at last, but already the Church was torn with controversy within its ranks. The old Rome was too republican for the pomp-loving Constantine, and also paganism was something there that could not be sloughed off like the skin of a snake. It would be better to start afresh—to create a completely new capital for the eastern part of the Empire; one that was nearer the vitally important northern and eastern frontiers, and in a sense at the cross-roads of the ancient world.

New walls were built, stretching from the Golden Horn across to the Sea of Marmara, which roughly trebled the area occupied by the old Greek city, while sea-walls were added, to link up with those rebuilt by Septimus Severus. On the site of his camp, on the Second Hill, from which Constantine directed the short campaign before the city fell, he ordered a magnificent forum to be built.

Elliptical in shape, it was paved with marble and surrounded with colonnades, and at either end were archways. In the centre stood—and still stands—his column. About 125 feet high (without the statue it is now ten feet less) it is on the top of the Second Hill, on the north side of the busy Ordu Street: of the Forum of Constantine itself nothing seems to remain above ground. Consisting of six large drums of porphyry, carved with encircling laurel leaves, it stands on a battered plinth, restored in 1779 by the Sultan, Abdül-Hamid I. Time and again in Istanbul one is left wondering how various monuments have survived at all. The Column of Constantine is no exception. Sixty fires have swept that city during its history, and they have left their mark on the Burnt Column, as it is aptly called. Calcined, blackened and split, it is now bound together with straps of iron: of the first importance historically, it cannot be called beautiful (page 20).

When the city had been Greek it was in the care of the goddess Rhea and Apollo, the sun god; and it was no accident that the statue which topped the column was a bronze by no less a man than the great Phidias—of Apollo transformed into Constantine himself. Here, in the base, the old and the new religions were entombed together. On the Emperor's orders the reputed Palladium of Troy, a wooden statue of Pallas Athene taken to Athens by Aeneas after the end of the ten-year siege, was placed in a cavity, together with a quite remarkable collection of more than doubtful relics, including the axe with which Noah made the ark, loaves from the Miracle at Cana, the stone from which Moses drew water, and the alabaster box which held the ointment with which Mary Magdalen anointed the feet of Christ. Apparently they are still there.

The statue of Apollo, now holding a sceptre in his right hand, a globe in his left and crowned with rays which incorporated small pieces of the nails used at Christ's crucifixion, survived until it fell in a storm in 1105, in the reign of Alexios I Komnenos. It was not restored, but replaced by Manuel I Komnenos with a gilded cross.

The walls of Constantine enclosed five other forums, along the course of the Mesé, the main street of the city, which ran its whole length from the Hippodrome erected by Septimus Severus to a gateway which also served as a triumphal arch, near the south end of the new land walls. These walls have quite vanished; after the city was enlarged for a third time—in the fifth century—they were demolished.

Even before Constantine came to Byzantium there was at least one church in the city: St Irene, north of the Hippodrome. Now another and much larger basilica was being built almost alongside (though today St Irene is separated from Santa Sophia by the fifteenth-century wall of the Seraglio). The first Santa Sophia would have been not unlike St Paul-outside-the-Walls in Rome (A.D. 386). It would have had a large nave with aisles, a timber roof, shallow transepts and a semi-circular apse. Decorating it were many statues, both pagan and Christian, including a nearly complete series of the emperors.

Across the city, on the top of the Fourth Hill, another church was being built, dedicated to the Holy Apostles, which was destined to become the Westminster Abbey of the Byzantine emperors. But paganism was by no means a thing of the past: for a number of years ceremonies would incorporate both pagan and Christian rites.

If Santa Sophia was to become the religious heart of the city, its secular one was the Hippodrome, which adjoined the new imperial palace—a large and unsymmetrical series of buildings spreading down the slope of the hill towards the Sea of Marmara. Originally built by Septimus Severus in A.D. 203, it was not large enough for Constantine. In shape it was rectangular, and to enlarge it at its south-west end meant building on a huge substructure of arches, for the hill falls away sharply towards the Sea of Marmara. With this new semi-circular addition the Hippodrome now had an overall length of about 1,300 feet and a width of approximately 490 feet. The number of tiers of seats was also increased, from sixteen to nearly forty. At its north-east end, towards Santa Sophia, was the Kathisma, the imperial box, looking down the whole length of the arena, and behind and below were the stables—the Manganon.

Down the middle of the Hippodrome was the Spina, around which the track ran. Built of stone, it was not more than a few feet high. At each extremity were three cones, marking the turning points, while just behind was where ovoid-shaped objects, to the number of seven, were piled one on top of another to indicate the number of laps run in the chariot races. It was not until the reign of Theodosius I (379–395) that the great obelisk from Karnak was set up in the centre of the Spina; but the so-called Obelisk of Constantine Porphyrogenitus may date from the time the Hippodrome was enlarged and embellished by Constantine. Very tall and very thin, it was originally covered with plates of bronze decorated with bas-reliefs. Today only the holes remain into which the pins fitted to clamp the plates in position, and its name, referring to the Emperor who ruled in his own right from 944 to 959, comes from the fact it was he who restored it.

Also on the Spina would have been the bust of the reigning

Emperor, surrounded by a laurel wreath, bronze statues brought from Greece, and most important from an archaeological point of view, the Serpentine Column from Delphi. This was a bronze column, originally about twenty-six feet high, which was set up on the Sacred Way leading up to the Temple of Apollo to commemorate the final defeat of the Persians at Plataea in 479 B.C. It consisted of three entwined serpents, and their heads supported a golden tripod: the latter was stolen by the neighbouring Phocians in the middle of the fourth century B.C., and then Constantine ordered its removal to his new capital, along with many other works of art from the Ancient World.

Through the centuries the Serpentine Column was regarded almost with fear by the citizens, and several attempts were made to mutilate it. One was made towards the end of the reign of Theophilus (died 842), and another after the Turkish conquest of 1453. Today all that remains is about eighteen feet of the column, jagged and broken at the top (page 20). This and the Obelisk of Constantine Porphyrogenitus, are all that are left of the vast one-time Hippodrome as it was in the time of Constantine the Great himself. It could seat forty thousand spectators, but now apart from the fact the tree-lined square, the At Meydani, conforms to its shape, it might never have been. Even the exact site of the imperial box is a little uncertain: it was probably on or near the position now occupied by the Kaiser Wilhelm II Fountain.

Chariot races were almost an obsession with all classes, who divided themselves into two factions, the Blues and the Greens. Originally there were four colours for the racing chariots, red, white, blue, and green, but slowly these became simply the Blues and the Greens. Here class did enter into it: the Blues were distinctly more fashionable than their rivals. These factions even had their own spokesmen who formed a link between the Emperor and his people, ranged according to their colour in the Hippodrome. The Blues sat on the right of the Emperor, and the Greens on his left, and their leaders, called Demesmen, acted as their intermediaries: they offered congratulations or criticisms as the situation demanded.

These factions were the nearest equivalent to political parties in the Empire, and a petty official did not need to expect rapid promotion in his job if he supported the one which at that moment was not dominant. They were responsible for the trained bands raised in time of trouble to defend the city, and when it was decided to build a new wall, in the fifth century, they were made responsible for finding the labour and seeing the work was done.

Chariot races were held in the morning as well as in the afternoon, twenty-four in all. Only four chariots could take part: the starting line was at the top end of the Hippodrome, to the right of the Emperor as he sat in the imperial box, and there were seven laps, making a course of about a mile and a half. The equivalent of bumping and boring was common, resulting from time to time in fatal accidents, as that of the young charioteer who was killed on the eve of his wedding. Sometimes the races were held after dark, by the light of torches: a most impressive sight beneath a star-filled sky. Between the races were entertainments such as wrestling, acrobatics, and fights with wild animals, though at least from the time of Constantine onwards the Hippodrome never saw gladiatorial combats. In Italy itself they lingered on for nearly another century before the protests of the Church were successful.

The charioteers were the public heroes of the city, better known and better liked than its real administrators. The prestige of winning was more important than the prize, about seven or eight pounds in money, a cloak, and a wreath. Together with the Leader of his faction the winning charioteer would go up the steps towards the imperial box to receive his rewards from the hand of the Emperor himself: this semi-divine man who for all that he was now a Christian was hedged in with a quite oriental magnificence and remoteness from his people.

It was Diocletian who began the cult of the semi-divine Emperor about the year A.D. 300, and Constantine the Great took it up wholeheartedly. The title 'Equal of the Apostles' speaks for itself. On his death the Emperor was supposed to 'bear joint rule with the Son of God', and automatically became 'of sacred memory'. Except, one presumes, when he had been deposed or murdered, a frequent occurrence. In theory the emperor was chosen from birth to fulfil the will of Heaven, and how he came to the throne was less important than the fact that he had got there: success was itself sufficient, and his accession was considered to obliterate automatically his past life, and in more than twenty cases that would mean blood from his hands and guilt from his soul.

Emperors were supposed to be elected, chosen by the senate and the army, with the agreement of the people. But since he had the right to crown a successor during his own lifetime (whilst still retaining all his own authority) he could build up a dynasty. Indeed, for length two dynasties are remarkable in the turbulent history of the Empire: the Macedonians who ruled from 867 to 1056; and the Palaeologi, from 1259 to 1453. Also, the Emperor had the status of a royal priest, having rights of entry to the sanctuary in church denied to other laymen.

When he passed through his city he rode in a chariot drawn by four white horses or mules and, if it was an important occasion, a religious or secular festival, the route was cleaned and decorated with myrtle, rosemary, box, ivy, and such flowers as were in season. The residents hung their best carpets and tapestries out of the windows, and the air was heavy with incense. Cheering and applause was forbidden: at intervals along the way choirs drawn from the Blues and the Greens were stationed, to sing the Emperor's praises. In the Hippodrome itself it was the custom to start with a hymn—reminiscent of 'Abide with me' before the start of the Cup Final!

Of all the events seen in the Hippodrome during its active life—by the year A.D. 1200 chariot races were a thing of the past—none could have been more arresting or ferocious than the scene which followed the return to power of Justinian II. At times quite mad, this Emperor ruled twice, from 685 until he was overthrown by his navy in 695. Physically mutilated, his nose was cut off, he was exiled to the Crimea, but in 705 he returned to Constantinople and a spectacular revenge on his usurping successors Leontius and Apsimar. Tightly bound, they were brought into the Hippodrome and laid on the ground by the imperial throne. For several hours Justinian II watched the chariot races, his feet firmly placed on the necks of Leontius and

Apsimar. Then they were taken to the old theatre of Byzantium, on the hillside below the present Seraglio, overlooking the Sea of Marmara, and there executed.

Since Constantine was creating a completely new city on the shores of the Sea of Marmara it was necessary to create a completely new senate, which would one day have a rank equal to that of the old Rome. At best it was a spineless body: perhaps all that need be said about it can be summed up in the words of one of its members to the Patriarch Anastasius: 'I have never learned to accustom myself to innovation, and I fear them above all else, for I know full well that in making innovations safety can in no way be preserved.'

To go with the new senate there was a new aristocracy and bureaucracy, with a new system of titles and modes of address: Your Sublimity, Your Magnificence, and Your Loftiness are only three of these Gilbertian prefixes to respectful speech. Each year on the 1st of January two consuls were elected, though like the senate they were little more than cyphers from the Empire's Roman past. About their only independent action was that which followed their installation in the Forum of Augustus (outside Santa Sophia). Then they each performed the act of manumission, the symbolic freeing of a slave.

It was the custom to send small ivory diptychs carved with the likeness of the consuls to all parts of the Empire, and a number of them are to be seen today in various museums in western Europe, in particular in the Victoria and Albert Museum in London. Quite small, these hinged panels show not only the consuls for that particular year, but also may include portraits of the Emperor and Empress, angels and allegorical figures, as well as lively little genre scenes such as men fighting bears in the arena (consular diptych of Areobindus; Landesmuseum, Zürich) or men leading horses (leaf of diptych of Flavius Anastasius, A.D. 517; Victoria and Albert Museum).

The actual direction of the new city was in the hands of the prefect; after the year 359, there were four of them. Unlike his fellow dignitaries he still wore the toga, and not military clothing, and formed the link between the senate and the Emperor. Under him he had numerous officials, responsible for various departments: the markets, the water supply, the harbours, etc. The old Roman custom of bread and circuses, in the form of free oil, wine, corn, and bread may have been continued in the New Rome, but it can have been only an indifferent compensation for the lives led by many of the poorer people. Living for the most part in tenements, they were tied to the class into which they were born: bakers were even forbidden to marry outside their own trade, as in medieval England farm-hands in the country were tied to their village for life. There was one law for the well-born, and another for those who were not. In the former category transgressors could only be executed after the sentence had been sanctioned by the Emperor himself, and they could not be condemned to penal servitude with hard labour in the mines.

Only six years after Constantine decreed Byzantium should become his new capital it stood complete, though much of the construction work was so shoddy it had to be rebuilt in the reign of his successor, Constantius. According to Gibbon the new city included, in addition to the first Santa Sophia and the Hippodrome, two theatres, eight public and one hundred and fifty-three private baths (including the magnificent Baths of Zeuxippus built in the time of Septimus Severus, which adjoined the Hippodrome and must have been a treasure-house of ancient bronze and marble statues), fifty-two porticoes, five granaries, eight aqueducts or cisterns, fourteen churches, fourteen palaces and 4,388 houses sufficiently well built to be enumerated. Then there were four basilicas for use by the senate, law courts, etc.

It must have been magnificent, but there were many who regarded it as little more than an upstart rival to Rome, Alexandria, or Antioch. St Jerome said it was clothed in the nudity of nearly every other city. Certainly Italy and Greece had been rifled for its embellishment, and the process would continue for centuries. An obelisk from Karnak, four bronze horses from Rome, the Serpent Column from Delphi, a bronze of a man driving a donkey from Actium, a colossus of Pallas Athene from Athens, parts of temples at Ephesus, Ba'albek and on the island of Delos: the list could be extended almost indefinitely.

Not only sculpture and parts of buildings were transported to the new capital but people as well. Members of the old Roman families were encouraged to emigrate: the money to pay for their fine new town houses was to come from the rents of estates in the country which they were given as a further inducement to make the move.

Then, on May 11, 330, came the great day on which the city would be inaugurated by Constantine as the new capital. At a magnificent ceremony in the Hippodrome the ancient town of Byzantium became New Rome, a Latin city with a Greek name —Constantinople, City of Constantine.

For centuries to come May 11 was kept as a public holiday, the then Emperor going to the Hippodrome, where a gilded wooden statue of Constantine the Great was carried in procession on a triumphal car surrounded by guards with white tapers. As it passed the imperial box the Emperor rose to his feet, and still standing saluted it and the memory of the man who had brought his city and Empire into being.

Chapter 2

324–361

Bloodshed within Constantine's family. Murder of his relatives after his death by the army. Constantius, Emperor. Religious controversies in Constantinople. Remains of the original Santa Sophia. Pagan survivals. The emblem of the city.

The beginning of Constantine the Great's reign in the city could not have been more bloodstained. Not long before the ceremonial laying of the foundation stone of the West Wall on November 4, 326, there had been a ghastly tragedy in the palace. Quite what the cause was is a mystery, but as a result Constantine's eldest son by his first marriage, Crispus, was executed and his second wife, Fausta, also. Apparently the Empress was put to death by being suffocated in the bathroom of the palace. Before that it had been his old rival and brother-in-law Licinius, together with his young son. Now it was his own wife and son, as well as a number of his friends. Great he may have been in many ways, but as St Constantine he is difficult to accept. The history of Byzantium had begun with violence, and the pattern would remain almost unchanged to the end.

More bloodshed followed his death on May 22, 337, when the army wiped out most of his family with the exception of the three sons who would actually rule, and two nephews, one of whom was considered so sickly that his execution would be unnecessary.

As co-Emperors there were Constantius, ruler of the East

Roman Empire; Constantine II, ruler of the West, and Constans who received North Africa as his portion. Constantine II was destined to be killed in an ambush of his younger brother Constans' soldiers (340); while Constans was himself murdered ten years later after being overthrown by his officers. That was not the end of the bloodstained catalogue. Gallus, one of the two nephews, spared because of his ill-health, was eventually beheaded by his cousin Constantius in 354.

Of the house of Constantine only two males now remained alive: Constantius, ruling the East Roman Empire from Constantinople (though he was seldom in the city), and his young cousin Julian, who would succeed him.

Campaigns far from the capital occupied most of Constantius's reign of twenty-four years. In the east there were the Persians, and in the north the barbarians, especially the Goths; while in the west there were the upheavals which followed the murder of Constantine II.

In Constantinople the city's religious life was hardly more edifying than the dynastic quarrels of its ruler. The Church was bitterly divided on the exact nature of Christ: there were those who adhered to the decisions of the Council of Nicaea (Iznik), called in 325 by Constantine, and the followers of Archbishop Arius. The Arians, as they were called, not only differed from the Nicenes on a crucial theological issue (page 151), but also embraced a certain amount of thought which, if not actually pagan, was non-Christian.

One patriarch, Paul, was driven from the throne no less than five times in fourteen years by his Arian opponents. The climax came when Hermogenes, the master-general of the cavalry, tried to expel Paul in a most ham-fisted fashion. Not only was he murdered and his body dragged through the streets, but his palace was burnt. The prefect of the city then took over, and used guile. He requested Paul to come to him in the Baths of Zeuxippus, which had a private entrance into the palace, the grounds of which stretched down to the Sea of Marmara, where a ship was waiting. Almost before he knew what was happening, the Patriarch Paul was hurried along corridors, across courtyards, down steps and onto the ship, which at once set sail for Thessalonika. While the crowd was still wondering what was going on, the gates of the palace opened and out drove the prefect in a chariot surrounded by guards with drawn swords. Beside him sat Macedonius, the Arian rival for the patriarch's throne.

Such was the crowd of people trying to get into Santa Sophia on the other side of the square that 3,150 were killed, trampled to death in the rush.

The beginnings of Christian Constantinople were not auspicious.

Only two buildings remain of that first cathedral and they are quite overshadowed by its vast successor. One is the Baptistery, on the south side near the present entrance. Almost square, with a shallow dome, and in front a narthex, it is octagonal inside, with an apse. In the seventeenth century it was converted into a mausoleum, and contains the tombs of the Sultans Mustafa I and Ibrahim. Unfortunately it is closed to the public, as is the other building, the Treasury; this is small and circular and, because of the surrounding wall, difficult to get near.

Among the trees to the west of the cathedral are fragments of Santa Sophia's predecessors: late Roman entablatures, capitals and even the top centre of a pediment, carved with a cross in a circle, the Labarum of Byzantium. It was a cross in a circle that Constantine and his army saw in the sky shortly before the Battle of the Milvian Bridge, when he decisively defeated Maxentius in 312. A year later came the Edict of Milan, giving toleration to Christianity, and for that matter to all other religions in the Empire.

But even now, in the middle of the fourth century, Constantinople was not completely Christian. Constantine the Great allowed two temples to be built, one to Castor and Pollux for the benefit of the Hippodrome employees, and the other to Tyche. To pagans Tyche was the genius or spirit of the city. The figure of Constantine which was paraded through the city each year during the inauguration festivities held a small Tyche in his outstretched right hand.

The emblem of Constantinople which appears on the reverse of early coins shows the city as a woman seated on a throne, one foot resting on the prow of a ship—symbol that it was a great seaport—while on the reverse of the silver coin struck to commemorate the inauguration of 330 the figure holds a large cornucopia, most suitable for a city whose harbour is called the Golden Horn. One detail concerning this emblem: there is nothing specifically Christian about it. An augury for the reign to come, that of Julian. He was an avowed pagan.

Chapter 3

361–378

Julian the Apostate (361–363). His character and habits. Reversion to the old gods. The Harbour of Julian. The Emperor Valens. His Aqueduct. Killed by the Goths at Adrianople (378).

For thirty-five years Christianity had been the religion of the state, but now at Constantinople the Emperor himself had reverted to the old gods. Abhorred by the Church, Julian the Apostate is an interesting and complex character. An intelligent, highly-strung boy, he felt from an early age that several of his family had been murdered simply because they had not embraced Christianity. His childhood lacked affection, spent as it was in the care of a tutor deeply versed in classical literature. When still young he was packed off from Constantinople with his elder brother Gallus to Macellum and Nicomedia where, though outwardly Christian, he became more and more one with the old gods. From there he went to Athens, and was probably initiated into the mysteries of Eleusis. Then, at thirty he was jolted from the world of Homer and Plato to try and save Gaul from the invading Germans. Astonishingly enough he beat them soundly at Strasbourg in A.D. 357.

At the beginning of 360 his troops elected him as Emperor, though Constantius still lived. But before Julian reached Constantinople his rival was dead, and he became sole ruler of the two halves of the Roman Empire.

In Constantinople he issued edicts against the Christians. Temple sites and lands for endowments given to the church had to be returned, while those temples actually demolished had to be rebuilt. No Christian teachers could take lessons in schools where the basis of the curriculum was classical literature. Christian emblems disappeared, and the imperial guard soon contained only pagans. Since the Church was split into warring factions Julian thought that by granting equal toleration to the Nicenes and the Arians alike they would consume each other, and the religion destroy itself.

Julian envisaged a restored Hellenic world, but the form of paganism which he tried to force on the city and the Empire was a version of his own concocting, quite removed from that of Athens and Olympia. It was open house for all the gods and goddesses of Europe and the Middle East. In this rather tawdry pantheon with its highly theatrical mysteries, Venus from Cyprus rubbed shoulders with the Persian Mithras, and Isis from Egypt with the Greek Zeus.

Julian saw himself as a philosopher, if not in a tub like Diogenes, at least living in very different style to his predecessors in the imperial palace. Almost vegetarian, he despised chariot races in the Hippodrome, and cut down the size of the army of servants. The story goes that when he asked for a barber he sarcastically wondered aloud who had been sent. 'It is a barber that I want, not a receiver general of the finances.' Obviously there was room for economies: this one man alone was allowed twenty servants and twenty horses. As Gibbon expresses it: 'The number of eunuchs could be compared only to the insects of a summer's day.' He goes on: 'The luxury of the palace excited the indignation and contempt of Julian, who usually slept on the ground, yielded with reluctance to the indispensable calls of nature, and who placed his vanity, not in emulating, but in despising, the pomp of royalty. But with the fripperies, Julian affected to renounce the decencies of dress; and seemed to value himself for his neglect of the laws of cleanliness.' Certainly he rejoiced in dirty hands, long nails, and a beard full of lice!

A republican at heart he elevated the senate in Constantinople to be of the same rank as that in Rome, and enthusiastically embraced the consuls, elected for a year on January 1. In view of his personal habits, that, and his liking to sit beside the judges hearing cases, and interfere with the verdicts, must have tried the susceptibilities of those who felt that cleanliness was next to godliness. Their Emperor had neither.

The only memorial Julian left in Constantinople—after only two years he died from an arrow wound whilst retreating from the Persians during an unsuccessful campaign—was the harbour of Julian which he commanded to be opened. Quite small, it was sited behind the walls of Constantine on the Sea of Marmara, about 325 yards west of the site on which the church of SS. Sergius and Bacchus now stands. He also commanded a crescent-shaped portico, called the Sigma, to be built along the quay for the benefit of the merchants who used the harbour. In 509 a mole was added, to check the tendency to silt up, and it remained in use until about 1510, after the Turkish conquest of 1453. Until filled in for the laying of the railway line in the 1870s it was said that under certain conditions of light you could see the hulls of several imperial triremes embedded in the mud at the bottom.

Nowadays, without a map showing the site it is impossible to believe there ever was a harbour in that area, and the same applies to the larger Kontoscalion harbour—a little to the west, which after the middle of the thirteenth century was used by the imperial navy. Then it was dredged and deepened, and closed with iron gates. In addition to a mole it had a natural and unseen defence, the current, which would carry enemy ships past the entrance before they could attack. Then the defenders could come out, and harry them from behind.

Though the reign of Valens was quite lengthy, for the East Roman Empire, from 364 to 378, apart from the great aqueduct between the Third and Fourth Hills, which still bears his name, he left little mark on Constantinople. Originally the aqueduct, one of several bringing water into the city, was three-quarters of a mile long with two rows of arcades, one above the other; though in the part which still stands there is only one. Today 800 yards remain intact, towering above the new Atatürk Bulvari—a much needed artery across one of the most congested parts of the city. The massive dark-coloured aqueduct, sometimes called in Turkish the Grey Falcon Arcade—a charming but one would think somewhat irrelevant name—was begun as far back as the reign of Constantine the Great, but only finished in 378, with the help of stones taken from old Roman baths. Frequently damaged by earthquakes, it was restored after the Turkish Conquest of 1453 on the orders of Mehmet II Fatih, and about a century later Süleyman the Magnificent instructed Sinan, his great architect, to rebuild it.

One action by Valens was to have dire consequences for Constantinople and the Empire. In 376 he allowed the Goths to cross the Danube and settle within the frontiers. If he and the barbarian leaders were well disposed towards each other, the rapacious way the imperial officials fleeced the Gothic settlers and reduced them to near famine inflamed them against their hosts. Two years later, the whole of the Gothic army, goaded beyond endurance, marched towards the south. On the plain outside Adrianople (Edirne) came a dreadful defeat for the Empire. Valens, badly wounded by an arrow, was burned to death in a hut to which he had been taken, and two-thirds of his army was killed.

Nothing, it would seem, could stop the Goths streaming across Thrace to Constantinople, only one hundred and fifty miles away.

Column of Constantine, A.D. 330.
'The Burnt Column'

Site of the Hippodrome. Foreground: remains of the Serpentine Column. Background: Obelisk of Theodosius I

Theodosius I attending chariot races in the Hippodrome. Obelisk of Theodosius A.D. 390

Basilica of St John of Studion (Imrahor Mosque), A.D. 463

Chapter 4

379–395

Constantinople in danger from the Goths. Theodosius I elected Emperor. Opportune death in the city of the Gothic leader. Paganism banned in the Empire. The sect of the Arians banished from the city. The Forum and Column of Theodosius. The Golden Gate (380). The Obelisk of Theodosius (390). Its erection. The bas-reliefs on the plinth. The four bronze horses now in Venice. Statue to a favourite charioteer.

The Emperor was dead, two-thirds of his army killed, and it looked as though the way to Constantinople was open for the barbarians. The Empire of the East Romans, not yet half a century old, needed a great man if it was to survive. He came, from the other end of the Mediterranean, to rule from the shores of the Sea of Marmara. But nearly a year was to elapse before he assumed the diadem in 379, and by then the Goths would come nearly to the walls of the city. Barbarians that they were, presumably hardened to cruelty and to atrocities, it was they who found their stomachs turned by the behaviour of one of the defenders. A number of Saracen troops, employed in the imperial army, made a sortie out of one of the gates. Shrieking and yelling, a giant Saracen who was completely naked, fell on one of the Goths, stabbed him in the throat with a dagger and drank his blood as it welled out. The Goths turned and fled.

For Emperor of the East, Gratian, ruler of the West nominated Theodosius, son of a Spanish general who in 368 came to England to try and restore order in the fast-crumbling island province. In 376 the older man was snared in an intrigue, and executed at Carthage. After that, until summoned by Gratian, his son lived the life of a gentleman-farmer on his estates in what is now Castile in Spain. By the time of his death, in 395, he was sole ruler of an Empire stretching from Hadrian's Wall to the Euphrates.

Now, of its own accord, the menace from the Goths was subsiding: they were falling out among themselves. Theodosius himself rode out seven miles from Constantinople to meet their leader, Athanaric (or Athanrich), and took him back as his guest. The elderly Goth could not believe his eyes, and said as much. Then, quite suddenly he died after he had been in the city for two weeks. Theodosius I appeared most distressed, and ordered a magnificent funeral, and even had a monument put up to the Goth's memory. The barbarian soldiers were most impressed at the high opinion the Emperor evidently had for their leader's memory—and enlisted in his army. If Athanaric's death was solely due to natural causes, it was remarkably timely for a number of people.

A grateful Orthodox Church first called Theodosius 'the Great'. There were many in the Empire who still clung to the old gods, and it was Theodosius who banned paganism, the restoration of ancient temples, and even that strongest of links with the pre-Christian world, the Olympic Games. The latter would not be revived until 1896. His reign also saw the end in Constantinople, if not elsewhere, of the Arians, the sect that believed the Holy Ghost could proceed from God the Father, but not from Christ.

This was dealt with by Theodosius immediately after his arrival in the capital. At that time the archbishop was an Arian, and Theodosius offered him the choice of giving up his office or accepting the Nicene Creed. The churchman chose voluntary exile. In his place the Emperor installed Gregory Nazianzen (380)—regarded as one of the founders of the Greek Orthodox Church. His installation in Santa Sophia was anything but peaceful, as much of the population were Arian in sympathy. On his way to the cathedral with Theodosius the hostile crowd had to be kept back with drawn swords.

Then, the next year came the Second Oecumenical Council, held in the church of St Irene. Only one hundred and fifty bishops attended, none from west of Thessalonika. Already the rift between the two halves of the church had begun. In St Irene the Nicene Creed was reaffirmed, Arianism condemned, and Theodosius demanded communion with Constantinople and Alexandria—not Rome and Alexandria. By 1054 the breach would be complete.

As a military commander Theodosius also deserved the epithet of 'great'. While the western half of the Empire was brought to its knees by the barbarian invaders, Theodosius stood firm in the east, and also in Italy. In 386 he repelled the Goths, trying to cross the Danube and enter the Empire, and to commemorate the victory a column was set up in 392 in the Forum of Tauri (or Theodosius), obviously modelled on the Column of Trajan in Rome which contains a spiral staircase and has on its outside a sculptured frieze, also winding upwards, depicting the Emperor's victories. Like so much else it has all but vanished, the top of the modern Ordu Street running across the site of the Forum.

Twelve years earlier, in 380, he apparently commanded the erection of the Golden Gate, Porta Aurea, about a mile and a half west of the land walls of Constantine, on the road to the west. Built of marble blocks so constructed that no cement was necessary, it consists of a triple arch set between two massive and squat pylons which contained chambers used by the garrison. Over the central archway stood a statue of Theodosius, brought down by an earthquake in the time of Leo III, perhaps the terrible one of 740. Also for decoration there were four bronze elephants. Theodosius made his triumphal entry into the city in a chariot pulled by them.

Some of the decorations still remain: they consist of sculptured panels set on the outer wall. An attempt in 1625 by the British Ambassador to have them stolen for six hundred crowns came to nothing. In front of the Golden Gate stood a smaller arch, with only one opening, now much ruined. Then, in 413, when the great wall of Theodosius II was added to the west of the old defences, the Golden Gate was incorporated into it, forming the most impressive of the entrances to the city. So it remained until 1203 or 1204 when the crusaders came to Constantinople. Mistrusting their intentions, the then Emperor Isaac II Angelus ordered the three archways to be walled up. They remain walled up to this day and, after the Turkish Conquest of 1453, Mehmet II ordered a fort to be built against it within the city: it was named Yedikule, the Castle of the Seven Towers. The two massive pylons which contained chambers formed its strongest part, and the south pylon in particular was to reek with fear and with blood. It was in the lower chamber that prisoners were beheaded straight into a disused well, while in a room above the Sultan Osman II was cruelly murdered in 1622. Certainly nothing in the Tower of London can rival that one brooding pylon for concentrated horror: perhaps the torture chamber in the Chateau Chillon runs it close.

Theodosius I did not despise the Hippodrome and all it stood for: no Emperor except Julian the Apostate was foolish enough to do that, to disregard the secular heart of Constantinople. To him the city owes its most important late Roman monument—it is still too early to call the art of the Empire Byzantine. On his orders the obelisk of Thutmosis III (1504–1450 B.C.) was brought from Karnak to Constantinople, to be set up on the Spina which ran down the centre of the Hippodrome. Carved from a single piece of Syenitc porphyry it is 65 feet high, without the pedestal. To transport it by water from Egypt to Constantinople must have been a major feat, but to bring it from the quayside to the Hippodrome was an even greater one. Whether brought ashore in the Boucleon harbour or on the other side of the city in the Golden Horn, the roads up the hill to the site are in places fairly steep.

Today the floor of the Hippodrome is some ten feet below the level of the grass-covered and tree-lined At Meydani, the square that covers the site of the old Hippodrome. As a result only half the marble plinth on which the obelisk stands appears above ground, though the lower part is visible in a stone-lined excavation. Its erection must have been fascinating, not to say nerve-racking, to watch and far more difficult than the setting-up of the Colonne Luxor or Cleopatra's Needle or even, for that matter, the obelisk in front of St Peter's in Rome. There at the critical moment the obelisk would not move the last few feet into the vertical, and though the crowd had been commanded on pain of death to keep quiet, a sailor cried out: 'Water on the ropes.' Water was thrown on the ropes, they tightened, and the obelisk moved into the vertical.

At Constantinople it took thirty to thirty-two days to set up this huge monolith carved with hieroglyphs glorifying the Pharaoh and the god Horus. The work was carried out under the direct supervision of Proclos, the prefect of the city (not a Greek engineer as is sometimes stated), who two years later fell from favour and was beheaded. Theodosius himself attended the operations. What makes it all the more remarkable is that the obelisk does not rest directly on the plinth, but on four bronze cubes, each about eighteen inches square. That it still stands after more than 1,200 years is in itself wonderful: but how much more so in view of the earthquakes that time and again have laid waste so much of the city.

Bas-reliefs are carved on the four sides of the upper part of the plinth, all connected with Theodosius I and the Hippodrome. One shows him supervising the erection of the obelisk, another attending a triumph: with him in the imperial box—the Kathisma—are Valentinian II (nephew, and Emperor of the West) and his two sons, Honorius (who would succeed Valentinian) and Arcadius, Constantinople's next ruler. Below them in the arena are kneeling prisoners offering gifts or tribute. The same royal group appears in a third bas-relief where they are watching the chariot races. In a fourth panel (opposite the Sultan Ahmet Mosque), Theodosius I is presenting prizes to the winners. He stands in front of the box, the hand holding a laurel wreath resting on the rail in front, while Honorius and Arcadius sit on either side. Obviously they are portraits. Arcadius had prominent ears, and there is a remarkable similarity between this bas-relief and a sculptured head in the Archaeological Museum which came from his statue in the Forum that bore his name (page 29). With the large expressionless eyes it seems to have more in common with Greek sculpture of the Archaic Period rather than late Roman imperial portraiture.

The bas-relief is interesting from an historical and architectural point of view, giving some idea of the appearance of the interior of the Hippodrome in its great days. In the background can be seen the wall with blind arches which ran round the top of the tiers of seats. The imperial box at least at this date looks quite small, its flat roof supported in front on two Corinthian columns.

It was Theodosius II, the Emperor's grandson, who had the four famous bronze horses, by Lysippus of Corinth, brought to Constantinople from Rome, and set either in pairs on either side of the box, or else all four on the roof. From Greece they had been taken to Rome by Nero to decorate his triumphal arch. From there they went to Constantinople, where they remained in the Hippodrome until carried off in 1204 by looting Venetian crusaders, who set them on the façade of San Marco. Then after Napoleon's troops entered the republic, the first enemy ever to set foot in the city, they were taken to Paris and placed on the Arc de Carrousel between the wings of the Louvre, and later returned after Waterloo.

On this same bas-relief of Theodosius and his family a dance is going on in the arena. Dances, juggling, and wrestling formed interludes between the chariot races, and here are scantily clad girls, and musicians, including what must be the oldest representations of the organ, invented in Byzantium. On either side two musicians hold these small portable organs—about the same size as a hurdy-gurdy. Another musician plays on the kind of pipes forever associated with fauns, satyrs, and and centaurs. Two pipes with, as it were, one mouthpiece. In out of the way parts of Roumania the peasants still make them, from straws, and the sound is surprisingly musical.

All in all, the Obelisk of Theodosius with the bas-reliefs on its plinth, is one of the most rewarding objects in Istanbul. Its erection is given as 390, though in that particular year the Emperor was in Milan, from where he ordered the shameful massacre of Thessalonika. It may have little bearing on the history of Constantinople, but it does show the place held by the charioteers in the daily life of the people. The star charioteer in the second city in the Empire disgraced himself by trying to have an affair with one of the city Governor's slave-boys, and was thrown into prison. The inhabitants rose up, demanding the release of their maladjusted hero, and murdered the Governor. In a fit of temper Theodosius I ordered a massacre, to take place in the Hippodrome. Then he repented, but his counter-command arrived too late. By then between seven and fifteen thousand inhabitants had been butchered at the races.

In Constantinople it was the custom to erect statues on the Spina in the Hippodrome to favourite charioteers, and the base of one survives: it is now in the Room of Christian Antiquities in the Archaeological Museum. It is to one Porphyrios, a handsome Alexandrian, though the bronze statue itself has long since disappeared: no doubt it was melted down by the crusaders. More than once he is shown in bas-relief guiding his four-horse chariot to victory, cheering figures in the foreground, and on one panel in addition to the names of famous horses eight or nine of them are carved, grouped about two small figures. This is vividly evocative of what occupied the thoughts of the citizens during many hours of drudgery, hard work, or gilded laziness.

Chapter 5

395–457

The Column of Arcadius. St John Chrysostom. The vices of the Court flayed in his sermons. Attempts to engineer his removal end in riots. Santa Sophia burnt. Constantinople ruled by a eunuch. The walls of Theodosius (413). Their architecture. The towers and gates. Damage by earthquakes. Rebuilding and addition of a second wall (447). Their appearance today. Threat to Constantinople by Attila (447). The imperial family. Plan to assassinate Attila misfires. Honoria, sister of the Emperor of the west, plans to marry Attila. Death of Attila. Pulcheria as Empress in her own right. The Column of Marcian.

'At length, in the thirty-fifth year of his age, after a reign (if we may abuse that word) of thirteen years, three months, and fifteen days, Arcadius expired in the palace of Constantinople. It is impossible to delineate his character; since, in a period very copiously furnished with historical materials, it has not been possible to remark one action that properly belongs to the son of the great Theodosius.' So wrote Gibbon about Arcadius, who occupied the throne from 395 to 408. If he himself was something of a nonentity three individuals, a man, a woman, and a eunuch, were not. The first was a saint, John Chrysostom; the second an Empress, Eudoxia; and the third Eutropius, the power behind the throne.

The only memorial the soft-living Arcadius left in his city was the column which in 402 he had erected in the centre of the forum bearing his name, the last one along the Mesé before coming to the Golden Gate. The column was his tribute to his father's victories over the Goths and Ostrogoths in 394–5, and was surmounted by a statue of Theodosius I, which however was taken down in 421 and replaced by one of Arcadius himself.

About 165 feet high, it must have been as tall or taller than the Column of Constantine. The plinth on which it stood was thirty feet high, and on the twenty-one drums of which the shaft was composed scenes from the campaigns of Theodosius and Arcadius were carved, like the Column of Trajan in Rome. But as a result of earthquakes it had to be taken down in 1715, and all that now remains is the plinth, next to a baker's shop.

Through sermons in which St John Chrysostom flayed the vices of his time, from the court downwards (page 92) we can see something of the luxury that had made Constantinople a by-word throughout the Mediterranean world. He singled out the lavishness of Arcadius and his entourage for a detailed catalogue: 'The Emperor wears on his head either a diadem, or a crown of gold, decorated with precious stones of inestimable value. These ornaments, and his purple garments, are reserved for his sacred person alone; and his robes of silk are embroidered with the figures of gold dragons. His throne is of massy gold. Whenever he appears in public, he is surrounded by his courtiers, his guards, and his attendants. Their spears, their shields, their cuirasses, the bridles and trappings of their horses, have either the substance, or the appearance, of gold; and the large splendid boss in the midst of their shield is encircled with smaller bosses, which represent the shape of the human eye. The two mules that draw the chariot of the monarch are perfectly white, and shining all over with gold. The chariot itself, of pure and solid gold, attracts the admiration of the spectators, who contemplate the purple curtains, the snowy carpet, the size of the precious stones, and the resplendent motion of the carriage.'

With his piercing eyes and high forehead, St John Chrysostom was not a man to be overlooked in a crowd. The son of well-to-do parents, living in Antioch, he spent six years meditating in the desert. But it was not long after his return to his home town that his sermons brought him to Constantinople, to become its archbishop. Here was a man who was different: many must have found him uncomfortably so. He used his personal revenues on the hospitals instead of trying to rival the Emperor in luxury, and from the pulpit of Santa Sophia attacked the female servants of many of the clergy in Constantinople, saying they afforded a perpetual occasion either for sin or for scandal.

He never hesitated to say what he thought, and to act accordingly. On one visitation he deposed no less than thirteen bishops in two provinces alone. Naturally, this behaviour made enemies, and the Empress Eudoxia invited the Patriarch of Alexandria to come to the capital, together with a train of bishops, to secure a majority vote against him in the Synod. They arrived with what amounted to a bodyguard of Egyptian sailors. The archbishop ignored four summons to attend the Synod, meeting over the water in Chalcedon (Kadeköy). In his absence he was deposed, and the good bishops suggested to Arcadius that St John should be punished for treason, which carried the death penalty, for attacking the Empress in one of his sermons. He had likened her to Jezebel. In point of fact there was some doubt whether Arcadius or one Count John was the father of her son, the future Theodosius II.

St John was arrested, led through the city and taken by boat up the Bosphorus and landed near the entrance to the Black Sea. Meanwhile there had been a popular explosion in Constantinople: the Patriarch of Alexandria just escaped with his life, but most of the monks and Egyptian soldiers who had accompanied him were cut down in the streets, and the crowd swept towards the imperial palace. Inside it was Eudoxia, instigator of the future saint's removal, who grovelled at her husband's feet, begging him to restore St John before they were murdered.

Only two days after his banishment the archbishop was back in his cathedral—denouncing women in general and Eudoxia in particular. He even said, or so his enemies told the Empress: 'Herodias is again furious: Herodias again dances; she once more requires the head of John.' She was furious too.

During the Easter baptisms, which in the ancient church only took place three times a year, the clergy were driven out, first to the Baths of Constantine, and then into the open country. More riots followed, and Santa Sophia, the senate house, and a number of other buildings burnt. The destruction of Santa Sophia was only partial, but it was not until 414 that it was completely restored.

This time St John Chrysostom really was exiled, leaving Constantinople, a city he would never see again, on June 20, 404. On the orders of his old enemy, Eudoxia, he was to go to the monastery of Cucusus, seventy days' march away in Armenia. Three years later he died while being transferred to Comana (near the modern Tokat, east of Ankara), and in 438 his body was brought back to Constantinople. Theodosius II, by then the Emperor, threw himself on the coffin, begging the saint to forgive his mother and father for what they did.

Eudoxia, the cause of nearly all his misfortunes, was beautiful and immoral, a not uncommon combination in the empresses of Byzantium. The real ruler was not the Emperor, but the career-conscious eunuch Eutropius, who became all-powerful after ousting Rufinus, his predecessor. During four years, 395–399, he ruled Constantinople and the Empire, the first of a long line of eunuchs who was to do so, both in Byzantine and Ottoman times. Extremely arrogant, with delusions of manliness, he had statues of himself erected in the senate, city and Empire with the legend that he was the third founder of Constantinople—and appeared on horseback and in armour at the head of his—or the Emperor's—troops. Much of his behaviour could probably be traced to his origins and early life: 'born in the most abject condition of servitude; that before he entered the imperial palace, he had been successively sold and purchased by a hundred masters, who had exhausted his youthful strength in every mean and infamous office, and at length dismissed him, in his old age, to freedom and poverty'. (Gibbon.)

Now the wheel of fortune had certainly turned. Governorships and high offices were his to sell, and he even brought in the most severe treason laws: it was a capital offence even to think treason, or to plead for those already accused. When his fall came it was hard. His eclipse was touched off by a revolt in Phrygia and the imperial army, sent to quell it, went over to the rebels; their chief in Constantinople declared that he could not subdue them by force of arms, but their terms for peace were simple, Eutropius's head. Eudoxia, who hated the insolent, wrinkled, and painted old man, went to Arcadius with a tearful story that the eunuch had insulted their small son Theodosius. Eutropius took himself off as fast as he could into Santa Sophia for sanctuary. (This all happened in 399, before the cathedral was burnt or St John exiled.) Quite what the archbishop's motives were for protecting the sexless tyrant against Arcadius and Eudoxia might be open to question, but while Eutropius literally hid under the altar, St John delivered a sermon in the packed nave—on the forgiveness of sins.

On the promise that his life should be spared, Eutropius came out from under the altar, and a little later out of Santa Sophia itself, to find he had been stripped of all ranks, his property confiscated, and condemned to perpetual exile in Cyprus. Hardly had he reached the island before he was ordered back to Constantinople by his enemies who would only be content with his blood. He was tried in Chalcedon, not in Constantinople itself, a twisting attempt to find a way round the oath by which his life had been spared, and sentenced to death. The crime which cost him his head had nothing whatsoever to do with his years of misrule. The ageing eunuch was found guilty of using mules to pull his chariot of a breed and colour which were for the Emperor's exclusive use.

Even in death—during childbirth—Eudoxia would seem to have resembled the Red Queen, forever crying 'Off with his head!' As her funeral procession was passing through the streets of Constantinople a servant girl spat out of an upper window and quite by accident hit the Empress's coffin as it was just below. She was put to death on the imperial tomb.

Though the Theodosian walls take their name from the Emperor, Theodosius II, when they were first built he was only thirteen, the credit should really go to Anthemius, the Praetorian Prefect of the east, who practically ruled the Empire during the boy's minority. By the fifth century Constantinople had burst its confines within the walls of Constantine. Since the city was surrounded on two of its three sides by water, it could obviously expand in only one direction: towards the west. Houses had sprung up in the fields, and soon the district became an important part of the city, and quite defenceless.

Then in 410 came the news, and it must have been almost unbelievable, that Rome itself had fallen to the barbarians. Less than a century before many had come from the old capital at the bidding of the Emperor to settle in his newly inaugurated city of Constantine. Now it was Constantinople itself that was threatened. In the north the Huns were already across the Danube.

The orders were given for a new line of walls to be erected about a mile and a half to the west of Constantine's defences. Looking at them today, stretching north from the Sea of Marmara for over four and a half miles to the Golden Horn it hardly seems possible the wall was built within twelve months. All the citizens had to help, either with money or by actually working on it. The labour force was under the direction of the two factions, the Greens and the Blues, who had been charged by Anthemius with the task of raising it. In addition to the professional masons, 16,000 of the inhabitants worked as they could never have worked before.

Limestone from quarries not far away was used, set in courses with bricks about thirteen inches square. Structurally it is as massive as it is long. The inner wall (the outer was added thirty-four years later) is on average thirty feet high on its outer side, and forty on the inner—the city side. Fifteen feet thick at the base, it batters down to thirteen and a half feet at the top. This parapet walk is reached by steps on the inside, usually set near the gates which punctuate its length, and guarded by a parapet on average four feet eight inches high. In all there are ninety-six towers, between 175 and 181 feet apart, with a height of sixty feet, projecting in front of the wall. Most are square, while the remainder are five, six, or eight sided. Each consisted of an upper and a lower chamber. The lower opened straight into the city, and in time of peace they were often rented out to the adjacent property-owners: otherwise they were used as guardrooms. Usually there was no direct access to the room above which could only be entered from the parapet-walk. Windows looked out from each wall of the towers, while another flight of steps led up to the battlemented roofs.

The gates and several smaller posterns gave access to and from the city. When the walls were built they were planned to incorporate the Golden Gate; built twenty-three years before by Theodosius I as a triumphal arch outside the city.

Actually standing on the shore of the Sea of Marmara near the west end of the sea walls, which had to be lengthened to join up with the new Theodosian walls, is the Marble Tower, taking its name from its foundations. Four stories high, it was used as a prison and has been identified with the Prison of St Diomed: a church of that name now quite vanished, stood nearby. Then, right at the southern end of the Theodosian walls stands Christ's Postern (Dabağhane Kapisi). A little further inland the modern breach for the railway line, then Yedikule (Castle of the Seven Towers), a fifteenth century Turkish fortress built behind the Golden Gate. Beside it is a small gate, used in Byzantine times by the ordinary public, who could not use its large neighbour. Tall and narrow, the arch of the Yedikule Kapisi is still surmounted on the inside by a bas-relief of a Byzantine eagle.

Continuing north past a well-preserved stretch of the walls, next comes the ruined Xilokerkos Gate (Belgrat Kapisi), then the Pighi Gate (Silivri Kapisi) which was used by the Emperors when going to visit a sacred spring nearby, or else to stay at one of their hunting lodges near the city. Beyond is the Sigma, the unexplained inward curve in the walls, which takes its name from the Greek letter Σ. After seven more towers have been passed there is the Rhegium Gate (Mevlane Kapisi), which once had a portcullis. After a small military gate comes the Gate of St Romanus (Top Kapisi). The name came from a nearby church, which contained reputed relics of the prophet Daniel: though Moslems who also claim him as one of their prophets, declare *his* remains are in a shrine in Persia—and far too sacred for Christians to visit.

Another military gate, and then the opening for the large modern road that leads to the airport and to Edirne. Beyond is the Edirne Kapisi, called in Byzantine times the Charisius Gate.

It was particularly badly damaged by the earthquake of 1894, and the upper parts of both towers on either side were much damaged and have been completely rebuilt. Nearby, the walls are in ruins, a memorial to the final assault—with cannon—by the Turks in 1453.

Next, after another military gate, the Kerko Porta is a small doorway in the wall through which fifty Turkish janissaries penetrated into the city itself on the morning it fell.

Originally the Theodosian walls continued in a straight line down the Sixth Hill to the shore of the Golden Horn: but in the twelfth century a new wall was built to enclose the Blachernae Palace which until then stood in the open country.

On numerous occasions the Theodosian walls have been damaged by earthquakes: in 542, 554, when the damage round the Golden Gate was serious and particularly in 558 when Santa Sophia also was shaken. In fact, the destruction in the city was such that for thirty days Justinian refused to wear his crown as a sign of mourning. Then in 740, when St Irene was wrecked (page 107), the tremors lasted for eleven months. Other severe earthquakes came in 975, 1032, 1033, with very severe shocks in 1344 when the walls had to be repaired from end to end, and more recently in 1894, when the oldest church in the city, St John of Studion, was completely wrecked.

But the most disastrous earthquake of all was the first. In 447 Attila, the Scourge of God, had defeated Theodosius II, and was advancing on Constantinople, laying waste to Macedonia and Thrace as he came. At that critical moment the city was hit by a series of violent tremors: damaging Constantine's Santa Sophia, but what was more important for the inhabitants, destroying the wall. No less than fifty-seven of the towers were brought down.

Desperately, the Byzantines bought time—with gold. Their foreign policy followed its usual course: Attila was bought off with a down-payment of 6,000 lbs of gold (£900,000 at present prices (1962)), and an annual tribute of a further 2,100 lbs. Time and again such methods gave the Empire an opportunity to get its second wind, or to engineer a falling-out among its enemies. Again the Greens and the Blues provided the labour:

16,000 men, while Constantine, the then Praetorian Prefect of the East, had absolute authority to see nothing hindered the work. Later, when peace had returned, Constantine issued a decree that the streets and shops of Constantinople should be lit at night. It was not until the fifteenth century that London could boast street lighting of a sort, while Vienna had to wait until the eighteenth century. But now it was the wall, and only the wall that occupied everyone's thoughts.

Two months only were needed to complete the work, to rebuild great stretches of the wall, fifty-seven towers *and* add a completely new smaller outer wall with towers of its own, making 192, together with a wide and deep moat. Two inscriptions on the inside of the Mevlane Kapisi record that all this really was done in sixty days: such was the fear Attila had over the minds of men. 'In sixty days, by order of the sceptre-loving Emperor, Constantine the Eparch added wall to wall' (Greek); and 'By command of Theodosius, in less than two months, Constantine erected triumphantly, these strong walls. Scarcely could Pallas have built so quickly so strong a citadel' (Latin).

The space between these two walls is about sixty feet; then comes the outer wall, about ten feet high, with towers between thirty and thirty-five feet high, usually set in front of the larger ones on the main wall. In front there was now a terrace, also about sixty feet wide; then the moat—of the same width—though today only a short stretch is full of evil-smelling water, the rest being either empty, or used as market gardens. Near the Golden Gate it is still twenty-two feet deep. On both sides the moat is lined with stonework, strengthened at intervals with buttresses.

In 510 yet another wall was added for the city's defence, though at a distance from it of about thirty-two miles, stretching from the shores of the Sea of Marmara to the Black Sea. This one was constructed chiefly of earth, and its relationship to the Walls of Theodosius is not unlike that of the Antonine Wall on the Solway Firth to Hadrian's Wall across Northumberland and Cumberland. Today practically nothing remains of this Long Wall.

These then are the bastions that for over one thousand years

Golden Gate (Porta Aurea), A.D. 380
Walls of Theodosius, with moat, A.D. 413 and 447

SS. Sergius and Bacchus (Küçük Aya Sophia Mosque) A.D. 527. Gallery over south-east exedra

Mosaic: girl with a pitcher, *c.* A.D. 565. Imperial Palace

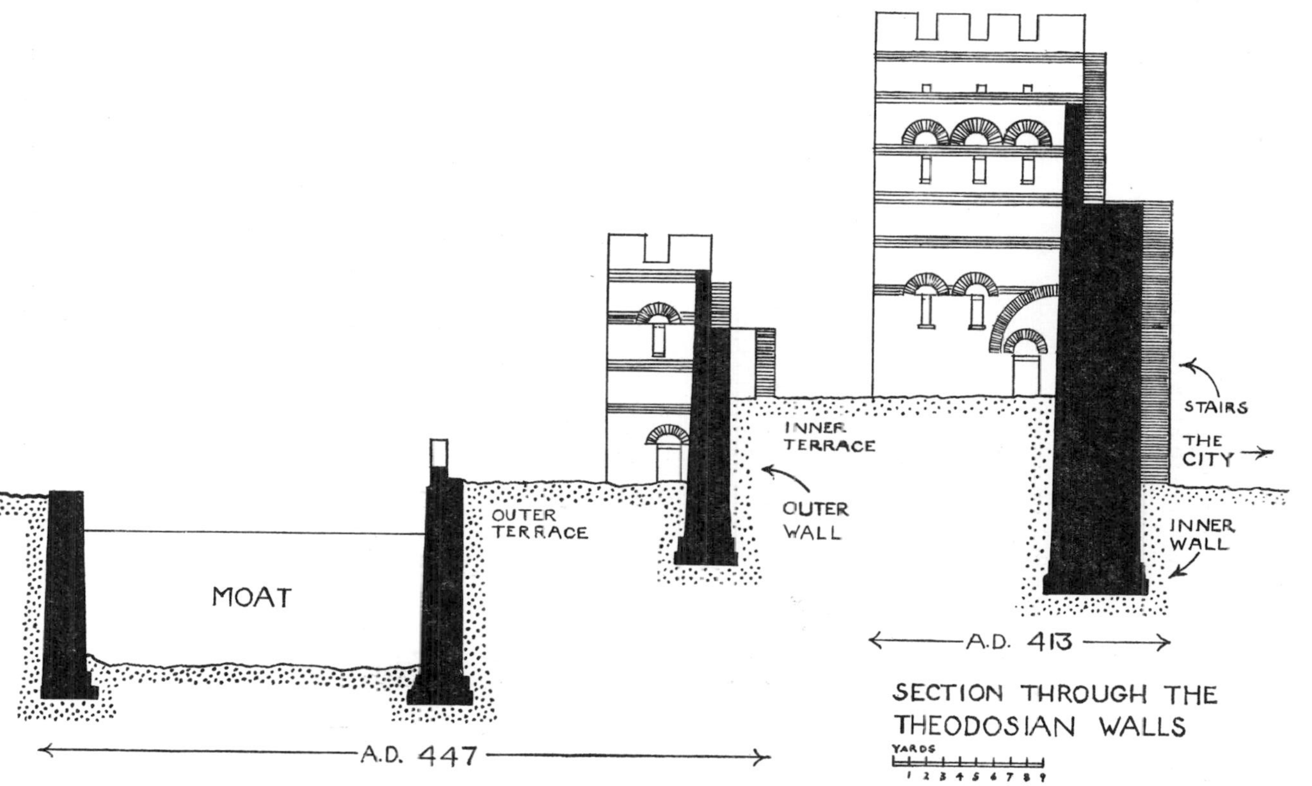

SECTION THROUGH THE THEODOSIAN WALLS

were to keep out the enemies not only of Constantinople, but of western civilization itself. Think of the sentries in the night-time, calling to the man on the next tower, and so on along the whole length of the great wall—to keep each other awake during their centuries-long vigil; and beyond in the darkness, the fires of the Bulgarians, the Avars, the Persians, the Arabs, the Crusaders, and lastly the Turks, watching and waiting.

Even at a distance the courses of stone and brick stand out: white and red-brown, almost dazzling in brilliant sunshine. Tower after tower, some intact, some ruined—riven from top to bottom with huge cracks caused by the earthquakes—stretching away over the rising and falling of the ground. They look noble and a little forlorn, bearing the marks of old age and the havoc of the Turkish siege, more than five hundred years ago. At the Gate of St Romanus Constantine XI would go out to die 'in the winding sheet of his Empire', killed alongside his soldiers, that morning in May, 1453; while through the adjacent Edirne Gate Mehmet the Conqueror would enter the city as it fell to his janissaries, riding a white horse. But before that day one thousand and six years of Byzantine history would unroll itself behind the walls of Theodosius.

Unfortunately, the man forever associated with these walls is not really worthy of the honour. The reign of Theodosius was long—forty-two years, and undistinguished. Weak, lazy, and always expecting to be entertained, he never bothered to read the state papers set before him, and only really stirred himself to go hunting. Extremely pious, he also spent much time psalm-singing.

More interesting as a human being is his wife, Eudoxia. Hers was a success story with an unhappy ending. The daughter of a Greek philosopher, Leontius, she was originally called Athenias. With the exception of one hundred pieces of gold he left all his money to her brothers, confident her looks and intelligence would take her right to the top. Although only left a small sum of money the jealousy and spite of her brothers was such she fled to Constantinople, where she asked the help of Pulcheria, sister to Theodosius II. Pulcheria summed up Athenias, and decided she should marry her brother. A portrait was shown to Theodosius, who was also told of her trials and tribulations. He fell in love with what he saw, and it was arranged he should hide behind a curtain in Pulcheria's apartment so he could see Athenias unobserved. Marriage followed. Athenias renounced the old gods, taking the name of Eudoxia at her baptism.

Like her husband and sister-in-law she was now deeply religious, among other things writing a paraphrase in verse of the first eight books of the Old Testament, and also the prophecies of Daniel and Zachariah. But even so she did not feel that the possession of worldly goods always implied vanity. On a pilgrimage to Jerusalem—more like a lavish progress—she all but reached the bottom of the treasury with her gifts to various shrines and religious institutions. Among the relics she brought back were the reputed chains of St Peter and an icon of the Virgin painted by St Luke. But now she was unwise enough to try to dispute supremacy as first lady in the imperial palace with Pulcheria. Theodosius might be the nominal ruler, but his sister, and the eunuchs, held the reins. The method used to deal with the interfering Eudoxia was ruthless and efficient. A rumour was circulated that the Empress was in love with the handsome Master of the Offices. He was executed, and finding her position impossible, Eudoxia asked to be allowed to return to Jerusalem. She went, but on Pulcheria's orders two priests in her train were murdered by the Count of the Domestics (imperial bodyguard). Eudoxia retaliated by having the Count assassinated, whereupon Pulcheria told her brother to strip his wife of her rank. She never returned to Constantinople, dying in Jerusalem at the age of sixty-seven, protesting her innocence to the end.

It was against the background of personal spite in the imperial palace that the menace of Attila grew to a reality. In 446 Theodosius II bought off the Huns with tribute, and in the palace a plan was hatched by the all-powerful eunuch Chysaphius—unofficial co-ruler with Pulcheria—to bribe their ambassador to assassinate Attila. The Hun ambassador appeared interested, and then told his master the whole scheme. Attila demanded two hundred pounds of gold as ransom for a

Byzantine envoy he held, and sent two ambassadors back to Constantinople, one with the purse containing the bribe hanging about his neck. His name was Orestes, and like his Argive namesake he wanted vengeance.

Theodosius heard the truth about himself and his ministers, but by sending an embassy laden with valuable presents he was able to appease Attila. Having been caught out in an assassination plot the weak Byzantine Emperor now metaphorically had to grovel at the feet of a hard-riding barbarian.

Next came a pathetic and most extraordinary episode concerning the Imperial Family and Attila. The tottering West Roman Empire was now ruled from the marsh-surrounded city of Ravenna on the east coast of Italy. There, at the age of sixteen, Honoria, sister of the Emperor Valentinian, had an unfortunate and all too obvious love affair with her Chamberlain. As soon as the child was born Honoria was packed off to Constantinople, and the care of the iron-minded Pulcheria. There she became a prisoner in the imperial palace, but after fourteen years she had had more than she could bear of the self-righteous behaviour of the sisters of Theodosius II, all dedicated virgins. Anything was preferable, even the embraces of Attila. Through one of the palace eunuchs she sent him a ring, asking the Hun to say they had been secretly engaged for some time. Attila refused her offer: the secret was out, and Honoria was sent back from Constantinople to Italy and perpetual imprisonment. Then —in 453—Attila demanded her, and said the next year he would come and ravage Italy, for the second time. He returned to his wooden palace beyond the Danube, where he married yet another wife, but on that same wedding night the Scourge of God died, from a burst blood-vessel. Only in the manner of his death was Attila the Hun a laughing matter.

Meanwhile the Emperor Theodosius II himself had died, in somewhat more decorous circumstances. When out riding he was thrown from his horse into the little River Lycus at the point near the Edirne Gate where it enters the city, to flow into the Sea of Marmara via the Harbour of Eleutherius. His spine was damaged, and on July 28, 450, he died.

Now it was Pulcheria, his managing sister, who became

Empress, in her own right, the first Constantinople had seen. After her death only three years later, in 453, she was canonized. But her first action as Empress was far from saintly. She turned on the eunuch Chysaphius—responsible for the humiliating episode concerning Attila's ambassador—and on her orders without any trial he was beheaded, near the Silivri Gate. Pulcheria's second action of note was to take a husband, though to the end of her life she rejoiced in her virginity. He was a soldier, Marcian: remembered if at all by the column he had erected in Constantinople, which stands in a side street not far from the west end of the Aqueduct of Valens. Smaller than the others, thirty-two feet high, it was carved from a single block of granite. The Corinthian capital remains, but the statue of Marcian has long since vanished.

According to tradition the column nods in a most familiar way whenever a single woman passes who has parted with her virtue, a state of affairs which no doubt could be traced back to Marcian's relationship with his wife. The situation must have been difficult: if a woman with a guilty conscience passed the column she risked being publicly shamed by it, and if she made a detour through the nearby streets the local gossips would soon notice, so either way she stood to lose her reputation.

Chapter 6

457–527

Foundation of the Monastery of St John of Studion (463). The Monastery and St Theodore, its greatest abbot. The Church of St John. The death of the Emperor Zeno (491). The Hippodrome: riots which began there. St Peter and St Mark (458). Why it was built. The Church of the Virgin of Blachernae. Rise of Justin I.

The real ruler in the capital after the death of Marcian (457) was an army clique, headed by Aspar, in origin belonging to the race of Alans, living in the Caucasus, who held the upper hand with his guards—also from the far end of the Black Sea. Apart from nominating a junior officer, Leo of Thrace, the principal steward of his household as Emperor, he left his memorial in the city in the form of the huge disused Cistern of Aspar, next the Sultan Selim Mosque. Five hundred feet square, and originally thirty-six feet deep it is now a garden, and ten feet shallower.

Leo, who was of Syrian origin, showed himself ungrateful to his puppet-master Aspar, undermined his authority and finally broke his power altogether, and nominated Anthemius (467–472), as Emperor of the western half of the Roman Empire. But the days of this dual system were numbered, and in the reign of Leo I's son-in-law Zeno the title was abolished altogether, and Zeno proclaimed sole ruler of the whole Roman Empire. As a capital city, Constantinople was paramount.

The reign of Leo I, and of his son Leo II, who came and went within a year, may not have been particularly memorable in the city, but it was in 463 that the most important religious house in Constantinople was founded. Studius was a patrician—probably a consul in the time of Marcian, who brought the Monastery of St John of Studion into being. Architecturally of the first importance, it is also a most peaceful and beautiful spot, just off the street that leads to the Golden Gate.

The monastery really was large, housing a thousand monks, origininally called the Acemetes, 'the sleepless ones', who twenty-four hours out of twenty-four celebrated the Divine Liturgy without ceasing. This was done by dividing them into three choirs, who in relays made the basilica of St John resound with the rising and falling of their voices: three hundred or thereabouts, chanting the praises of God. In later centuries it became almost customary for the Emperor's children to receive some of their education there, and a number of disillusioned—or deposed—rulers retired to it from the dangerous intrigue-ridden world of the imperial palace.

Theodore the Studite, died 826, was its most famous abbot, who stood out against the Iconoclast emperors, for which he was scourged and exiled, after leading a procession round the monastery gardens carrying icons when they had been forbidden. Eighteen years after his death in exile his body was brought back to Constantinople, and buried at the east end of the south aisle of the church. Feeling that the monks in his monastery were becoming too lax and worldly, St Theodore introduced the rule that no female living thing could enter its precincts. The worldly distraction of women coming and going was obvious, but Theodore also strongly objected to the way some monks were breeding animals and selling them for private profit in the outside world. To this day the ruling is still observed most strictly on Mount Athos, the holy mountain where the Virgin Mary is the only woman. There no female may set foot on the peninsula where twenty monasteries live out their existence, outside time, as though the Byzantine Empire had not ceased to exist on May 29, 1453.

St Theodore did much to stop monasticism in the East Roman Empire sliding into an easy sheltered life in which the wherefore of a monk's life tended to be overlooked. Meat was only allowed if absolutely necessary for the health, and the meals consisted mainly of vegetables cooked in oil. Much of the monks' time was spent in copying manuscripts, and there were graduated punishments for mistakes: fifty genuflections for smudging a page; one hundred and fifty for omitting accents and punctuation; thirty for losing the temper or breaking a pen —while if the copyist omitted part of the original he would find himself on bread and water for three days.

Situated about three hundred yards from the Sea of Marmara, at the south-west corner of the city, it was easily accessible by water through a gate (Narli Kapisi) in the sea walls, and once a year on the Feast of the Decapitation of St John the Baptist (August 29), the Emperor used to come in great state by boat from the harbour of the palace, to take part in the service. At its climax it was he who had the privilege of censing the monastery's most precious relic, part of the skull of the Baptist (page 198), enshrined in the south side of the Bema, the tiers of seats for the priests set in the apse behind the altar.

The church is a basilica, the Christian adaptation of the pillared hall of justice of ancient Rome, with its apse at one end— and the only church adhering to that plan which remains in the city. Originally it was preceded by an atrium with an ablutions fountain in the centre; in front of the church itself was a narthex and, adjoining the aisles, north and south there were cloisters.

Today the atrium is like a pleasant courtyard, shaded with fig and nut trees and full of Turkish tombstones, for in the time of Beyazit II (1481–1512) it was converted into a mosque, now called Imrahor Camii. Like gondola posts, they lean at all angles, topped by the type of turban the man would have worn in life to indicate his professional status. Only the north wall of this atrium goes back to Byzantine times, but at least the narthex, of three bays, with—long since vanished—a timber roof, is still reasonably intact, though much damaged by Istambul's twin enemies, fire and earthquake.

Four columns, with beautiful Corinthian capitals, stand on either side of the three entrances: above them the entablature; architrave, frieze, and cornice—in what Wren would no doubt have described as 'a good Roman manner'.

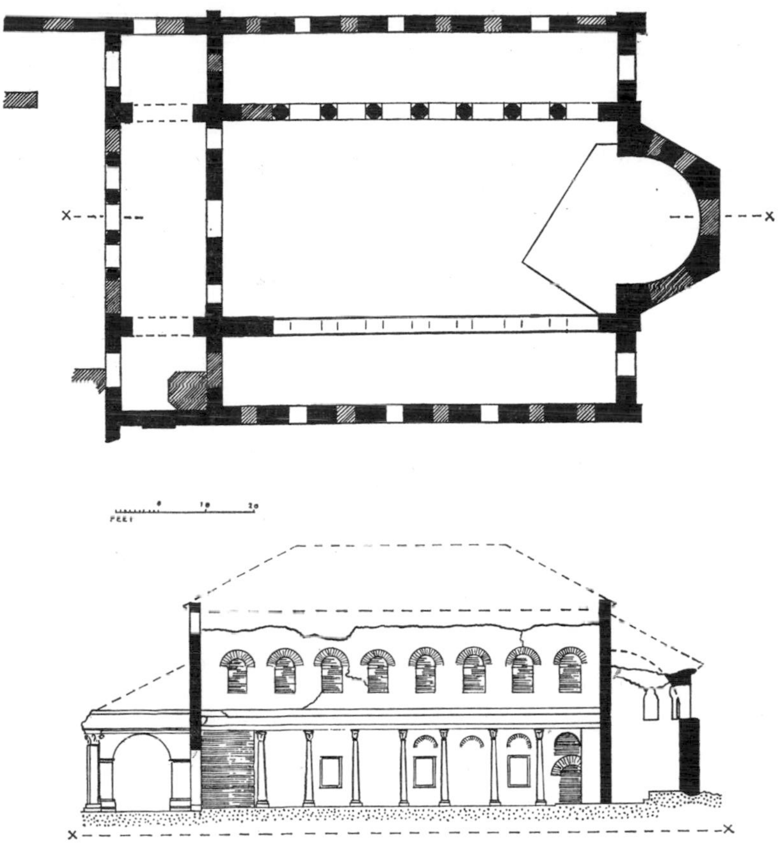

St John of Studion A.D. 463 Imrahor Mosque

Beyond the door from the narthex the ancient church is quite open to the sky: the west front still stands to its full height, and so do the outer walls of the aisles; while to the east the apse (largely Turkish) remains to the springing of the vaulting. The walls are of alternate courses of roughly squared blocks of stone and layers of thin red bricks. In the wide nave, still with its floor of coloured marble added after the city had been recaptured from the Latins in 1261, when the monastery was nearly in ruins, all that remains is the arcade of seven verd-antique columns, surmounted by calcined and weather-beaten capitals and an architrave. There was a gallery above the aisles, also with seven columns, supporting the open timber roof, but like so much else it has quite vanished. Badly burnt in 1782, the basilica was completely wrecked in the terrible earthquake of 1894, which wrought so much havoc to the Theodosian Walls.

An immense peace seems to have settled over St John of Studion, flooding it like the strong sunshine which etches in sharp relief little shadows on the uneven surface of brick-work and time-worn sculpture, and in a city where so much violent history seems to have permeated the very walls of so many of its buildings, that is a noticeable quality; peace and a sense of goodness.

The time of the Emperor Zeno—like Leo I a Syrian—was not particularly memorable, except perhaps when he died. Death came suddenly from epilepsy in Easter week, 491. As soon as the news spread through the city the leaders of the Blues and the Greens, the imperial guards, and the people flocked to the Hippodrome, calling out: 'Give an Emperor to the Romans.' Zeno's widow, a heavy-faced woman not unlike Queen Anne in looks, went to the Kathisma where she was greeted with: 'Ariadne Augusta, may you be victorious! Lord have mercy on us! Long live Augusta! Give an orthodox Emperor to the Romans, to all the earth.' Through a crier she told them the court, the senate, the army and the church would choose a successor. She ended with a warning to the people to keep calm, and abide by whoever was chosen. In the imperial palace one Anastasius, an elderly bachelor, once nominee for the See of Antioch, was chosen. Then there was a slight delay while they buried Zeno. But apparently he was not really dead, and the story later arose that he had been buried alive.

For two days a soldier on guard at the tomb in the Church of the Apostles heard moaning, and finally: 'Have pity, and let me out!'

'But we have another Emperor,' said the soldier, evidently incapable of rising to the situation.

'Never mind, take me to a monastery,' said Zeno, most accommodatingly. But the widow Ariadne would not allow the tomb to be opened at first. Finally it was opened, and Zeno, by now very dead, was found to have eaten his boots, of imperial purple. Or so the story goes.

The true political centre of Constantinople was not so much the Senate, at best of times a cypher which praised and ratified the whims of the emperors; but the Hippodrome. There the people assembled to let their opinions be known in no uncertain way. But in the reign of Anastasius (491–518) a riot there was not political, but started by rowdies who threw stones into the arena during the races. The crowd demanded their release, and when the Emperor refused and ordered the imperial guards to arrest the ring-leaders he himself had to flee from a hail of stones. At this date most of the benches were still of wood: these were set on fire. The flames spread to the part of the palace which adjoined on the east side, while to the west the blaze reached as far as the Forum of Constantine.

Then in 512 there was another riot, this time religious in origin. Anastasius suggested that the words 'Who was crucified for us', should be added to the Trisagion: Holy God, Holy Mighty, Holy Immortal.' This, the people thought, smacked of Monophysite heresy, and they set fire to the houses of those they considered suspect, beheading a monk who first put the suggestion to Anastasius, and paraded through the streets with their trophy on a pole, demanding a new and orthodox emperor. Anastasius, looking as terrified as he must have felt, appeared in the Hippodrome without his crown, and abjectly promised that the offending phrase should not be added to the Trisagion.

From pre-Christian times the pool outside the Theodosian Walls at its northern end had been sacred, and since the building of the Holy Shrine, dedicated to the Virgin of Blachernae (the name of that district), the spot was doubly so. Attention was really focused on the district as a result of some exceedingly dishonest dealings by two patricians: Galbius and Candidus. These two went on a pilgrimage to Jerusalem, and one night they put up at the house of a Hebrew woman who had fitted up one room as a chapel to contain a most sacred relic: the Robe of the Virgin, kept in a chest. The two men wanted it for themselves, put their heads together, and when in Jerusalem had a chest made which was identical. On their return journey they again stayed at the house, and substituted it for the one containing the Robe. Back once again in Constantinople Galbius and Candidus built a little church (458) on land they owned at Blachernae, just outside the walls. As a blind it was dedicated to SS. Peter and Mark, as they wanted to keep the relic all to themselves. But the secret leaked out, the Emperor made them give it up, and placed it in his own nearby church of St Mary of Blachernae.

A church dedicated to SS. Peter and Mark still stands; not the original, and now the Koca Mustafa Mosque. Very simple and small—just over fifty feet long, it is a cross in square without galleries, and with three apses at the east end. Much altered and repaired throughout the centuries, the shallow dome, roof, and cornices date from Turkish times.

The Church of the Virgin soon became a centre of pilgrimage for the court, and Anastasius was the first to build a palace there. At this date quite modest, it later grew until by the middle of the twelfth century the Palace of Blachernae was the principal residence of the Emperor—the old palace by Santa Sophia being almost abandoned.

Among the imperial guard in Constantinople was a Dacian peasant, whose nephew was destined to be Byzantium's greatest Emperor, and give the city its most wonderful building, Santa Sophia. With two others, three young shepherds set out for the capital from their village near the modern city of Sofia in Roumania. Tall and strong, they were soon enrolled in the guards of Leo I, and fifty years later Justin, the Dacian peasant, had worked his way up to the rank of senator and commander of the guards. In 518 Anastasius died, leaving no sons to succeed him. The real ruler in the palace was Amantius, a eunuch. He wanted the throne for one of his family, and gave Justin a large sum with which to encourage the guards to see things his way. Justin saw his opportunity to bribe them to support his claim—and at sixty-eight he became Justin I, Emperor of the East Romans.

Obviously he could not expect to have a loyal subject in the enraged and flabbergasted Amantius. A charge was trumped up, and he was beheaded. The law of the jungle also applied in the marble and mosaic halls of the imperial palace, and the next to be removed was Vitalian, a popular consul and general. At an imperial banquet in the presence of Justin I he was stabbed 'not thirty-two times but seventeen', and into his shoes stepped Justinian, nephew of Justin I.

Justinian was as self-seeking as his illiterate uncle, and set about buying popularity—with public funds. His term as consul, which would only last one year, cost 288,000 pieces of gold. Knowing what would appeal, he gave the charioteers really fine horses and expensive trappings. On one occasion he financed a spectacle in the Hippodrome; during which twenty lions and thirty leopards were introduced into the arena at one time.

Through the senate, who were in his pocket, the proposition was put to his old uncle that Justinian should become his co-Emperor. Justin was not enthusiastic, but when he realized time was treading on his heels he agreed: 'The life of Justin was prolonged about four months, but from the instant of this ceremony he was considered dead to the Empire which acknowledged Justinian, in the forty-eighth year of his age, for the lawful sovereign of the East.' (Gibbon.)

Chapter 7

527–565

The Emperor Justinian I and the Empress Theodora. The background of the Empress. Her marriage to Justinian. Their appearance. Her conduct as Empress. Justinian's character.

A.D. 527 was momentous for Constantinople and the Empire, Justinian was now Emperor, together with his wife Theodora. It could with truth be said that the most glittering throne in the world was open to all comers. Justinian was the nephew of a Macedonian shepherd, while Theodora was—literally—the prostitute daughter of the keeper of the wild animals at the Hippodrome.

It was off the shores of Cyprus that Aphrodite was born out of the waves—and it was from Cyprus that Theodora's people came. The goddess would have been proud of her fellow-islander. In the time of the old Emperor Anastasius the Cypriot Acacius was paid by the Green faction to look after the wild animals at the Hippodrome: bears for fighting, etc. He died, and instead of choosing a man suggested by his widow, who had hoped to marry him, someone else received the job, and she and her three small daughters were left destitute. In desperation the widow decided to appeal to the compassion of the crowd. During a festival the three girls, the oldest only seven, were sent into the arena dressed in suppliant's clothes. Catcalls and derision came from the left side—from the Greens who once had employed their father. Such sympathy as there was came from the Blues, on the right side. The memory of that day, with its humiliations and rebuffs, must have burnt deep into the little girl's mind: when Empress, Theodora always showed favour to the Blue faction at the expense of the Greens.

There was nothing for it, when older the three girls went on the stage, with all that could and did imply. In Constantinople there was no serious theatre as the Athenians would have known it, only farce of the crudest kind and revues that were more than suggestive. Women and children were not admitted. Erotic songs and 'artistic' dances by troupes of girls wearing only the thinnest of gauze drapery was the fare offered to the tired businessman. Since women and children were forbidden there was nothing to inhibit the actors and actresses: indeed the latter were synonymous with prostitutes, and no one above the rank of clarissimus (a grade of nobility) was allowed to marry a theatre girl.

Dancing was not Theodora's chief attraction; she was a natural comedienne in slap-stick farce: complaining with dramatic gestures and a fatuous voice about her hard life and blowing what can only be described as raspberries were two of her histrionic specialities. Another, which no doubt appealed greatly to her audience, consisted of lying down, covered only by flimsy drapery over which corn was scattered: then several hungry geese were let loose on the stage.

From time to time the church tried to get Sunday shows banned, and if any bishop was reported as having been present at such a performance he could expect to be deposed, and spend at least three years in a monastery as a simple monk. Hardly surprising.

Even in Constantinople, which had and deserved something of its Babylonian reputation, Theodora was notorious. Many men wishing to avoid scandal would cross to the other side of the street rather than risk being greeted by her. As Gibbon expressed it in a footnote: 'At a memorable supper, thirty slaves waited round the table: ten young men feasted with Theodora. Her charity was *universal*.'

To the relief of many she left the city, with one Ecebolus, who however abandoned her in Alexandria. While in Egypt she was careless enough to have a son, who was brought up in Arabia. Years later when she was Empress he learnt who his mother really was, and set off for Constantinople. In the imperial palace he was ushered into her presence, said who he was—and was never seen again.

When she returned to the capital from Egypt she was a changed woman. It really does seem as though she had some foreknowledge of her extraordinary destiny. She gave up prostitution and took to spinning wool, and living most respectably in a small house, on the site of which she later ordered a church to be built.

In due course Theodora attracted the attention of Justinian, ruling in the name of his uncle. Already he was middle-aged, of average height, round-faced, going bald, clean-shaven but with a suggestion of five o'clock shadow. In modern clothes he would look like a typical Greek businessman to be seen enjoying the cool of an Athenian summer evening at one of the outdoor cafés in Constitution Square.

Before long the future Emperor wished to make her his wife, but was barred by the law which forbade anyone above the rank of clarissimus to marry an actress. There was only one thing to do: change the law, which he did in the face of bitter family opposition—leaving the way open for a glorious repentance for actresses who could now marry into the best families.

When the time came for their coronation, in the palace, she too received a diadem from the hands of the patriarch. Her rank was nearly equal to that of Justinian; her throne certainly was, and oaths of allegiance were taken to both of them. She even demanded that she should be called 'Mistress', implying that the people were her personal slaves.

In appearance she was below average height, not beautiful, with big eyes and a large nose that probably became fleshy as she grew older. In an attempt to preserve her looks she spent many hours, both day and night, on her couch in the palace on the Asian shore which she preferred to the imperial palace in the city itself.

Her behaviour was autocratic and thoroughly ill-bred. Important people were kept waiting in a stuffy ante-chamber, and when they were allowed to kiss the imperial shoe, they did not know whether they would be received with remote arrogance or flippancy: possibly a light kick in the teeth. So it is said, she even had her own dungeons beneath the palace, where those who fell foul of her could be flogged or racked under the supervision of a terrible woman gaoler. If Theodora wanted someone removed from this life she would send her assassins about their business with the words: 'If you fail in the execution of my commands, I swear by him who liveth for ever, that your skin shall be flayed from your body.'

While in Egypt Theodora came to sympathize with the Monophysites, the heretics who believed that Christ had only one nature, a divine one—with the result that orthodox churchmen regarded her as tainted with false dogma. Good works now interested her, and she converted an old palace on the Asian side of the Bosphorus into a home for fallen women, five hundred of whom were deported thence from the streets and brothels of Constantinople. However, some were sufficiently ungrateful as to throw themselves over the wall into the sea rather than have good done to them by their august sister-under-the-skin.

In A.D. 549 this extraordinary woman died, killed by cancer.

Justinian, who was to give Constantinople three buildings which are among the most remarkable of its possessions, was the exact opposite of Theodora. He lived simply, slept little, was not promiscuous, and as a man could be easy-going, affable, patient—or a raging despot. Like a number of earlier and later emperors he never led his army into battle, not even from behind, like the celebrated, cultivated, underrated Duke of Plaza Toro. But in fairness, in Belisarius he had a superb general to win his wars.

Chapter 8

527–565 *(continued)*

SS. Sergius and Bacchus (527). The Nika Riots (532) between the two Circus factions of the Greens and the Blues. Santa Sophia burnt. Green faction massacred in the Hippodrome.

At least as far as the city of Constantinople is concerned, Justinian began his reign with an act of thanksgiving—the building of the enchanting little church of SS. Sergius and Bacchus. When he was no more than an obscure army officer—in the time of Anastasius—he was sentenced to death for his supposed part in a treason plot, and in a dream the two saints, Sergius and Bacchus (themselves Roman army officers who were martyred in the reign of Maximanus), appealed to the old Emperor to spare Justinian's life, which he did.

The church once stood just beyond the wall that enclosed the imperial palace, today separated from the Walls of Constantine and the Sea of Marmara by the railway line. With its shallow dome and minaret, the latter an addition after the Turkish Conquest of 1453, it is a most exotic-looking little building (page 148). The foundations were laid in A.D. 527, the year Justinian came to the throne, and completed before 536. Originally it was joined to the church of the Apostles Peter and Paul, a basilica which has quite vanished.

After the year 547 the custom seems to have started of placing the twin churches at the disposal of the Latin clergy in the city. The most famous churchman from the west who came to celebrate Mass would have been Gregory the Great, when he

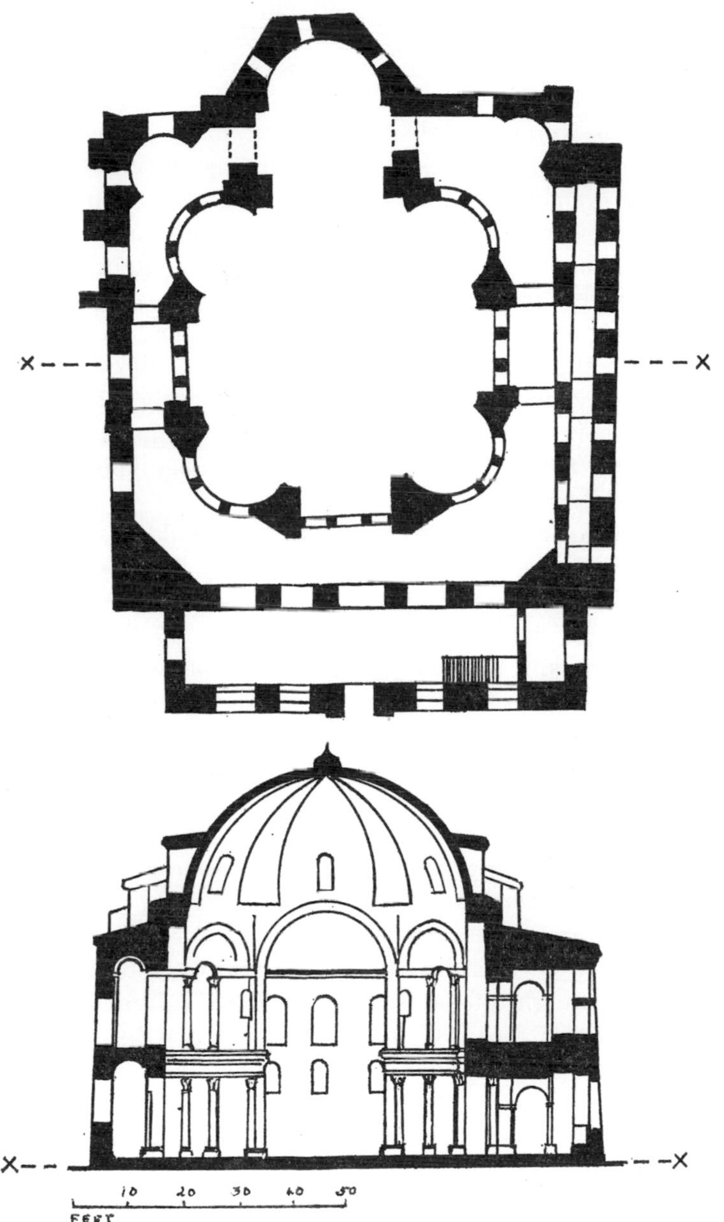

SS. Sergius and Bacchus A.D. 527–536 Küçük Aya Sophia Mosque

was Papal Nuncio. In 597 he sent St Augustine to England to begin his missionary work.

The massive outer walls of the church make a most irregular rectangle which encloses a dome standing on eight piers. In front stood an atrium, long since in ruins, and in Turkish times alterations were made when it was turned into a mosque. The structural inaccuracy which is to be found in a number of Byzantine churches, particularly in Constantinople, is most marked here. None of the outer walls is at right angles, the apse is not exactly in the centre, while the dome is fifty three and a half feet one way, and only fifty and a half feet another. But when in the church itself the structural defects pass almost unnoticed: there is so much to delight the eye: whether knowledgeable about architecture or not.

SS. Sergius and Bacchus is one of those buildings that by its proportions give an impression of being far larger than it actually is. The central space is all-important: octagonal, and covered by a dome of sixteen compartments. Constructed of light materials, it also looks light, almost buoyant, rising from directly over the arches, there is (inside) no drum, the eight windows curving with the surface of the dome. Though nearly semi-circular in section, because of the way the outside walls of the octagon are built up to form a drum supported by large buttresses, the dome with its melon-like ribs is quite shallow. The angles of the octagon are formed into exedrae—semi-circular bays with columns. The church is in two storeys, the upper part round the large open space of the dome forming the gallery which was usually used by the women. Between the eight piers taking the weight of the dome are pairs of columns, except in the archway of the apse: two above and two below, making twenty-eight in all. They and the entablature are the most beautiful feature of SS. Sergius and Bacchus. The carving makes a whole chapter in the history of Byzantine sculpture. The capitals of the lower order are the melon variety: that is with pronounced ribs, and covered with abstract and floral design—including vine leaves, with the monogram of Justinian and Theodora, quite deeply and crisply cut. Above comes the entablature: a most elaborately carved piece of work with dentils, egg-and-dart ornament and acanthus leaves, as well as a long inscription (in Roman lettering: a few centuries later and it would be in Greek) to the royal couple.

'Other sovereigns, indeed, have honoured dead men whose labour was useless. But our sceptred Justinian, fostering piety, honours with a splendid abode the servant of Christ, Creator of all things, Sergius; whom nor the burning breath of fire, nor the sword, nor other constraints of trials disturbed; but who endured for the sake of God Christ to be slain, gaining by his blood heaven as his home. May he in all things guard the rule of the ever-vigilant sovereign, and increase the power of the God-crowned Theodora whose mind is bright with piety, whose toil ever is unsparing efforts to nourish the destitute.'

Above, two more columns support small round-headed arches, with capitals showing their Ionic origins, together with a design of acanthus leaves—though the result is nothing remotely like a composite capital as Vitrivius or Wren would have known it (page 37). They are in fact cushion capitals: that is, comparatively narrow below where they meet the top of the column itself, but becoming much wider above to support the masonry of the archway itself. In other parts of the Empire, to the west, including Ravenna and Thessalonika, a large slab of stone called a pulvino or dosseret was inserted to help spread the weight and reduce the risk of the capital splitting: but it does not seem to have been used in Constantinople itself. A year before the church was begun in the capital the eight-sided church of San Vitale at Ravenna was erected (526), possibly by the same architect, which has had the good fortune to retain all its wonderful mosaics. In SS. Sergius and Bacchus the last of the mosaics disappeared about one hundred years ago.

A detail that could be taken as representing the change from Roman architecture to one that is specifically Christian can be read into the arcades between the piers. Below, the columns support a flat classical architrave, while above they support round arches.

The little church is beautiful, as well as being important architecturally—and the two do not always go together—for by uniting a domed church such as this with a basilica like St

John of Studion the architect arrived at Santa Sophia, a domed basilica.

Once a year the imperial couple used to come to the church, going up to the gallery normally used by women. First the Emperor would light tapers, opposite the altar, then go to pray in the chapel of the Virgin and lastly take part in the service from one of the exedra on either side of the apse. After receiving the Sacrament he and the Empress were served with light refreshments, still in the gallery, before they returned up the hill to the palace.

Today, like nearly all the other Byzantine churches in the city, it is a mosque. The Turkish alterations are slight, apart from the minaret and the portico in front of the narthex, which with its arcade of columns supporting pointed arches is charming. The praying area beneath the dome is raised about ten inches by a boarded floor which hides the bases of the columns. Traces of rain have stained the plaster work in the eastern exedrae and part of the dome, where a few feet of one of the ribs have come away, and some cracks are noticeable; though to the west, judging by the smooth surface and new whitewash they have been recently dealt with.

In the reign of Anastasius and Zeno there had been trouble caused by the Greens and the Blues: riots and killings. But they were to be nothing compared with the clash between the factions of the Hippodrome which came about in 532. The whole city was divided into two camps, no less violently opposed to each other than the Royalists and Parliamentarians in seventeenth century England. The Greens were out of favour—largely because of the way they had humiliated and rebuffed Theodora when she and her sisters had been sent into the arena that day years before to seek their charity. For their part the Blues, sure of themselves in Justinian's favour, became completely out of hand. Their supporters even had their own form of dress, wore their hair long like the dreaded Huns, and spoke in loud and deep voices. By night they roamed the streets in bands, brawling with their rivals, murdering 'and it was the boast of assassins, that their dexterity could always inflict a mortal wound with a single stroke of a dagger'. Because of their power in the city, and throughout the Empire, for the plague was not confined to Constantinople, justice seldom if ever caught up with them. One prefect who tried to punish several of the Blues had to flee to the Holy Sepulchre itself in Jerusalem for sanctuary, while a governor of Cililia (southern Turkey), who condemned and had executed two of that faction after they murdered his groom and attempted his assassination, was himself hanged on their grave—by order of Theodora.

And yet it is to these two murderous factions that the world owes one of its greatest glories, the cathedral of Santa Sophia.

In 532 Justinian attended the races in the Hippodrome to celebrate the Ides of January. From the start there was continuous barracking from the Greens, which Justinian ignored until the twenty-second race; then through a crier he answered them. While wishing the Emperor long life and victory, the Greens complained about the oppressive behaviour of some of his ministers. 'Be patient and attentive, you insolent railers!' cried Justinian's mouthpiece. 'Be quiet, you Jews, Samaritans, and Manicheans!' But the Greens would not be quiet, and the slanging match between the Emperor and a section of his subjects continued. The Greens called out how they dare not walk through the streets, and in general were thoroughly persecuted. Justinian continued to abuse them until the point came when they renounced their allegiance, regretting that his father had ever been born, called him a murderer, an ass, and a lying tyrant.

'Do you despise your lives?' asked Justinian, and the Blues rose up threateningly in their seats. The Greens also got up, and fled. Just then seven assassins from both factions were being paraded through the city as a warning to others before being taken to Galata to be hanged. There five were executed, but the last two escaped when the rope broke, and some interfering monks from the Monastery of St Conon gave them sanctuary. Since one man was a Blue and the other a Green the two factions called a truce, until the couple had been restored to their own parties. The palace of the prefect who had ordered the hangings was burnt and his officers and guards massacred. The prisons were burst open and the rioters' numbers swelled with the dregs of the city. At the head of the rioters were priests with holy relics. They were manhandled by the heruli, near-barbarians in the imperial army—and the issue became a religious one. Women on the roof-tops threw stones down at the soldiers, who retaliated by setting fire to the houses.

The flames swept through the narrow streets, involving the timber-roofed Santa Sophia, part of the palace including the long portico opening onto the Forum of Augustus, Sampson's Hospital for incurables—together with its wretched inmates (it stood between Santa Sophia and St Irene), many public and private buildings, among them the baths of Zeuxippus: what bronzes and marbles must have been destroyed.

As the heart of the city blazed both the factions kept calling 'Nika, Nika!' Victory, Victory! from which the riots took their name. Law and order had quite broken down. As many as possible of the well-to-do fled over the Bosphorus to the Asian shore, to look back on the pall of smoke hanging over the city, and for five days Constantinople was given over to the rioting factions, forever calling 'Nika!'

From Justinian's point of view, in the past the rivalry of the two factions had the effect of diverting attention from himself, and in particular his extortionate Finance Minister, John of Cappadocia. When the city was in flames he was removed from office and Justinian himself went to the Hippodrome to confess his own errors of judgement, and accept the repentance of his subjects. However his subjects were feeling far from humble, and loudly doubted the sincerity of his gospel-sworn oaths. He retreated up the winding corridor and private staircase from the Hippodrome back into the palace.

Now there was the suspicion that the Greens were supported by two nephews of the former Emperor Anastasius. During the five days of rioting Justinian held them, Hypatius and Pompey, as hostages. Then, fearing they might assassinate him, he ordered them back to their palaces. On the morning of the sixth day Hypatius was taken by the mob to the Forum of Constantine where an elaborately jewelled collar, in lieu of a diadem, was forced on him.

Neither Justinian nor his General Belisarius knew what to

do, and it was Theodora, that woman of the people, who saved the Thirteenth Apostle when he could not save himself. She made a magnificent speech, worthy of a greater and better sovereign: 'If flight were the only means of safety, yet I should disdain to fly. Death is the condition of our birth; but they who have reigned should never survive the loss of dignity and dominion. I implore Heaven, that I may never be seen, not a day, without my diadem and purple; that I may no longer behold the light, when I cease to be saluted with the name of queen. If you should resolve, O Caesar! to fly, you have treasures; behold the sea, you have ships; but tremble lest the desire of life, should expose you to wretched exile and ignominious death. For my own part, I adhere to the maxim of antiquity, that the throne is a glorious sepulchre.'

Soon enough the Blues began to repent their alliance with the Greens, leaving the latter alone and uneasy in the Hippodrome with their newly proclaimed Emperor, Hypatius. Three thousand of Justinian's veteran troops marched quietly out of the palace, which overlooked the whole of the south-east side of the Hippodrome. At a pre-arranged signal they burst open the gates at either end on that side and streamed in. That day, it is said, thirty thousand of the Green factions were slaughtered in the arena and on the tiers of seats.

Hypatius and Pompey were dragged before Justinian, and together with eighteen patrician so-called accomplices, were privately executed by the imperial guards. Now the Nika Riots, like the fire itself, had burnt out, and came the huge task of making good. Santa Sophia, and the adjoining church of St Irene, stood in ruins. It was a magnificent opportunity to give the city a cathedral worthy of it, and whatever the Emperor's other failings, he proved himself worthy of his name—Justinian the Builder.

Chapter 9

532–537

The building of Santa Sophia. Description of the building by contemporaries. Its appearance and architecture. Damage by earthquakes. Materials used from older buildings. The Sweating Column. Mosaics. The clergy. Services. The fittings.

There are so many things about Santa Sophia that are amazing: not least that after 1,425 years it still stands, despite earthquake, fire, revolutions, wars, a change of religion, and the heavy passage of time.

Justinian claimed the idea for the cathedral came to him from an angel. In reality it was designed by two Greek architects, Isidorius of Miletus and Anthemius of Tralles, and according to the historian, Procopius, the plan was ready in thirty-three days. Anthemius was one of five talented brothers from Tralles (south-east of Izmir), whose fame reached the Emperor's ears, and who ordered him to come to Constantinople. Brilliant architect that he was, as a man he must have been most objectionable. When he fell out with his next-door neighbour over walls and windows, he invented a primitive form of pump which forced steam through leather tubes into the adjoining roof. It rumbled and the ceilings shook so that his neighbours thought it was an earthquake. On another occasion he annoyed them by flashing dazzling mirrors at them as they sat at table.

Justinian commanded, and his subjects obeyed. Marbles were brought from all parts of the Empire, and nearer home, in the city itself even the lead conduits were broken up to make the coverings for the domes. Taxes were imposed, and according to the historian Zonaras even the schools were closed, the teachers receiving no wages and dying of hunger. Justinian laid the foundation stone, and for five years, eleven months and ten days 10,000 men worked unceasingly to complete the building. Every day the Emperor came, dressed in a simple linen tunic, to supervise the work. Over a thousand years later the young Sultan Ahmet I would do exactly the same when building his mosque which today stands on the site of part of the imperial palace, across the square from Santa Sophia.

The foundations rest on a bed of concrete twenty feet deep, the walls are of brick, while the huge piers which support the dome are of blocks of limestone, apparently fixed together not only with iron ties, but also with molten lead poured between to act as a cement. The columns are of marble and the whole of the interior was covered with marble revetments and gold mosaic. For the dome and semi-domes light-weight bricks were made in Rhodes, twelve of them weighing only as much as one ordinary specimen. Each was stamped with the words: 'God founded this work and God will come to its aid.' Faith as well as cement was used in its construction; every twelve courses relics were inserted: preferable to the heretics who were walled up during the construction of the fortress-cathedral of Albi in southern-central France.

Then on December 26, 537, while its dedication to the Divine Wisdom was taking place, Justinian exulted: 'Glory to God who has judged me worthy to accomplish this work; I have surpassed you, Solomon!' Justinian had wanted to give his city 'the most magnificent church since the Creation,' and in so doing he had eclipsed Solomon's Temple.

The writers of the day were driven to poetic parallels to describe the interior. The groups of columns in the exedrae were likened by Procopius to 'dancers in a chorus', and by Paul the Silentiary to 'well-greaved warriors from Thebes'. Procopius considered it beyond his powers to describe, and then proceeded to do so. Theophile Gautier likened Seville Cathedral rising above that city to an elephant among a flock of recumbent sheep; Procopius had his own simile for Santa Sophia: 'It rises almost to the skies and dominates the surrounding edifices as a warship dominates the waves. The dome is as though suspended from Heaven by chains of gold.'

Brooding, massive, and weighed down by the huge buttresses added through the centuries, the sense of relentless grandeur is not altogether offset by the minarets added after the Turkish Conquest of 1453. Magnificent, but until the eye reaches up to the semi-domes and the great dome, now surmounted by a glittering crescent, not exactly beautiful in the accepted sense of the word. Fascinating and exciting to look at, the building seems as though poised on the razor edge between ugliness and beauty. But framed between the leaves of the plane trees, and against a background of blue sky and slowly moving clouds, the lead covered domes of both cathedral and the türbe—imperial tombs—of the Sultans and their families which nestle against the south side, it can look indescribably romantic. Everything that the words Constantinople or Istanbul can conjure up in the mind's eye.

Structurally the cathedral *is* unique in Byzantine architecture; and it was not until after the Turkish Conquest that it was copied in their mosques both in Constantinople and in Cairo. It is the perfect fusion of the basilica and the domed church, and for the first time on a large scale pendentives were used to convert the square central area into a circle to support the dome. These pendentives consist of curving masonry (forming part of the surface of a sphere) approximately triangular in shape. Those in Santa Sophia must overhang by at least twenty feet, and are more than sixty feet from top to bottom: higher than the dome, which is only fifty feet high.

The ground plan—without the accretions of buttresses added to prevent the whole structure from foundering—is nearly square: 253 feet by 234 feet. To the west stood a large atrium, now destroyed, which contained an ablutions fountain: carved on it was the inscription, 'Wash your sins and not only your face' which, in Greek, forms a palindrome. This atrium joined an inner and an outer narthex, which still stand. Both these structures are of nine bays with cross vaulting: the outer being of one story only while the inner has a large gallery which connects the

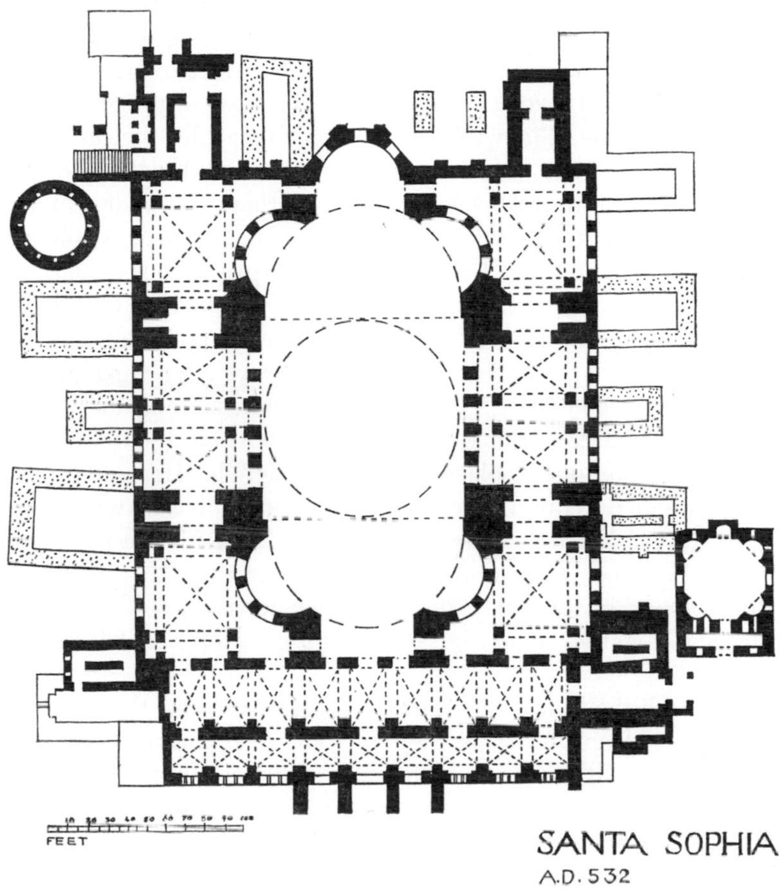

gynecaeum—women's galleries—over the north and south aisles of the church itself. The outer narthex has three doorways, no longer used, and is whitewashed: all the mosaics have vanished. Today the entrance is by the south porch, leading into the inner narthex. Almost fifty feet long, it retains the mosaic-work on the vaulting: abstract and floral designs in blues and greens on a gold ground, while above the inner door is the mosaic, which must date from after the Iconoclastic Controversy which ended in 842 (probably late tenth or early eleventh century), of the Virgin and Child, with Constantine on her right offering his city, and on her left Justinian offering his church. Austere and grand, it is a fitting introduction to Santa Sophia and Byzantine art itself. The inner narthex is two hundred feet long, twenty-six feet wide and forty-two feet high, a foretaste of the grandeur and size to come. The walls are lined with marble: the care and accuracy to cut the sheets without cracking or breaking must have been infinite. Above, on the vaulting, there are more mosaics similar to those in the south porch. The greens, blues, and golds a cool delight to the eye. Nine great doors—dating from after the crusaders looted and almost wrecked the cathedral in 1204—lead into the nave: so big they seem more suitable for giants. With flat lintels (as all the doorways have throughout the building) and frames that batter slightly, making the openings a little narrower at the top than the bottom, the doorways would not look out of place in a Roman temple. Here as in SS. Sergius and Bacchus the architecture looks both backward and forward. Plain black crosses on a gold ground fill the heads of the arches over the doorways: while in the centre over the Royal Door is the early tenth century mosaic of Christ Enthroned, together with the suppliant figure of Leo VI (page 85).

Through the Royal Door which must have seen the coming and going of seventy-three emperors and also empresses ruling in their own right, the immenseness of Santa Sophia is visible at one glance: an uninterrupted space 253 feet long by 101 feet wide. At either end a semi-dome and in the centre the cupola, itself with a diameter of 101 feet (Bannister Fletcher gives it as 107 feet), with its key almost floating 180 feet above the marble pavement. If the whole of the centre dome was omitted and you joined the two semi-domes together you would have a church exactly like a larger edition of SS. Sergius and Bacchus, complete with exedrae.

In Santa Sophia the weight of the dome is borne on the four great piers at the angles of the central space, the thrust being transmitted to them by the great pendentives already mentioned. To the east and west the thrust is also taken by the semi-domes which form a continuation of the arches. North and south the weight is taken on the semi-circular arches, fifteen

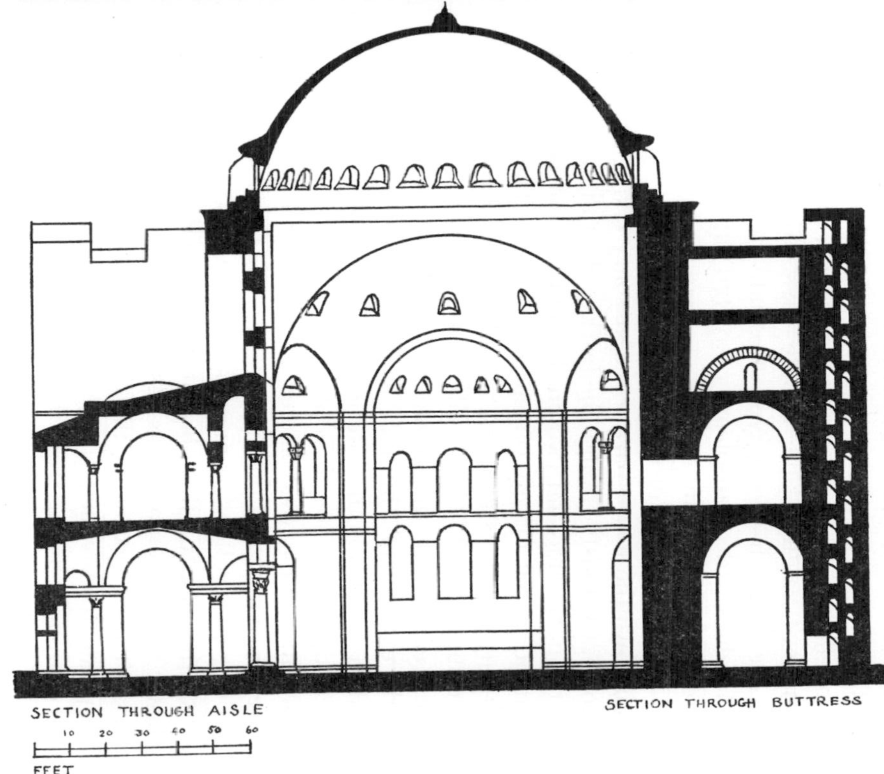

Santa Sophia. Section through nave, looking east

feet thick, which form part of the upper side walls, and are visible on the exterior. The great buttresses, north and south, give additional support to the four piers which carry the weight of the dome. Their east-west walls are between four and seven feet thick. Since these massive abutments are pierced with openings at floor level and also for the galleries above, it converts them, in effect, into vast flying buttresses. The aisles and galleries have vaulting, the middle bays cross-vaults, while those in the angles have the type of pseudo-dome vault used in Galla Placidia's little mausoleum (A.D. 420) at Ravenna. After the earthquake of 558 the excessively massive buttresses were built up above the level of the galleries, enclosing stair turrets, to weigh down the lower part of the masonry taking the thrust of the dome. Curiously enough the brickwork of these additions, two on the north side and two on the south, is not bonded into the main fabric, but merely cemented against it. They were the first of many additions made to Santa Sophia which were structurally to support and aesthetically to weigh down the exterior.

At this early date the Byzantine architect still seemed to regard the exterior of a building as little more than an unnecessary evil: a casing for the interior. At first the brickwork was left exposed, though now it is plastered over. In the middle of the last century this was painted in red-and-white stripes to simulate the courses of stone and brick, while today it is colour-washed egg yolk yellow. It must be admitted that a dull day is kinder to the exterior than bright sunshine. Perhaps one day the plaster will be removed, as has been done on the adjoining church of St Irene, exposing the warm brickwork.

The pendentives which support the dome each have a six-winged cherubim; dating from the time of Basil II (976–1025). Because of their celestial nature they have no legs and, since Turkish times, no faces either: those are covered with gilded discs. Islam forbids the portrayal of the human form (though outside the religious sphere the ruling was more honoured in the breach than the observance), and it was believed that the craftsman would have to spend all eternity trying to animate his creation. This applied even to the animal kingdom. The lions supporting the fountain in the Court of Lions in the

Santa Sophia, A.D. 532–537. Minarets added by the Turks after 1453
Santa Sophia, west front

Santa Sophia. The interior looking south-east. It is in the gallery over the south aisle (originally the Gynecaeum, for women only) that a magnificent series of mosaics, including Imperial portraits, is being brought to light from beneath plaster with which they were covered by the Ottoman Turks. The four columns which support the gallery are some of those brought from the Temple of Diana at Ephesus. The circular marble paving (enclosed by a wooden railing) marks the site on which the Emperors were crowned

Alhambra in Granada are almost abstract, to avoid trouble in the hereafter.

Above the pendentives floats the dome, the effect of lightness being enhanced by its shallowness: only 50 feet. Forty small windows ring its base, and these are separated by as many ribs. The special light-weight bricks are 27 inches square at the bottom, diminishing to 24 inches square at the top, and only two inches deep. The cement between was of the same thickness. The whole dome itself is only two feet thick, and covered on the outside with lead. Within, the mosaic of Christ in the centre has long since vanished, to be replaced with painted plaster. In the catastrophe of 558 part of the dome was brought down, the remainder hanging perilously, while part of the eastern semi-dome also collapsed. Justinian was still alive, and Isidorius, nephew of the architect of that name who helped design the building, advised that the cupola should be made twenty to twenty-five feet higher: the steeper curve would make it more resistant to such shocks.

In 975 a further earthquake severely damaged the western semi-dome and arch, which took six years to rebuild: as long as the whole cathedral itself took to erect. Then in 1346, during the civil war, and at a time when the Empire was nearly bankrupt, the eastern semi-dome and arch fell. It too took six years to rebuild. But only just over a century and a quarter later in 1475 the Turks had to rebuild it. In a city with at least thirty-six major earthquakes between A.D. 366 and 1894 it is remarkable the damage is not worse. Like St Peter's, Rome, and St Paul's, London, the dome of Santa Sophia has an iron chain about its base, inserted in 1847 by the architects Fossati, two Italian brothers called in by the Sultan to advise, and supervise, very necessary repairs.

Throughout the building all the windows are round-headed, for the most part filled with plain glass. Black and white photographs do little justice to the interior: invariably they make the great nave appear too dark. To the top of the galleries the overall impression is of a smoky grey, while above, the plaster-covered curving surfaces of the arches, dome and semi-domes are golden-yellow. Once gold mosaic would have been used. Up to the springing of the vaulting, the walls are completely covered with sheets of marble, cut thin and set side by side so the veining matches, in frames which are carved.

The north and south walls of the nave have magnificent colonnades: four columns on each side at floor level and six in the gallery above. As already mentioned, materials were brought from all over the Empire. The temples of the classic world were rifled for the Glory of God and of Justinian.

The columns on either side of the nave are of verd-antique (green brecchia), and came from no less than the Temple of Diana at Ephesus—one of the true wonders of the ancient world. Perhaps they looked down on St Paul when he came to preach in that city and infuriated the inhabitants who rioted, crying: 'Great is Diana of the Ephesians!' Then in the four exedrae, on plan opening out of the semi-domes, the eight porphyry columns —dusty purple in colour—came originally from the temple of Jupiter Heliopolitan at Ba'albek, though after Aurelian defeated Queen Zenobia they were taken to Rome. Aurelian himself came to a sad end: murdered by his entourage, quite near Byzantium, whilst on a campaign against the Persians.

Other temples, famous in pre-Christian times, were made to give up their columns: from Delos—that island so sacred to Apollo that none were allowed to be born or to die on it: from Cyzacus (Erdek), a once great city on the southern side of the Sea of Marmara, and even from the temple of Pallas Athene in Athens.

The remaining columns in the aisles of Santa Sophia are of Egyptian granite: twelve on each side, making forty columns in all on the ground floor. There are said to be one hundred and seven in the whole church. Perhaps as beautiful in their way as the mosaics are the capitals of these columns. Melon, wind-blown acanthus, Byzantine Corinthian, cushion capitals: nearly all types are represented. All are exquisitely carved, and many have that peculiar form of decoration, drilling, which the Byzantine craftsman carried almost to excess. For example, the surface of a capital decorated with acanthus leaves is drilled with small holes, an eighth or a quarter of an inch across. When seen close to—there are a number of capitals lying on the ground in the Mosaics Museum (page 84)—it can look fussy and mannered, but when seen as the sculptor intended, perhaps twenty feet up on top of a column it is most effective, adding to the richness of the scheme. Another form of decoration for capitals was to carve the surface with a design like woven basketwork.

Most magnificent of all are the eight identical capitals, four on either side of the nave, with the monogram of Justinian and Theodora. A distant echo of the composite order, they have Ionic volutes and acanthus leaves, which instead of standing upright are as though blown sideways by wind. Above them the flat surfaces of the spandrils between the arches are covered with an abstract tendril-like decoration: shallow carving of a design that must surely have come from the Sassanid Persians, just beyond the Empire's eastern frontier. Looking at those great arcades at close quarters, with their fascinating and unfamiliar sculpture, they seem an epitome of this massive and glittering and yet almost alien Christian civilization that was Byzantium.

To the faithful, both Christian and Moslem, the pier in the north-west angle of the north aisle has special qualities: the Sweating Column of St Gregory. For most of its height it is covered with sheets of bronze, but in the middle of one side is a hole, and behind a cavity in the stonework as deep as the second knuckle-joint, worn by millions of fingers placed there through more than fifteen centuries. One day when Justinian was afflicted with a splitting headache, so the story goes, he paused and rested his head against the cool surface of the column, and the pain vanished. Because it is porous, and therefore damp, it acquired its name. The damper it feels to the touch, the better your character. Also, it is supposed to help in the cure of eye diseases, and the hopeful still come to it, such as an elderly Turkish woman putting her fingers first in the cavity and then onto her eyelids.

The exedrae, each nearly as big as the central apse, have two columns below and six smaller ones in the gallery above, which apart from the increased number of columns looking down into the body of the church is identical on plan with the aisles below. These large galleries formed the Gynecaeum, for women only, where they were quite separated from the men in the nave below. It was in the south gallery not so many years ago that a whole series of mosaics came to light beneath the plaster with which they were covered by the Turks after converting Santa Sophia into a mosque. In fact work on them is still in progress, and unfortunately both galleries, north and south, are closed to the public. Among the mosaics there are Christ with St John and the Virgin, damaged but most beautiful (late thirteenth century), and ex-votos; portraits of various sovereigns presenting gifts to Christ and the Virgin, including Constantine IX Monomarchus and the Empress Zoë; between them an impressive figure of Christ—the face reminiscent of the celebrated Christ Pantokrator in the dome of the convent church at Daphne, outside Athens, though the latter must be some forty years later in date than the one in Santa Sophia (between 1028 and 1050). Another is of John II and his wife St Irene, and a son, Alexis (page 171), between the Virgin and Child. Superb quality colour photographs of these mosaics, and many others in Istanbul, can be found in the lavishly illustrated *Byzantine Painting*. (See bibliography.)

Recently uncovered mosaics that can be seen from the body of the church include the Virgin and Child, the robe a brilliant blue, in the semi-dome of the apse: though originally dating from the ninth century, it was largely restored in the fourteenth. The face of the Virgin has a humanity of expression not found before the twelfth and thirteenth centuries: the golden age of mosaics in the city. High up on the north wall beneath the dome three full-length portraits of saints have been restored to the light of day, Ignatius Theophorus, St John Chrysostom, and St Ignatius the Younger. Though about eighty feet up (glasses are almost a necessity), even at that distance it is possible to make out the fine features of St John Chrysostom with his burning eyes and high forehead.

Of all forms of Christian art, the true Byzantine mosaic is the most remote and timeless, completely in harmony with the mystical nature of the Orthodox Church. The very dedication of Santa Sophia and St Irene, the one to the Divine Wisdom and the other to the Divine Peace, demonstrates at a superficial level this mystical approach. Distance is a handicap to the spectator: it is difficult to contemplate a mosaic such as the Virgin and Child in the apse, at least one hundred and fifty feet away from the spectator, in the same way that one can regard an icon in the Byzantine Museum in Athens, or an ivory in the Victoria and Albert Museum in London. The very distance makes it impossible to look at the object, and the object alone, to the exclusion of all else. Surely it is by looking at and returning to colour photographs such as those just mentioned, that these mosaics can best cast their spell. The nearest parallel in another sphere is perhaps the last movement of Stravinsky's Symphony of Psalms: austere and yet supremely beautiful.

It is in the aisles that the spirit of Byzantium still seems to linger. To a large degree the great vestibules, corridors and chambers of the palace shared this architecture, its oppressive magnificence a fitting setting for the Court, and also an architecture made for conspirators and violent, cruel happenings.

One of the loveliest views in the whole one-time cathedral is through the south door of the inner-narthex into the south aisle, when the brilliant mid-day sun catches the gold mosaic of the vaulting, making it stand out—a glittering many-faceted sheen—above the capitals and columns that support the massive sweep of the groins and arches. Then, another time, in the late afternoon of early autumn, the lengthening shadows make it seem almost a different building. Fewer people about, the vast nave almost empty. The aisles dark and brooding, the light coming weaker now, filtered through the columns of the gallery over the south side. It was up there, in the south-east exedra, adjoining the apse, that Theodora with her attendant women used to participate in the services. Impassive faced, robed in purple and glittering with jewels that must have flashed at every slightest movement, she could look down into the nave where her husband was seated on his throne of gold.

The patriarch, ten bishops, eight hundred priests, a choir of one hundred castrati, two hundred choirboys and even one hundred women—most unusual. For accompaniment an orchestra of harps, mandolins, zithers, cymbals, drums, and tambourines played by three hundred musicians in red silk. The whole church ablaze with lamps and candles. The iconostasis (screen) supported on gilded columns, and in the sanctuary the patriarch's chair of ebony inlaid with ivory, set next the Emperor's throne. The altar, freestanding, also of gold set with stones, and surmounted by a baldachino supported on four silver columns, topped with the cross triumphant over the globe of the world. In the apse behind the altar the semi-circular tiers of seats were occupied by the bishops: in the centre the patriarch's throne of silver inlaid with gold.

Beneath the east piers supporting the dome stood a large ambo, a pulpit from which the Gospel was read. At different times Santa Sophia possessed four: the second, described by Paul the Silentary, was circular, raised on columns and reached by two flights of stairs. It was there in full view of the congregation that after the seventh century the patriarch crowned the Emperor (page 69). Today all that remains is the inlaid marble floor which was beneath. In the bare, echoing cathedral which became a mosque and is now a museum, one is all too aware of the truth of Keats's line: 'When old age shall this generation waste.'

Soon the cathedral is left to itself, fast filling with shadows, and to its memories and to its ghosts: few of them happy.

Chapter 10

532–565

The Underground Cistern. General Belisarius and his wife Antonina. Triumphs in Constantinople to celebrate victories. The fall of Belisarius. Justinian revises the laws. Plague. Danger from the Bulgarians. Death of Justinian I.

Were it not for the fact that it is below the street, the third of Justinian's additions to Constantinople would lie almost literally in the shadow of Santa Sophia. The Greeks knew it as the Cisterna Basilica, the Underground Cistern, while the Turks call it the Yerebatan Sarayi—the Underground Palace. Possibly first built by Constantine the Great, the present structure is the work of Justinian, the date given as A.D. 532, the one in which Santa Sophia itself was begun.

If not altered out of recognition, Santa Sophia would look very different to that Emperor, could he see it now; but if he went down the steps from the street into the underground cistern, it would be exactly as he last saw it, one thousand four hundred years ago. In its way the cistern is one of the most impressive sights in all Istanbul. Three hundred and thirty-six columns, all with well carved Corinthian capitals, set in twelve rows of twenty-eight, supporting beautifully constructed vaulting. Although it could never see the light of day and would be visited by a very few people, the quality of workmanship could not be higher.

The cistern, fed by the aqueducts of Valens and of Hadrian, was not intended for everyday use, but as an emergency water supply in the time of siege. Rings of discolouration on the columns, some nearly as high up as the capitals, show the depth of the water at different times. Today there is about a metre of water, reflecting the columns, receding into utter obscurity beyond the reach of the electric light (page 149); the only sound the dripping of water percolating through the vaulting from the world above. Whichever way you look there are rows of diminishing arches and columns—like some underground Mosque of Cordova, and as large.

At much the same time that Santa Sophia was being built Justinian's general, Belisarius, was covering himself with glory—and consequently making enemies at home more dangerous than those abroad. Apparently brought up among Thracian peasants, his secretary-biographer Procopius is tellingly silent about his early years. Like Pallas Athene he would seem to have sprung fully grown, and the first we really hear of him was as a member of Justinian's bodyguard. In 533, with two successful campaigns in Persia behind him, he was chosen to direct the war in North Africa to win back the part which had fallen to the Vandals. It may have been that his appointment was influenced by his wife Antonina, who was alternately the friend and enemy of Theodora.

Herself of a foul reputation which she justified nearly to the end of her life, it was Belisarius who was the virtuous partner in the marriage. The daughter of a charioteer, Antonina, like the Empress, began life as an actress-prostitute. Twenty years older than her husband, she had several illegitimate children, of whom Photius was as old as his step-father.

The preparations for the campaign went ahead and by June, 533, the fleet was assembled at Constantinople: 500 transports of between 30 and 500 tons, with 35,000 soldiers and 5,000 horses on board: the ships manned by 22,000 sailors and escorted by 92 light galleys rowed by 2,000 of the city's strongest youths. 'The whole fleet of six hundred ships was ranged in martial pomp before the gardens of the palace. The patriarch pronounced his benediction, the Emperor signified his last commands, the general's trumpet gave the signal of departure, and every heart, according to its fears and wishes, explored with anxious curiosity the omens of misfortune and success.' (Gibbon.)

In the autumn of 534 Belisarius returned to Constantinople, having destroyed the Vandals and conquered his way along the North African coast until opposite Gibraltar. Not even a rumour spread by his enemies in the capital that he intended to become king of North Africa could spoil his triumph. The procession marched from his palace to the Hippodrome, displaying battle-trophies, armour, golden thrones, chariots of state, vases, gold, and vessels from the Temple in Jerusalem. Also in the procession were a large number of the handsomest Vandals, among them their leader, Gelimer, still in purple. Into the Hippodrome at their head marched Belisarius, to prostrate himself before Justinian and Theodora.

A vestige of Ancient Rome that had not yet vanished was the office of consul—an empty honour though, and it was bestowed on the general. The day after his triumph came a second procession: his chair was carried by Vandals while some of the loot brought back from North Africa, gold cups, etc. were thrown into the crowd. Gelimer, the one-time Vandal king probably had the best of it, being granted a large estate in Galatia where he lived out his days in comfort surrounded by his friends and relatives.

Not only was Belisarius accompanied by his wife Antonina on his North African campaigns, but also by his illegitimate step-son Photius. The latter tried to break up an affair between his mother and a youth she and her husband had adopted, by imprisoning him in a fortress in Cilicia. But he reckoned without Theodora. When Antonina returned to Constantinople, minus her lover, a surprise awaited her in the imperial palace. 'I have found', said the Empress, 'a pearl of inestimable value; it has not yet been viewed by any mortal eye; but the sight and possession of this jewel are destined for my friend.' A bedroom door was opened, and there was the young man, rescued from the Cilician fortress by the imperial eunuchs. For placing him there Photius was racked and flogged in the palace dungeons, while his mother feasted with the Empress. Twice Photius escaped from his completely dark prison to sanctuary in Santa Sophia and the Church of the Virgin (presumably the church which stood on the flat ground at the bottom of the hill below the cathedral, near the sea shore). His third attempt was successful, and he escaped to Jerusalem, where he became a monk.

Even so great a man as Belisarius was destined to fall. While campaigning against the Persians he heard a rumour of Justinian's death, and said what he really thought of him. This was carried hot-foot to Constantinople, and to the Emperor. A commission set out to seize his treasure, and his personal guards were disbanded and absorbed by the imperial army. In the capital he was received coldly by Justinian and Theodora, and with contempt by the crowd. He went to his palace and threw himself down on his bed, terrified of the future, while Antonina paced up and down and would not speak to him. Long after dark a messenger brought a letter from the Palace; not from Justinian but from Theodora. 'You cannot be ignorant how much you have deserved my displeasure. I am not insensible to the services of Antonina. To her merits and intercession I have granted your life, and permit you to retain a part of your treasures, which might be justly forfeited to the state. Let your gratitude, where it is due, be displayed, not in words, but in your future behaviour.' Belisarius was fined a huge sum, and with the rank of count, ordered to go and direct the war in Italy.

The greatness of Justinian himself was on the wane, though it was a great achievement when he ordered the laws to be brought up to date. All the imperial edicts since the time of Hadrian were gathered together in the Codex: the Digest classified the rulings of the Roman jurists—boiling down three million lines into 150,000. The Institutes consisted of a reference book for law students, while all new laws promulgated after the Codex came out were gathered together in the Novels. Roman law, as it applied to a Christian society, had been standardized.

For four months, in 542, plague raged in Constantinople. The glands were affected: in the groin, under the armpit, and under the ear. With it went black pustules, and it seems to have been a form of bubonic plague, similar to the Great Plague of 1665. Indeed Constantinople must have resembled London, with plague pits and deserted houses and streets. Justinian himself contracted it mildly, and recovered.

Then in 559 when the Bulgarians invaded Macedonia and Thrace, Constantinople was glad enough that it had Belisarius to defend it. The seventy-seven year old Justinian ordered the gold vessels in the churches such as St Mary of Blachernae to be moved into the city itself, and the inhabitants lined the walls to watch Belisarius leave; his soldiers mounted on horses commandeered not only from private citizens but even from the imperial stables.

By raising great clouds of dust by day and by lighting huge fires by night they deceived the Bulgarians into believing that their army was much larger than it really was. When the fight came the Bulgarians charged straight into two ambushes, and after losing only four hundred men, turned tail and fled. Belisarius returned a victor to Constantinople, but such was the mischief-making that had gone on in his absence that Justinian hardly even thanked him for saving the city.

The long reign was ending in disorder, and natural disasters —earthquakes such as the one in 558 which wrecked the dome of Santa Sophia. Two discontented courtiers, Marcellus and Sergius, planned Justinian's assassination at a banquet. They even had black slaves stationed in the vestibule to announce the death of a tyrant. But the secret came out and the two were arrested, with daggers beneath their clothes. Marcellus committed suicide, but Sergius implicated two officers in Belisarius's household, who in their turn implicated the general.

On the 5th of December, 563, Belisarius was brought before the Council, which spared his life but confiscated his property. Six months later his innocence was established, but in March the following year he died (565), and the rapacious old Emperor appropriated his trophies from his campaigns against the Vandals. As for Antonina, she devoted her old age to good works, and even founded and endowed a convent.

Only eight months after the death of Belisarius, Justinian himself died, on November 14, 565, in his eighty-third year. Under him the Byzantine Empire may have reached its peak, but it is for building Santa Sophia that the world should best remember him, with gratitude.

Chapter 11

c: 550

Constantinople. Its renown. At the centre of trade routes. The Mesé, the principal street. Housing laws. The Imperial Palace. The Boucleon Harbour. Archaeological survivals. The Mosaics Museum. The Forum of Augustus and the Baths of Zeuxippus. The Forums of Constantine and Theodosius. The Barracks. The State Prison. The University. Timber Stores. Forum of Amastrianum. The Church of the Apostles. Forum of Arcadius. St John. The Golden Gate.

Constantinople had reached its zenith: nearly twice the size of the city Constantine had inaugurated that day in May, 330. Now it stood complete behind a circuit of walls no less than twelve miles round: on two sides lapped by the tideless waters of the Sea of Marmara and the Golden Horn, and on the third by the double line of the Walls of Theodosius. Those walls were the breakwaters on which wave after wave of barbarians literally dashed themselves, only to have to withdraw back into the forests and mountains of the Balkans.

Constantinople: from a position at the crossroads of the civilized world its name and wonders were carried to the furthest corners—and beyond. When, at Sutton Hoo on the banks of the Deben, the subjects of one of the last pagan kings of East Anglia prepared the funeral-ship for their lord and master, the vessels of silver that they laid in the cenotaph had been fashioned by a silversmith who could have called himself a citizen of the 'New Rome that is Constantinople'.

From the Golden Gate that road led eventually to the old Rome beside the Tiber. Across the Bosphorus one route would take the traveller south towards Damascus, Jerusalem, and Alexandria—with the knowledge that at the end of every day's journey he would find a caravanserai where he could get food, and a secure night's lodging for himself and his animals. Not only that, but he could travel the main roads of the Empire in the knowledge that they were patrolled by a special police force. If the traveller set his face to the east after crossing the Bosphorus from the city that was in the especial care of the Virgin Mary, the way would eventually bring him after a march of perhaps sixty days to Armenia, the little kingdom that adopted Christianity in A.D. 300, twenty-five years before it became the official religion of the Roman Empire. Beyond the mountain-encircled city of Ani the arid heart of Central Asia stretched away before the traveller. Later generations would know that route from Constantinople into the rising sun as the Golden Road to Samarkand.

Both in a physical and a spiritual sense the city was dominated by the newly completed Santa Sophia: it must have towered over the shapeless group of buildings that was the imperial palace, covering the slope down to the sea walls. Visible alike from the Asian shore and from far out to sea, according to the eye of faith the dome can be seen in an exceptionally clear sunset—floating over the city—from as far off as the summit of Mount Athos: 6,670 feet up and two hundred and fifty miles away.

As the old Rome waned, so Constantinople waxed. In 410 the old capital had been sacked by the Visigoths, and it was now dwindling into a provincial city, while its eastern successor could boast a magnificence which perhaps even outshone the great days of Augustus.

In this city beside the Sea of Marmara the main streets, such as the Mesé, had a width of about fifteen feet, with a colonnade on either side—inherited by such Italian cities as Bologna. These colonnades frequently contained booths which in the most exclusive areas had by law to be fronted with marble. Not only were these arcades frequented by the ladies of the town, but also by the homeless. In the very severe winter of 933 the Emperor ordered some of the openings to be filled in with windows and doors, for the comfort of the latter.

Opening off the main thoroughfares were the residential streets, about ten feet wide, with projecting balconies. At ground level the houses had no glass in the windows; instead there were thin sheets of marble or alabaster, though in the poorer districts where marble would have been an unheard-of luxury wooden shutters were used. By a housing act of A.D. 447, new streets had to be twelve feet wide, with the balconies ten feet from the one opposite. As in ancient Rome, there were huge tenement blocks—The Buildings—limited by law in Constantinople to a height of one hundred feet.

The houses of the well-to-do usually stood in their own grounds: two storeyed and with façades ornamented with pilasters. Inside, such mansions had a pillared central hall, marble lined walls and elaborate gilded ceilings.

In style the buildings of the imperial palace resembled the classic lines of a Greek temple, or rather a series of them. The entrance was directly opposite Santa Sophia in the Forum of Augustus, dominated by a huge arch surmounted by a figure of Christ: the whole structure covered with a roof of gilded tiles which gave its name: the Chalké or Brazen House. Directly behind the Chalké were the quarters occupied by the imperial guards, called the domestics, who were composed of four companies: scholars, excubitors, protectors, and candidates, numbering three thousand in all.

Nearby was the banqueting hall—the Triclinium of the Nineteen Couches, and the Throne Room, which contained the throne set at the top of a small flight of porphyry steps. Made of ivory, jewels, and gold and silver, it stood beneath a silver baldachino, with two eagles, also of silver, on its dome. A great curtain hung in front of the throne, which could be pulled aside to reveal the Emperor to those privileged enough to be received in audience.

Near the Chalké was a small court with the church of St Stephen, and opposite an octagonal hall containing a statue of Daphne, which gave its name to the whole of that part of the palace. The terrace and balconies of the Daphne overlooked the Hippodrome, while to the south of this part of the palace was a small court used for equestrian exercise. To the east was the sacred or God-guarded palace, which contained the Emperor's sleeping apartments. Here order was kept by the Silentaries, a troop of nobles. Some idea of the sheer size and magnificence of this semi-oriental palace can perhaps be gathered from one detail of life there. No less than thirty Silentaries paced back and forth in front of the purple hangings before the Emperor's bedchamber as he slept.

The population of the Seraglio of the Turkish Sultans was in its great days no less than ten thousand, and the numbers in the imperial palace of their Byzantine predecessors was probably about the same. Many of these were eunuchs, under the orders of the Praepositus of the Sacred Cubicle. Also in this, the God-guarded palace, were the numerous dressers, both men and women, who waited on the Emperor and Empress.

At the bottom of the hill between the palace and the walls stood the imperial garden. There, where now the railway line runs round Seraglio Point and where Turkish soldiers drill on the dusty squares of the Gülhane Barracks, ibis, peacocks, and pheasants wandered among the shrubs and flowers of the gardens.

Along the walls to the west was the Boucleon Harbour, though in Justinian's time its marble quays had not yet been decorated with the sculpture—including a lion and a bull in a death-struggle—which gave it its name. Behind stood the detached Porphyry palace. Perhaps it should be explained that in Greek purple and porphyry are the same word: just as red and beautiful are the same in Russian. There it was the custom for the imperial children to be born, taking the title of Porphyrogenitus, Born in the Purple.

And today? Pathetically little remains of all this magnificence. A few shapeless masses of brickwork, and semi-circular vaults, some above and some below ground. The site of the Chalké is covered by an open park, bright with salvias, while the cliff-like walls of Santa Sophia rise up over the plane trees that soften its massive architecture. To the west the infinitely beautiful Sultan

Ahmet mosque stands on the site of the Daphne palace, overlooking the green openness of the At Meydani which covers the Hippodrome. At the bottom of the hill there are some remains of the Sea Palaces, which formed part of the walls of the city itself, overlooking the Sea of Marmara. At the south-west corner of the palace grounds a flight of stone steps remains which connected the Harbour of the Boucleon with the palace, and farther along, to the east, a whole façade remains (page 149). Five round-headed arches, and in the three centre openings the stone frames of flat-topped doorways are still nearly intact, and just below, there are the corbels or brackets which supported a balcony. To the right, overhung with ivy, two columns with cushion capitals stand out amid the crumbling brickwork. The appearance of this façade fits in with the facts known about the murder of a tenth century Emperor, and may well have seen the first act of the tragedy (page 138).

A little beauty does remain inside the site of the palace: the mosaic floors, discovered just after the Second World War, behind the Sultan Ahmet. Some experts believe they date from the years 565–578, and were added to decorate a long portico. The museum is contained in several of the crypt-like substructures of the palace, where several mosaics have been placed after removal from their original sites; genre scenes and fabulous monsters. But the best and largest are still *in situ*, forming what appears to have been the floor of a long corridor, dating from before the time of Justinian. Subsidence and later alterations have damaged the mosaics, but even so they are most impressive. Here again the scenes are genre and mythological: the secular marriage of pagan art into a Christian society. Each scene is complete in itself, and does not form part of an overall design, which tends to give a lack of unity to the floor. Most charming is the boy offering a basket or nosebag to a donkey, who looks in two minds about accepting. Also there is a monkey fetching dates; a leopard catching a lizard—which manages to maintain a stiff upper lip in a difficult situation; two felines bringing down a deer; men fishing; shepherds; a boy with a lamb; a beautiful but fragmentary mosaic of a girl carrying a pitcher (page 37), and two gladiators fighting a tiger.

Mosaic over South Door, Santa Sophia. On the left Justinian presents his church to the Virgin and Child, while to the right Constantine the Great offers his city. Eleventh century

Late tenth century mosaic over the Royal Door, Santa Sophia. Christ Enthroned, with the suppliant Leo VI (886–912)

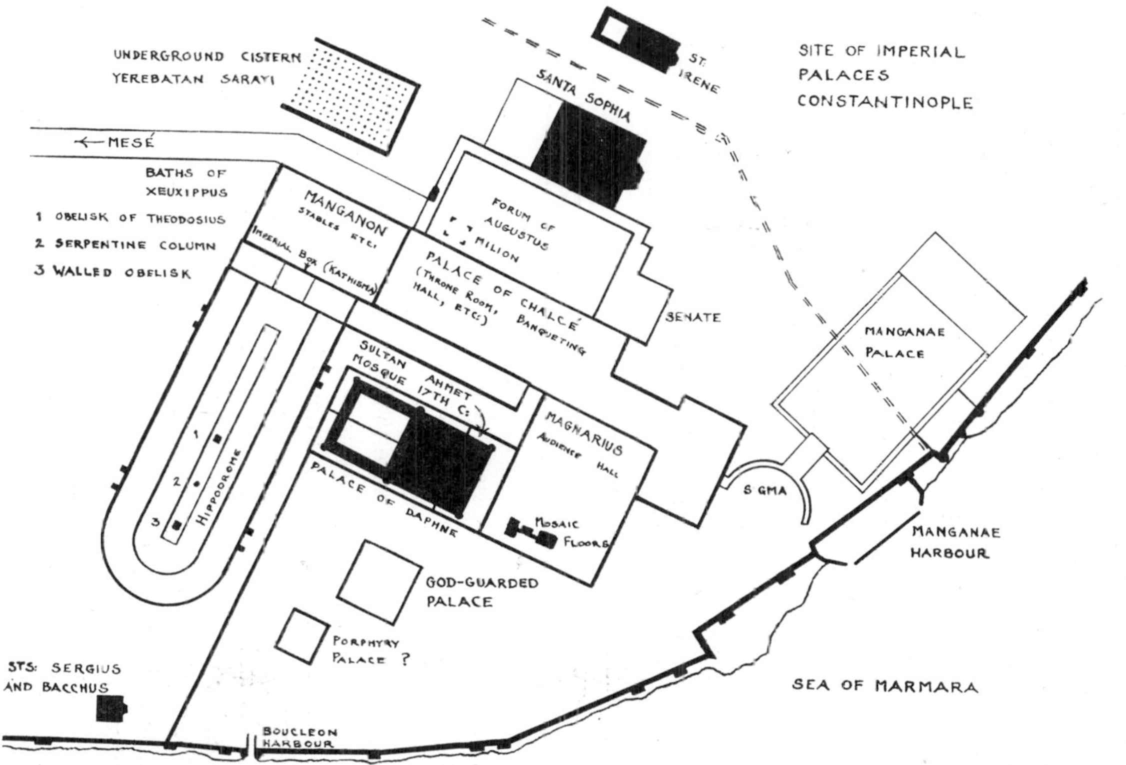
SITE OF IMPERIAL PALACES CONSTANTINOPLE
UNDERGROUND CISTERN YEREBATAN SARAYI
ST. IRENE
SANTA SOPHIA
←MESÉ
BATHS OF XEUXIPPUS
1 OBELISK OF THEODOSIUS
2 SERPENTINE COLUMN
3 WALLED OBELISK
MANGANON STABLES ETC.
IMPERIAL BOX (KATHISMA)
FORUM OF AUGUSTUS
MILION
PALACE OF CHALCÉ (THRONE ROOM, BANQUETING HALL, ETC.)
SENATE
MANGANAE PALACE
SULTAN AHMET MOSQUE 17TH C.
MAGNARIUS AUDIENCE HALL
S GMA
HIPPODROME
1
2
3
PALACE OF DAPHNE
MOSAIC FLOORS
MANGANAE HARBOUR
GOD-GUARDED PALACE
PORPHYRY PALACE ?
STS. SERGIUS AND BACCHUS
SEA OF MARMARA
BOUCLEON HARBOUR

In one part of the excavation the base of a column is still in place, and several large, but very battered Corinthian capitals remain. Wonderful as it is one cannot but regret all that has vanished, and speculate on what illustrious feet, clad in shoes of imperial purple, must have crossed and recrossed these floors. The spider has indeed spun his web in the palace of the Caesars.

Imperial magnificence must have been the overall impression of the Forum of Augustus: to the north Santa Sophia, to the south the palace, to the west the archway leading into the Mesé—the main street of the city—and to the east the senate house, set behind plane trees. There are still plane trees in the square, though except for one tall almost shapeless piece of masonry on the corner of the modern Divan Yolu (the streets still follow the course of the old Mesé), the great colonnaded square has quite vanished. Dominating the Forum was an equestrian statue of Justinian, clad most unsuitably as Achilles in armour. In the south-west corner, near the archway into the street, stood the Milion, the Golden Milestone from which all distances were measured. The actual milestone, the heart of Constantinople as well as of the Empire itself, was a gilded column set beneath a triumphal arch of four openings, with figures of Helena and Constantine supporting the Cross on its top.

Just outside the entrance to the Forum, next the Hippodrome to be exact, were the baths of Zeuxippus, built by Septimus Severus, and recently burnt down in the Nika Riots of 532. On the opposite side of the street was a most expensive store selling cloths and fabrics, called the House of the Lamps, from the number used to light up the window displays after dark. Next door, going up the hill, was the Octagon, where lectures were held and a group of monks (frequently consulted by the Emperor) used to meet. Close to that was the royal porch, containing a library: not an old collection, as in the time of the Emperor Zeno it was burnt, 120,000 manuscripts being destroyed.

Nearly the whole length of the Mesé was flanked with porticoes, and punctuated at irregular intervals with great forums: five of them. The first the traveller came to after walking up the hill away from Santa Sophia was the Forum of Constantine, enclosed by curving colonnades and with arches at either end where the Mesé entered and left it. In the centre stood Constantine's column, topped by the statue of Apollo masquerading as the Emperor.

A few hundred yards away to the north-east, behind the eighteenth century Nurosmanyie mosque, stood the Strategium, a barrack square with an obelisk in the centre and an equestrian statue of Constantine close by. According to tradition it was the spot where Alexander the Great reviewed his troops for the last time before setting out against the Persians. On one side of the square was the Praetorium, the state prison, used only by those awaiting trial. Today a Byzantine tower, about eighty feet high, which formed part of the group of buildings, rises up out of the seventh century Valide Han, a large caravanserai.

If the traveller had continued his walk along the Mesé, he would next have come to the Forum of Theodosius, with the university at its north end. In the centre stood that Emperor's column, modelled on Trajan's Column in Rome with a spiral staircase inside. At the beginning of the thirteenth century a usurping Emperor would be thrown to his death from its top. Battered remains, like stumps, are all that are left of columns on the south side of the modern Ordu Street*, but of the Forum little or nothing remains—at least above ground. On the site stands Beyazit Square and the Mosque of Beyazit II, one of the oldest in Istanbul, and behind it the magnificent new buildings of the university, a living link with the city's more distant past.

Between the university—which in the days when the city was called Byzantium was the Capitol—and the Golden Horn was the red-light quarter; appropriately enough grouped about a statue of Venus. Today she has moved her address to a certain street in Beyoğlu, on the other side of the harbour. Along the Golden Horn, adjoining the quays were such places as the cattle-market and at the Zeugma the timber yards, where the city's fuel was stored. Timber yards are still to be seen in the Fener District, but it is on the other side of Istanbul, in Langa, that huge stocks of wood, much of it for charcoal, are kept in piles twenty feet high and more.

On, down Ordu Street, where the traffic is like a mill-race

* Part of the triumphal arch of Theodosius.

hurtling towards the eastern extremities of Istanbul. At the bottom of the hill, where there is a traffic roundabout stood yet another forum, the Forum of Amastrianum. Over the entrance arch two severed hands, in bronze, had been set up. They were symbolic: anyone who had passed beyond on his way to execution was also beyond hope of a reprieve. In the eleventh century a man was literally saved at the last moment as he was about to pass beneath, thanks to the entreaties of the Emperor's favourite daughter. For the Forum of Amastrianum was to Constantinople what Tower Hill was to London.

If the traveller had turned right in the Forum, instead of following the course of the Mesé, he would after about a mile come to the Church of the Apostles, standing in a huge courtyard on the top of the Fourth Hill. Architecturally, it was second only in importance to Santa Sophia, and historically of the first rank. There from Constantine the Great onwards the Emperors were buried. In the centre of the church stood the porphyry sarcophagus of the founder of the city, and his mother, St Helena. Also buried there were his sons, as well as Theodosius I and II, Arcadius, Marcian, Pulcheria (sister of Theodosius II), Leo I and Zeno. In design this Westminster Abbey was one of the first of all churches to be built in the form of a cross, with a dome over each of the arms and one in the centre. St Mark's, Venice, is said to be modelled on it; while the present front of St Saviour in Chora is supposed to have inspired the original façade of the Italian cathedral.

Even if the Church of the Apostles had not been demolished in 1463, to make way for the imperious Fatih Camii—the Conqueror's Mosque, it is unlikely that it would have survived to the present day. Even before the Turkish Conquest of 1453 it was partly ruined, and would probably have been totally destroyed in the earthquake of 1677 which brought down most of the Fatih Mosque, one of the most massively built in Istanbul.

From near the Church of the Apostles the great Aqueduct of Valens strode across the valley between the Third and Fourth Hills, carrying one of the city's water supplies. More usual, though less spectacular, were the lead or earthenware pipes that fed the numerous cisterns such as those of Aspar, Moscus, the so-called Cistern of the One-Thousand-and-One Columns, or the Yerebatan Sarayi. The running expenses for maintaining the supply were met out of the wharf dues paid by merchants along the Golden Horn. In those days the water was free, which is more than the little bottles of drinking water are now.

If the traveller, determined to follow the Mesé to its end, returned to the Amastrianum Forum, and then continued his way, he would come next to the Forum of the Ox, and after that to the Forum of Arcadius. Of the column of that Emperor which once stood there only the base remains, next a baker's shop. Soon he would pass the remains of Constantine's land walls (now quite vanished), and still have a long walk in front of him before reaching the Golden Gate in the Walls of Theodosius. On his way he would pass on his left hand the Monastery of St John of Studion: the simple tiled roof of the basilica rising above the buildings that housed a thousand monks. The land is flatter here, hiding the sea from the traveller behind the walls which followed the line of the shore, until they reached the Marble Tower, and a little beyond Christ's Postern: the small gate in the southern end of the land walls. At the Golden Gate the traveller could admire it and its sculptures from inside or outside the city, but not pass through the triumphal arch itself. That was for the Imperial Family only. He must use the gate (Yedikule Kapisi) on its north side. Beyond the walls of Theodosius, stretching away over hills and valleys for four and a half miles to the north, the open country was dotted with market-gardens. They are still there: on the long slope down the Sixth Hill towards the Golden Horn, where there is no moat, reaching right up to the city walls. It would seem the living things, like plane trees near Santa Sophia or vegetable gardens outside the Theodosian walls, are the least subject to change: and give an unexpected continuity to the city's history.

Chapter 12

c: 550 *(continued)*

Life in Constantinople in the sixth century. In the imperial palace. Robes and regalia. Daily routine. Titles. Fashions of the well-to-do. Their palaces. Eunuchs. Marriage customs. Relations between classes. The army. The shops. Foodstuffs. Inns. Currency.

At the heart of life in the imperial palace, a hive if ever there was one, were the Emperor and Empress, surrounded by nobles, guards, attendants, servants, and slaves. Tyrian purple—a dye from a shell-fish, which smelt—was a colour reserved for the imperial household alone. So for that matter was silk. It was Justinian who gave instructions that silk cocoons should be smuggled out of China, so that the industry could be started in the Empire, instead of having to pay the high prices demanded by the Chinese.

If a lesser mortal dared to go out and about in purple-coloured clothes he would soon have had the heavy hand of the law on his shoulder. Also for the Emperor's exclusive use were scarlet shoes, sewn with jewels, that, like the scarlet buskins or leggings, were emblems of imperial majesty. Over white tunic and purple hose he wore a purple robe opening on the right side, which had a large square of cloth-of-gold embroidered on the back and front.

Bejewelled head-dresses might be a better description for the crowns and diadems worn by the sovereigns. Crowns as emblems of royalty came originally from Persia, and must have been far removed from the comparatively sober creations of west-European goldsmiths. One type worn by the Emperor consisted of a black hoop, expanding above, which was edged with pearls and quite covered with stones, while at the back strings of pearls hung down as far as the nape of the neck. That worn by the Empress was even more magnificent by the addition of sprays of jewels, and strings of pearls which hung down to the shoulders.

The nobles who attended the sovereign, called the Fathers of the Emperor, wore white robes with purple squares on the back and front, while the imperial guards—the domestics already mentioned—wore green tunics with red facings, black-and-white hose, and carried an oval shield; red, covered with black stars and with a blue border. To wait on the Empress, usually clad in a purple robe with a gold-embroidered border, was a train of ladies-in-waiting headed by three noblemen.

In the palace the daily routine began at seven a.m., when the grand janitor went with the guards and the noble Silentaries to open the main doors onto the Forum of Augustus. Then at eight a.m. the captain of the watch went to the door of the Emperor's sleeping apartments in the God-guarded palace, and knocked. The Emperor, surrounded by eunuchs, would come out, pray before a figure of Christ, and go through the palace to the throne-room. Then the grand janitor fetched the steward of the royal household, followed by senators, patricians, and prefects, who came forward to confer with the Emperor as he required them. Patricians were allowed simply to bow, and in return received an imperial kiss. If a document needed signing, the Emperor did so in purple ink, another of his exclusive privileges. A number of documents, relating to lands or rights granted to various monasteries by Byzantine emperors survive, in comparatively large numbers, in the libraries of some of the monasteries on Mount Athos. One, rather more accessible, is in the Byzantine Museum in Athens: the faded signature of the thirteenth century Andronikos II.

At ten a.m. the grand janitor walked through the antechamber of the throne room, jangling his keys as a signal that the audience was over. Then until two p.m. the palace was closed to such of the public as had business there, then it remained open until five p.m.

In addition to such titles as the Thirteenth Apostle and the Equal of the Apostles, the Emperor was called the Autokrator, Lord and Master, and after the seventh century the Basileus (Greek: King); while his heir, whether nominated or by blood, was called the Augustus or Caesar.

By the time of Justinian the Roman toga had been discarded in favour of a long brocaded coat and, since the barbarians just beyond the frontiers wore long beards, it was *de rigueur* for the smart citizen bent on keeping up with the Demitrii to be clean shaven. If not wearing a long coat, upper-class men wore a long-sleeved tunic of silk, reaching to the knees, with an expensive girdle round the waist. Over this, when it was cold, went an ankle-length cloak fastened with a jewelled clasp at the shoulder. Coloured hose and very elaborate shoes completed the outfit. A century before these expensive fashions had infuriated St John Chrysostom, who thundered against them from the pulpit of Santa Sophia (his sermons, being full of references to the customs, follies, and vices of his times are of interest to the social historian), much as nine centuries later the clergy of Old St Paul's were taking the same line against the fantastically elongated shoes worn in the reign of Richard II. The sight of fashionable youths teetering round the streets of Constantinople in the *dernier cri* was the last straw for the saint. 'If you cannot bear to use them for their purpose, why not hang them about your neck or stick them on your head?' Another fashion that rankled were the ostentatiously large ear-rings worn by well-to-do women: 'You bore the lobes of your ears, and fasten in them enough gold to feed ten thousand poor persons.' With the ear-rings went heavy necklaces, angle-length gowns, and if the wearer was going into the streets, gloves, a shawl, and a hood.

Many of the men could be identified in their callings by their clothes: physicians wore blue; philosophers wore grey; ascetics wore scarlet—and also they bound their hair with a fillet; while church-workers wore black hoods, grey mantles, and black shoes.

The luxury to be found in the houses of the very rich must

have rivalled that of Ancient Rome itself. Gold plating and ivory veneers were used lavishly, and no doubt the silver chamber-pots counted as status symbols. (That on display in the Seraglio which belonged to one of the sultans is twenty-four carat gold.) In these large households meals were served in much the same way as in the days of Augustus: a large semi-circular table around which the diners reclined on couches. In fact the banqueting chamber in the imperial palace was called that of the Nineteen Couches. In a really large establishment the servants and slaves could number as many as two thousand (slavery was something that remained until the very end of the Empire), while the eunuchs were to be found in droves. Nearly all came from a tribe living between the Black Sea and the Caspian; the operation to fit them for their peculiar role in life was usually carried out when they were youths, and the casualty rate, presumably from infection, was appallingly high.

Not only were the eunuchs employed, as their Greek name implies—keepers of the bed—in the women's quarters, but in many of the highest public appointments in the city. Right up to the fall of Constantinople a number of the patriarchs were eunuchs, and also fashionable doctors who attended women patients. When the Empress Irene (wife of John II) founded a convent, St Saviour Pantokrator, in the early twelfth century she stipulated that the priests must be eunuchs. Most of the highest court officials, such as the chamberlain, belonged to this typically oriental brotherhood. For one thing it gave them access to the innermost and most jealously guarded parts of the palace, and also it meant that the running of the Emperor's affairs could not pass into the hands of a hereditary clique. In later centuries in western Europe eunuchs were chiefly employed in the musical world, by the Church to augment boys' choirs, and later in opera, Naples being the centre of the infamous industry. Perhaps it does not seem such a laughable paradox that according to the conventions of opera-seria in the eighteenth century (as late as Mozart's *Idomeneo*) heroic roles had to be sung by a male soprano, that antithesis of virility, when it is remembered that Narses, one of Byzantium's greatest generals was himself a eunuch.

In the sixth century the well-off matron with time and money spent much of both choosing new clothes and jewellery, making up her face most carefully, and chatting with her friends at such places as the luxurious baths of Zeuxippus. Her daughter, however, was kept at home and only allowed out if strictly chaperoned. Marriage, in which the girl had no say, was usually arranged when she was about fourteen or fifteen, brought about by a professional broker. Curiously enough, in the sixth century marriage by Christian rite was not compulsory, nor did it become so until after A.D. 800. In the most shameless and brutal manner possible did the hitherto closely guarded girl discover the facts of life during a wedding feast that was nothing less than an obscene debauch; while in Constantinople what even today would be considered indecently crude details of their intimate life were openly discussed by married women at social gatherings.

At the other end of the social scale from the Emperor were the slaves and the poorest of the working class. They wore a short-sleeved tunic which reached to the knees, of undyed wool, a girdle at the waist, and in cold weather a hood. As like as not the wretched man or woman did not possess a pair of shoes. Although the throne was theoretically—and also in fact—open to all comers whatever their social background, the class system was fairly rigid, but one in which a title and breeding were not necessarily to be found in the same person. There was the hereditary nobility, but also titles were given as a reward for service, or lavished on the favourites of the moment. In the eleventh century the Emperor Constantine IX cheapened the whole system by bestowing titles right, left, and centre on the most unsuitable people.

It may have been due to the fact that life in the city and the whole Empire was so closely organized, and supervised, that class conflicts were almost absent. If an established order was overthrown, it was by a whole section of the population, united against something religious or political of which they disapproved. It was only towards the end of the Empire that there were notable outbreaks of class friction. In the fourteenth century, during the Civil War which lasted six years, there were attacks by the working class on the upper at Thessalonika, the second city of the Empire, which roughly coincided with similar outbursts in the west, the Jacquerie in France, and the Peasants' Revolt in England.

As important to the safety of the city as the merchants were to its prosperity was the army. It had no highly developed code of chivalry on the battlefield, or in the imperial palace, one might add. Single combats in front of their respective armies were not unknown, but extremely rare: the average Byzantine officer would merely have raised a slightly pitying eyebrow at the knight-errant, ready and willing to risk his life for the honour of his lady or in settlement of some real or imagined slight. The army never fought hot-headedly. It would feign flight, use night attacks, ambushes, or parleys to win time. Since almost all its battles were fought against non-Christians, they had the character of crusades, and victory was heaven's approval of the righteousness of the cause regardless of the methods used. The latter is typical of the reasoning of this oriental-Christian civilization.

The soldiers that the citizen saw riding or marching about Constantinople were divided into three types. The heavy cavalry who wore a steel cap, a long mail shirt reaching to the thighs, gauntlets, and steel shoes. In summer the cavalryman wore a light cloak over his armour, to prevent the sun making it unbearably hot, while in winter or wet weather he covered himself with a long woollen cloak. For arms he had a broadsword, a dagger, a long lance, and on his back a bow and quiver full of arrows.

Then there was the light horseman, usually a mounted archer, while the heavy footsoldier wore a mail shirt and steel helmet, and carried a sword, lance, and axe with a blade on one side and a spike on the other. If the footsoldier was an archer he was armed with forty arrows and a small round shield.* This army was organized with disconcertingly twentieth century efficiency. Mounted deputati were the equivalent of the R.A.M.C., and it was their duty to bring in the wounded to the doctors, while the crossing of rivers presented no insuperable problem: the army travelled with its own prefabricated boats.

* No slave could become a soldier: recruits had to be eighteen years of age, five feet eight inches in height—and were branded where it could be seen easily.

The points of contact between Constantinople and the contemporary scene were several. On the shores of the Bosphorus charioteers were public idols, much as footballers are today—one of their privileges was exemption from corporal punishment if they fell foul of the law. Also there was a system of compensation for injury and loss of work, and free medical treatment. By the eleventh century the monastery of St Saviour Pantokrator contained a most efficient little hospital, the organization of which would not be a disgrace today (page 175).

From time to time the erection of new buildings in the city led to trouble, and by law owners of property had their rights to direct views of the sea, gardens, or public monuments—though, in the case of the latter, the contestant in a case had to prove he possessed sufficient education to understand them.

As befitted the city whose harbour is still called the Golden Horn, the shops were numerous and well stocked—with fixed prices and no undercutting. Meat and poultry were for the better-off, while salted fish was the basic food of the poorer people. At the grocers the citizen-housewife of the New Rome that is Constantinople could shop for most of her requirements: cheese, salt fish, meal, honey, olive oil, vegetables, and even meat. The inns also sold wine and foodstuffs, but by law were not allowed to do so before eight a.m. on festivals and Sundays. It was required, also by law, that the bust or plaque of the Emperor must be prominently displayed wherever business was transacted: much as Kemal Atatürk's bust or portrait presides over shops, offices, and homes in present-day Istanbul.

For over seven hundred years the gold Byzant (or Solidus) could have been described as the hardest currency in Europe and the Middle East, accepted and respected from one end of the Mediterranean to the other. In Justinian's day the Byzant consisted of the 72nd part of one pound of gold, the pound being then approximately 11½ ozs, so at present rates each of these little coins, smaller than a sixpence, would be worth £2 while the follis, the smallest copper coin, would have a value of about 2¼d. Then, from the beginning of the eleventh century onwards it was debased in ever-increasing amounts, until it became quite worthless. Nothing, they say, is new under the sun.

Chapter 13

565–711

Justin II. The Emperor Maurice overthrown by a centurion, Phocas. The age of sieges. Constantinople in danger from the Avars (from South Russia). The Emperor Heraclius (610–641). The city besieged (626) by the Avars and the Persians. Triumph to celebrate the defeat of the Persians. Greek fire. Siege by the Arabs (668–674). Eyüp, the last of the companions of the Prophet, dies outside the city.

It was in the middle of the night that the Senate woke Justin (November 14, 565) with the news his uncle was dead, and that he—one of seven nephews—had been nominated by the old man as his successor. 'After composing his countenance to surprise, sorrow and decent modesty' (Gibbon), Justin II put on the red leggings, white tunic, and purple robe. He was then seated on a shield and hoisted aloft by four young men. The procession to the palace had begun.

After his coronation by the patriarch he went to the Hippodrome where he promised to put right any wrongs committed during his uncle's reign. Then and there a train of porters entered the arena carrying bags of gold which were distributed to the dead Emperor's creditors. At least Justin II would have the people on his side from the start.

But before many years had passed, though not actually insane, he realized that the diadem his uncle had worn for nearly forty years was too heavy for him, and on the far from high-minded advice of his wife Sophia raised Tiberius, a captain of the guard, to the rank of Augustus or Caesar, during the course of a tear-stained speech delivered in the portico of the imperial palace. Sophia's motives were not of the best. She saw he had not long to live, and hoped to remain Empress by marrying Tiberius. However, no sooner had Justin died than she discovered that Tiberius was secretly married already, and what was insupportable, insisted on calling her Mother. After that it was necessary to intercept her correspondence, reduce the number of her retinue, and guard against conspiracies.

The great burst of building activity in Constantinople was followed by a lull: there was neither the need nor probably the funds for further work. Tiberius II came and went (578–582), and was succeeded by his son-in-law, Maurice. He was a noble Roman, capable but unemotional, with a round face and an antiseptic character that inspired affection neither in the palace nor among his soldiers on the battlefield. The army had gone soft, and at the thought of wintering in hostile territory in what is now Roumania, killed a number of their staff officers, elected an illiterate centurion, Phocas, as their leader, and marched back to Constantinople, where they halted outside the walls. Maurice had never heard of Phocas and on being told he was not particularly brave, remarked: 'Alas, if he is a coward, he will surely be a murderer.' Prophetic words.

Inside the city, almost in a state of siege, Maurice ordered bigger and better games to be given in the Hippodrome, but already the Green faction was in touch with the mutineers. A few days later stones were thrown at him as he walked barefoot in a religious procession. Still he was undecided what to do. Then with his wife and nine children, some grown up, he took a small boat from the Boucleon harbour across to Chalcedon. From there he sent Theodosius, the eldest son, to get help from the Persians. Whilst he waited, racked with sciatica, the Greens—and now some of the Blues as well, left Constantinople to go to Hebdomon, about three miles along the coast from the Golden Gate, where Phocas had set up his headquarters in what was the Aldershot of the Byzantium.

Drawn in a chariot by four white horses, Phocas entered Constantinople, as its new Emperor. Games were given in his presence in the Hippodrome, during which some of the Blues called out: 'Remember that Maurice is still alive.' That same day, November 27, 602, Maurice and five of his sons were beheaded at Chalcedon. Theodosius, on his way to the Persians, was overtaken at Nicaea, and also executed. At first the Empress and her three daughters were spared, but after two counter-plots were uncovered they too were put to death. Phocas had wiped out eleven members of one family.

This tyrant in the tradition of ancient Rome had little in his appearance to commend him. He was small and deformed, with heavy eyebrows, red hair, no beard, and a large scar on one cheek. His temper, like his lust, was uncontrollable, and it is ironic he should have been the first Emperor to be crowned in church by the patriarch (from this century onwards in Santa Sophia). Before then it had been performed by the prefect of the city.

Eight years later Phocas watched from one of the Sea Palaces as a fleet sailed towards the city. Under Heraclius, Military Governor of Africa, it had come to dethrone him. All was over even before it dropped anchor. In chains and wearing only a filthy robe Phocas was taken out to Heraclius in his galley. 'Will you do better?' were his last words before the sword fell.

The new Emperor Heraclius (610–642) found Constantinople and the Empire faced with a terrible situation. Ostensibly to avenge the murder of Maurice, the Persians had crossed the frontiers into Egypt, Syria, and eastern Anatolia, and now showed no sign of getting out again, while right across the Balkans the Avars were active on the northern frontier—invading as far as Constantinople itself. So bad was the situation that Heraclius (himself from North Africa), prepared to move to Carthage, but the patriarch made him go to Santa Sophia and swear to stay in the city with his people. Had he left, and had Constantinople fallen to the barbarian Avars it would without doubt have been the end of civilization in the eastern Mediterranean.

Their leader, the Chagan, asked Heraclius to come to talks with him at Heraclia, a town on the north shore of the Sea of Marmara. Equestrian games were held to celebrate the occasion, but at a crack from the Chagan's whip, the Scythian cavalry encircled the Hippodrome, and only by riding hell-for-leather did Heraclius escape back to Constantinople: the imperial diadem wrapped round his arm. So closely were the Avars following that some nearly entered through the Golden Gate before it could be closed. Even so, when the Avars withdrew from Thrace into what is modern Bulgaria, they took with them 270,000 prisoners.

Now Heraclius found himself pressed by the Persians. They did not make open war but demanded tribute: 1,000 talents of gold; 1,000 talents of silver; 1,000 silk robes; 1,000 horses—and 1,000 virgins. Obviously the war had to be carried into their camp. In one of the least known and most brilliant campaigns in military history (622–625) Heraclius penetrated as far as Ispahan, via the Caspian Sea.

But a year later, in 626, the Persians themselves were in the suburbs of Constantinople: Chrysopolis and Chalcedon—on the Asian shore of the Bosphorus. Whilst awaiting the arrival on the European side of 30,000 Avars they spent the time looting and destroying. That was on June 29, 626. Just a month later the city was besieged by 80,000 barbarians—if it is fair to call the Persians barbarians.

Magistrates came out of Constantinople to meet the Chagan, with Persian envoys at his side. The Chagan did not mince his words: 'Your wealth and your city are the only presents worthy of my acceptance. For yourself, I shall allow you to leave, each in an undergarment, and a shirt.' Constantinople prepared for a siege.

The Avars brought up their weapons, including twelve siege-towers, the tops of which were level with the ramparts. For ten days they attacked, attempting to sap the walls from beneath a tortoise, a portable armoured roof under which men could advance in safety. At this date and for several centuries to come the Byzantine navy was a reality and not just a figment of a charitable imagination. Its biremes and triremes patrolled the Bosphorus, keeping the Persians on the Asian side, and so prevented them linking up with their allies the Avars. In the Golden Horn they destroyed a fleet of canoes, and soon the Chagan realized the operation was futile. After burning his siege weapons he gave the order to retreat.

When Heraclius returned to Constantinople in 628, after smashing the Sassanid Persian Empire so that it never recovered, he could enjoy a triumph to celebrate no less than six campaigns. But before then his actual return to the city was extraordinary. He never lacked courage on the battlefield, but he had an almost uncontrollable fear of water. When he arrived on the Asian side of the Bosphorus on his return from Persia nothing would induce him to get in a boat and cross over to the city. Eventually a bridge of boats was placed across the Bosphorus, with high sides made of branches and foliage, and he was induced to ride across on his horse. When he reached the suburb of Galata he did not follow the road which ran along the shore of the Golden Horn, but made a detour inland, finally crossing over to the city by the stone bridge built in Justinian's day, at the north-west corner of the walls.

Outside the Golden Gate was the starting point for such processions, with a march of about four miles right through the city to the imperial palace. First to move off across the dusty waste-land and onto the road that led into Constantinople were the prisoners and their guards. Then came the soldiers carrying the captured weapons and banners and trophies. Now it was Heraclius himself, riding in a chariot drawn by four elephants, who moved towards the central opening of the triumphal arch-cum-city gate. To use the gate for a triumph was the privilege of royalty which no general below imperial rank could claim.

When the chariot reached the great gate it would stop, the Emperor dismount, prostrate himself three times to God, and remount. Inside, the authorities would be waiting to present him with a golden crown and a laurel wreath: the Christian and pagan heritages of the city. Then the two factions, the Greens and the Blues, would be there to chant their dutiful praises. 'Glory to God, who restores our sovereigns to us, crowned with victory! Glory to God, who has magnified you, Emperor of the Romans! Welcome victors, most valiant sovereigns.' Where the elephants picked their way, and the ground shook to the tramp of marching soldiers, is now the large courtyard of the late-fifteenth century Yedikule, the castle of the Seven Towers, covered with coarse grass and rubble, and the only sound the chipping of Turkish stonemasons at work restoring the massive heavy pylons of the Golden Gate.

After the long and strenuous wars the Emperor now celebrating Byzantium was weak and wasted, and Heraclius himself declined into slippered ease. Perhaps the most important event of all for Constantinople passed unnoticed among its citizens. Far away to the south, on the edge of Syria, the Saracens pillaged a village. In itself it was of no consequence, but for the first time the enemy was fighting in the name of Islam.

The seventh and early parts of the eighth centuries were some of the most dangerous times in the whole history of the city. It was the age of sieges: by the Persians, the Avars, the Bulgarians, and now the Arabs. A huge fleet put its army ashore at Hebdomon (Bakirköy), and the citizens knew what to expect, though not how long it would last. Behind their wonderful walls they now had a new secret weapon.

The secret weapon was Greek fire, the most deadly invention before the advent of the crossbow. The brain-child of Callinicus of Heliopolis in Syria, he deserted to the Byzantines, taking his secret with him, and a state secret it remained for hundreds of years. Then in the eleventh century it was discovered by the Saracens, who naturally used it against the Greeks themselves. Even today its exact components are not known for certain. Practically inextinguishable, like a modern phosphorus bomb, it is thought to have been made from naphtha, sulphur, and resin. Burning fiercely, it would cling to any surface on which it landed, including those that were vertical. Greek fire was either tipped from the ramparts onto the heads of those below, catapulted in red-hot balls of stone or iron, or fired on arrows round which flax or tow dipped in the stuff had been wound. At sea it was either catapulted from fire-ships, or blown through copper tubes fitted to the prows of conventional warships.

Unable to breach the walls, the Arabs pillaged up and down both sides of the Bosphorus, and from April to September 668 quite blockaded the city. Then as winter approached they drew off to the near-island of Cyzicus (Erdek), eighty miles away on the south side of the Sea of Marmara, which they made their headquarters. For six summers they besieged Constantinople, returning each winter to Cyzicus, but the city remained uncaptured. Thirty thousand Moslems died before they finally withdrew through the Dardanelles and out of the Aegean Sea. Among those they left buried outside the walls was Eyüp (670), the last surviving companion of the Prophet.

Eyüp fell and was buried near the Heraclean Wall, that stretch at the bottom of the Sixth Hill, near the Golden Horn, which in 628 had been added by Heraclius to protect the Blachernae Palace and the Church of the Virgin, which the Avars had attempted to destroy. After the Turkish conquest of 1453 the grave was rediscovered: a mosque sprang up on the orders of Mehmet II, and today Eyüp is one of the holiest pilgrimage centres in Islam.

Chapter 14

711-741

Chaos in Constantinople, and danger beyond the walls. Siege by the Arabs and Persians (716–717). Enemy fleet destroyed. The beginning of the Iconoclastic Controversy (*c.* 725). Its causes and effects. Decline of art in Constantinople. St Irene. Its architecture and appearance today.

Chaos followed the death of Justinian II, the last of the Heraclean dynasty. Never was the principle that the throne was open to all comers better, or worse, illustrated than in the years A.D. 711–717, when three emperors were deposed in succession in the imperial palace. It would not be the first or last time in the history of Constantinople that it would seethe with internal strife, while outside the walls its very existence was threatened by a powerful enemy.

Far away in Egypt and other lost provinces the Arabs (or Saracens) were preparing another siege of the city. That earlier one, beginning in 668, had lasted intermittently for six years. But before their ships were once again sailing up the Dardanelles, the Emperors Philippicus Bardanes (711–713), Anastasius II (713–716), and Theodosius III (716–717) had come forward, and vanished nearly as quickly as the succession of spectral kings who helped spoil Macbeth's appetite at the banquet.

Once again Constantinople prepared to stand a siege. A decree was issued by Anastasius II that everyone who did not possess the means of subsistence for three years should evacuate the city at once. The granaries were filled to the top, the walls strengthened and repaired, and the artillery—the catapults for throwing stones, darts, and Greek fire—mounted on the ramparts or fixed to the decks of light craft in the harbour.

At the time when in the west the lamps were being relit one by one to pierce the long night of the Dark Ages it looked as though the brilliant flame in the east that was Constantinople might be extinguished. 120,000 Arabs and Persians advanced into Anatolia, and crossed the Dardanelles so as to attack Constantinople through Thrace, from the land side. For the first time since the days of Marathon in 480 B.C. Persian soldiers had set foot in Europe.

This was the moment when Theodosius III was removed, only too willingly one suspects, from the throne by Leo, the leader of the oriental troops. Either discontented army officers or plotting eunuchs seem to have been the principal scene-shifters in the imperial palace in Constantinople.

Like Justin I, the new soldier-Emperor Leo III the Syrian, was of humble origin. But he was not destined to be the begetter of a ruler of the stature of Justinian the Great. If any characteristic marked the later members of the Syrian dynasty (and their successors), it was cruelty. Possibly the son of a Syrian grazier named Conon who had settled in Thrace, Leo bought his place in the imperial guard for five hundred sheep.

Hardly had he time to find how heavy were the robes of imperial majesty than he had to face up to his enemies. First he tried to buy off the invaders with gold, but the Arabs and the Persians rejected the offer out of hand. Before long they would be reinforced by the Syrian and Egyptian navies: no less than 1,800 ships. They came, and like a 'moving forest' sailed across the mouth of the Bosphorus towards the water-girt city. They could not believe their eyes and their luck. On the Emperor's orders the great chain across the mouth of the harbour had been removed. They swept into the Golden Horn. Then the Byzantine fire-ships, light and manoeuvrable, darted among the Syrian and Egyptian ships, unable to take evasive action in the confined waters. Their destruction was total.

Now the siege by land and by water began in earnest. It

continued all through the incredibly bitter winter of 716–7, when the snow lay on the ground for a hundred days. At last spring returned, and with it came two fleets of 760 vessels bringing corn and reinforcements for the besiegers. Again the fire-ships went out, causing havoc, and a number of the Egyptian transports actually went over to the Byzantines. The confidence of the Arabs had been badly shaken. The fleets had been destroyed, while the great walls remained unbreached. Their morale sank even lower when faced with famine and plague. If Leo III was unable to buy them off with gold, it brought a Bulgarian army to his assistance, and between them they killed 22,000 Arabs. That, coupled with a completely untrue rumour that the Franks were coming from the west to help the city, broke them and, after a siege of thirteen months their armies withdrew from along the length of the Theodosian Walls. Back through Thrace they marched, recrossed the Dardanelles and were out of Europe. Of the fleet only five galleys reached their home port of Alexandria.

For some years now feeling had been building up in the Asian parts of the Empire against the Church. Islam's successes were blamed on its corruption, and in 729 it came to a head with a popular movement against monasticism and image worship. That the cult of images had got out of hand can be summed up in one episode: the custom of making a famous and miracle-working icon a godparent at a child's baptism. Leo III, himself semi-Asian, had little sympathy with such superstition, and behind him were ranged the army and the Asian parts of the Empire, against the Church and his European subjects.

The Iconoclastic Controversy, destined to drag on for over a hundred and twenty years, had begun. Before it was over Constantinople would have lost nearly all its finest art treasures. First icons were taken off the screens in the churches, and placed too high for the congregation to kiss. Then their wholesale removal was ordered. The breaking of images had begun in earnest. Thousands, perhaps hundreds of thousands, of icons were burnt or destroyed in Constantinople alone, many of them going back to the earliest days of Christianity. Not only were these painted panels attacked, but the mosaics, the glory of

Byzantine art, as well. Anything which portrayed the human form was taboo in church.

All this was not achieved without riots, bloodshed, and repression, and men of the calibre of St John of Damascus were driven into exile, and persecution was widespread.

Since the time of Phocas (602–610) art had been on the decline. The glorious burst of creative activity which coincided with the reign of Justinian the Great had quite spent itself. Now there was no incentive to create, and what must have been lost to the world in the way of art treasures is incalculable. It would be safe to say that during the Iconoclastic Controversy, over four hundred years of religious art in the world's most civilized city was swept away, so that today no mosaic of a religious subject remains in Istanbul that is older than the middle of the ninth century, when the dispute ended. Even the one of Constantine and Justinian making their offerings to the Virgin and Child, in Santa Sophia, is post-controversy. To see 'picture mosaics' of Justinian's day it is necessary to turn to Ravenna, the one-time capital of the West Roman Empire, for so long almost isolated from the rest of Italy by the marshes that time and again saved it from capture and destruction.

A typical form of decoration during this period is the black outline of a cross on a gold ground. Eight remain in Santa Sophia (page 66), while another, though damaged, survives in the apse of St Irene.

That great church, today separated from Santa Sophia by the late-medieval wall of the Seraglio, took on its present form at the very end of Leo III's reign, as the result of an earthquake. One feels there must have been two malign fairies at the inauguration of Constantinople in A.D. 330: fire and earthquake.

At eight p.m.—when it was closing time by law for the taverns and they would have been turning out their customers and dousing the fires for the night—on October 22, 740, the city was hit by an earthquake. Many churches and public buildings were wrecked and even the great Theodosian Walls were damaged. One of the towers, the seventh from the south end (next the gap made for the railway line), contains a Greek inscription recording the event. 'Leo with Constantine [his son and at that date co-ruler], wielders of the sceptre, erected from the foundations, this tower which had fallen.'

But it was St Irene that suffered most. A church had stood on the site when the city still had the resounding name of Byzantium, and until the first Santa Sophia was completed in A.D. 360 it probably served as the cathedral. Like Santa Sophia it was destroyed by fire during the Nika Riots of 532, and only thirty-two years later, in 564 it was again burnt. Now it was the turn of earthquake. All the vaulting and upper part of the walls seem to have been brought down and it was not so much a matter of restoring, as rebuilding on the original foundations.

By any standard St Irene is large: in Istanbul it is the second largest church after Santa Sophia, and consists of an atrium to the west (not shown on the plan opposite), a narthex, a nave with aisles, a short bema (chancel), and a large single apse. Recently it has been completely restored, the plaster that covered the exterior has been chipped away, while inside it has been removed up to the level of the springing of the vaulting. All the battle-trophies, guns, muskets, lances, swords, etc., with which it was filled, have been removed. For centuries the church, standing as it does in the vast first courtyard of the Seraglio, was used as an armoury. It was one of the very few churches in Constantinople which was not turned into a mosque after the Turkish Conquest (St Mary of the Mongols was another: page 212). Outside, the walls of reddish brick have little to decorate them: the need for external ornament had not made itself felt, and the eye is drawn straight to the dome. At St Irene the drum stands on a square base, though its corners are rounded off, and it (the drum) has twenty round-headed openings and sloping buttresses.

Though much altered and rebuilt in Turkish times the atrium —the cloister at the west end—is singularly interesting: the only one to remain reasonably intact in the city. At St John of Studion it is so ruined, and full of Turkish tombstones, that it is difficult to appreciate what it is simply by looking. Since the time of Leo III the ground outside St Irene has risen so much, no less than fifteen feet on the north side, that a long ramp leads down from the present entrance, into the north aisle: a long

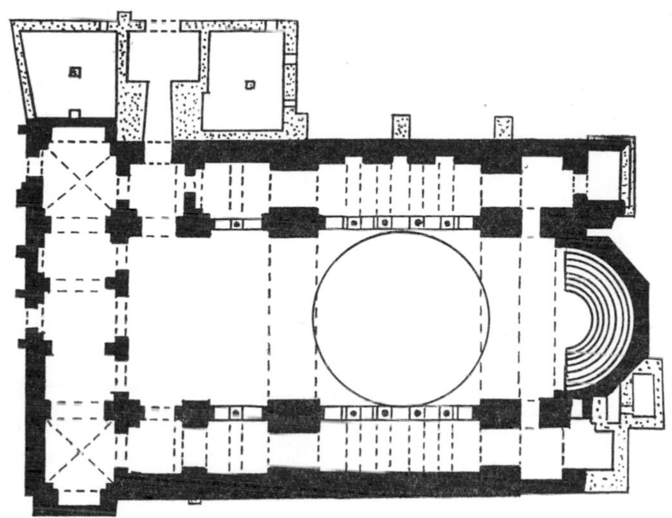

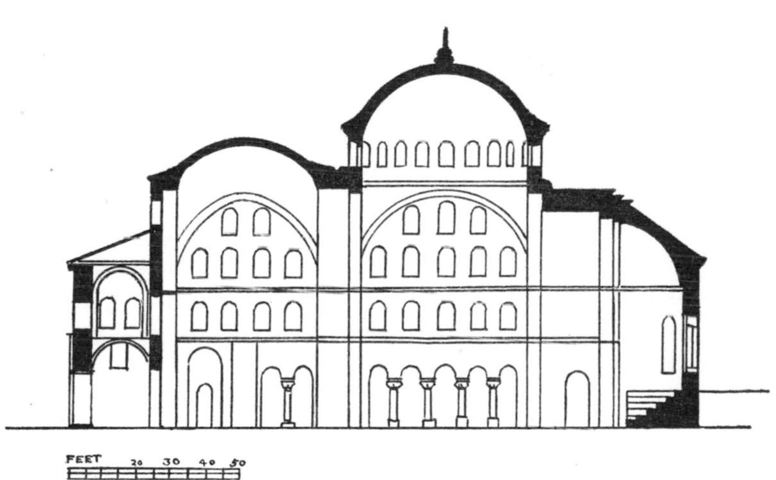

St Irene, a large fourth-century church rebuilt after the earthquake of A.D. 740

dark tunnel ending in the light emptiness of the great church itself. The narthex has five bays: at either end with cross-vaulting, while the three central bays are domical. The main body of the church is divided into two large bays. The bay to the west is separated from the aisles by two columns, one on either side, and covered with a most extraordinary piece of vaulting. The bay is not quite square: while the arches on its east and west sides are semi-circular, those to the north and south are stilted—elliptical—so their tops should all be level. Over this is set a covering that is really neither vault nor dome. You feel it was by sheer brute force that the masonry was made to fit. A cross-vault has been moulded into a domical vault. From the outside it appears as a very low drum, capped with a conical roof of negligible pitch.

The east bay is covered with an orthodox dome with pendentives supported on arches that are so thick they become barrel-vaults, and north and south cover the embryo-transepts. These transepts, if they can be so called, are separated from the space beneath the dome by an arcade of four columns on either side. A most curious detail has come to light about them during the recent restoration. For centuries their bases had been enclosed in wooden casings: now these have been removed, to show that the columns are all of odd lengths. Presumably they were taken from an older building for use in the restoration of St Irene, and the only way the architect could make their tops level to support the capitals was by standing them on bases of unequal height. One column stands on a very battered Corinthian capital, another on a roughly squared stone as big as a butcher's block, and so on. That the capitals themselves have been re-used from the earlier church is borne out by the monogram of Justinian and Theodora (obviously they date from the rebuilding after the fire of 532) which face into the aisles, and not into the nave where everyone—including the imperial couple—could see them. Once again, in the aisles, the architect seems to have had trouble with his vaulting, which is very stilted not to say slightly botched to make it fit the spaces between the ribs, which spring from just above the capitals of the arcades across to the outer walls (page 148).

St Irene, the name means the Divine Peace, has lost all its marble veneers, and apart from the sombre mosaic in the apse there is none of the exotic colouring of Santa Sophia with its great sheets of green, purple, and grey marble, only the soft tones of the brickwork. As you wander in the aisles it might be some early Romanesque abbey church in France rather than a great basilica on the shores of the Sea of Marmara.

Excavations have been carried out in the nave, showing two, if not three different levels of flooring. The lowest, about eighteen inches down, is of a mosaic pavement of classic design, presumably from the first church; while at a depth of about eight to ten inches is a floor of squared stone—evidently the level before the earthquake of 740. But most interesting of all is the apse, with its mosaic and bema. The bema are the tiers of seats, brick and stone, which make a semi-circular amphitheatre at the very east end of the church, with the bishop's throne in the centre. In the earliest days of the Church the celebrant faced the congregation over the altar—as he still does in St Peter's, Rome. At floor level there is a passage-way running right round inside the bema, with small openings looking into the church. For processional purposes, perhaps? Another bema remains in the eleventh century basilica at Torcello on one of the islands north of Venice; while there is a distant echo north of the Alps, at Norwich. There the bishop's throne is raised high up in the centre of the apse, facing down the cathedral (or did before the screen was built).

Above in the semi-dome of the apse is a large mosaic, partly restored in painted plaster, dated from this time of the Iconoclastic Controversy. Quite simple, it consists of a black cross on a gold ground (page 148). Mosaic also survives on the soffit of the arch in front of the semi-dome: a black and gold geometrical design and an inscription in Greek: '. . . in the good things of thy house. Holy is thy temple. Thou art wonderful in righteousness. Hear us, O God our Saviour: the hope of all the end of the earth and of them who are afar off upon the sea.'

Not only was the sea the defence of Constantinople, but also its life-blood.

Chapter 15

741-867

Constantine V. His supposed character. Cruel streak in the Byzantines. Damage to the harbour walls by icebergs (764). St Andrew in Crisi. Dissensions within the imperial family split by the Iconoclastic Controversy. The Empress Irene has her son Constantine VI blinded. Her reign. Arabs reach the Bosphorus. Siege by the Bulgarians (812). Walls of Leo V. Treason in the palace. Leo V murdered in the imperial chapel. Theophilus, the iconoclast Emperor. Sharp practices of businessmen in Constantinople. Denderis, the court fool. Monastery of Manuel St Nicholas. St John in Trullo. Kilise-Camii (St Theodore). Palaces rebuilt by Theophilus. The throne room. The mechanical throne. Reception of foreign embassies. The worthless Michael III. Damage done to the Serpentine Column. Gastria Convent. Murder of Michael III.

After a reign that apart from the beginnings of the Iconoclastic Controversy was remarkably free from upheavals in the city and farther afield, Leo III died in his bed in the palace (741), and was succeeded by his son Constantine V. If the portrait painted of him by his contemporaries is true he was a worthy successor to Nero. Not only was he godless and sadistic, but ran the whole gamut of sexual aberration. At least, all these failings were attributed to him by the enraged or embittered monk-chroniclers (both in the east and the west they seemed to possess a remarkable knowledge of the sexual frailties of man), who because of his iconoclastic sympathies to them seemed the devil himself. His nickname, by which he is still called, Constantine V Copronymus (Font-Defiler), arose from an unfortunate episode at his christening.

There was a credit side. He led his armies in battle against the Bulgarians, and redeemed 2,500 of his people who had been captured. But there is something undeniably odd and unpleasant about an emperor who showed pleasure on receiving a dish containing human noses, cut off as a punishment. To the iconodules he was a fiend, to the iconoclasts a saint.

An unpleasant streak of sadism formed part of the Byzantine make-up: half European, half Asian, with an entirely oriental disregard for human life. It could be summed up in their attitude to the throne. If a usurper overthrew the sovereign, God must have wished it, and been on his side. If however he failed that was also God's will, and the man deserved the horrible death that undoubtedly awaited him; an example of Byzantine double thinking. It has been suggested that calculated cruelty could be traced to the strain which Constantinople lived under. Always the fear of the enemy beyond the frontiers and frequently beyond the walls. For example, the sieges of the Arabs, one lasting six years and another thirteen months, never knowing when they might return, must have had their effect, and served to build up nervous tension over the generations.

During Constantine V's reign the walls of Constantinople had to withstand a new and most unexpected assault, by icebergs. According to the historian Theophanes in the winter of 764 the Black Sea froze for a distance of one hundred miles from the shore, and to a depth of sixty feet. On top of that snow piled up to a height of forty-five feet. When spring came again and the ice started to melt the current carried the floes down the Bosphorus. They piled up in the entrance to the Sea of Marmara and quite filled the Golden Horn. One huge iceberg was swept against the quay below the old Acropolis, shook the defences, and was itself broken in three. Even then it still towered over the city walls.

As in the previous reign the Iconoclastic Controversy gave Constantinople a martyr, and later a church dedicated to the saint. A man by the name of Andrew came all the way from Crete to rebuke personally Constantine V for his policy. He was arrested for his pains, ill-treated, and dragged through the streets as an object of derision. During this humiliation he was stabbed to death by a half-mad fisherman. The iconodules managed to get hold of his body, which they buried in or just outside the church of St Andrew (today the Koca Mustafa Paşa Mosque) on the Seventh Hill, not very far from the Silivri Gate. Later a convent grew up around the church, by then dedicated to St Andrew in Crisi (Crete). Begun by Pulcheria, the sister of Theodosius II in the fifth century, it was restored in the reign of Michael VIII (after 1261), and then extensively rebuilt in Turkish times. Originally rectangular in plan, with three apses to the east (the north has gone), the church consisted of two narthexes, an inner and an outer, which are only about half the height of the main part of the church, and occupy nearly half its length. The main area is as usual covered with a dome, and on either side there are semi-domes, and to the east quite a long bema (chancel) ending in an apse. Unfortunately, possibly the result of earthquakes, the main dome and the two semi-domes are only Turkish work. Had the original dome survived, it would have been possible to date it reasonably closely by the height of the drum on which it stood. The windows too only date from after the Conquest: nearly all windows in Byzantine churches in the city were round-headed, which the Turks converted to square, filling in the top with brick or stone. During the restoration work on St Irene, described in the previous chapter, the windows were restored to their original size and shape.

In 775 Constantine V went either to heaven or to hell, and was succeeded by his son Leo IV, unsound in mind and body. Aware of the fact, he agreed that his young son Constantine VI should be crowned, together with his mother, the Empress Irene. An oath was administered: in the palace, in Santa Sophia, and in the Hippodrome: the three estates of Byzantium. The first to swear were the five sons of Constantine V by a second marriage, who had received a rather raw deal from their half-brother Leo IV. But three times they plotted treason. On the first occasion they were forgiven; on the second instructed—or condemned—to enter the Church; but the third time they were punished with mutilation. The eldest was blinded and the others had their tongues cut out.

After five years in close confinement they escaped to the sanctuary of Santa Sophia. Nicephorus, the only one with a tongue, spoke for them all: 'Countrymen and Christians, look at your Emperor's sons, if you can still recognize our faces in this miserable condition. A life, a mutilated life, is all that the malice of our enemies has spared. It is now threatened, and we throw ourselves on your mercy.' It looked as though their pathetic appearance might lead to a popular uprising: so with lying words a court official lured them out of the cathedral, across the Forum of Augustus and into the palace. From there they were put on board a ship for Greece, and after arriving at Athens quite disappeared from history.

Now the Iconoclastic Controversy had even split the imperial palace. The regent for the young Constantine VI was his mother Irene, a beautiful Athenian who as a seventeen-year-old orphan came to Constantinople, and was married by Leo IV. While her son was manipulated by the Iconoclasts, Irene's sympathies were in the opposite direction. When he grew up he resented her domination (and capable government) and, urged on by friends, planned to banish her to Sicily. Irene heard what was afoot, and banished his friends instead. But then the Armenian guards in the palace refused to take an oath of loyalty to her alone, and recognized Constantine VI as the lawful sovereign.

Whatever affection Irene may have had for her son, it turned to a terrible hate, and she set about discrediting him with his subjects. His first marriage had ended in divorce, because he wanted to marry Theodote, his mistress, appropriately enough a lady of the bedchamber. The Church disapproved of all this, and Irene inflamed the affair until it appeared the second union was no marriage, but just an adulterous association. For eight months Constantine VI knew nothing of a conspiracy against him, but finally sensing something was afoot fled cross the water to the Asian shore.

Irene was not quite ready to strike, so sent a letter asking his forgiveness—after warning his so-called friends that if they contacted Constantine she would tell him of *their* treachery. The Emperor was brought back to Constantinople, and confined in the Porphyry palace, where he had been born, while his frightful mother decided in council how to render him unfit for the throne. On her orders, as he slept, Constantine was stabbed in the eyes with daggers—blinding being the legal punishment for adultery and thereby barring him from the throne.

For many years Constantine VI lived on, a prisoner forgotten by everyone, in the God-guarded palace.

Now the tide had turned—temporarily, against the Iconoclasts. Icons were once again exposed for public adoration, and hundreds of miracles were reported, or reports of miracles were circulated. Irene made her own secretary Patriarch, and the monasteries were revived. At St John of Studion, which once had a thousand monks, only twelve remained, and to repopulate it men were drafted in from houses in the provinces. For abbot it had the redoubtable Theodore the Studite. For his opposition to the Iconoclast emperors he would be scourged, and die in exile.

A curious little memorial to Irene, the restorer of the icons and friend of the Church, is in the Byzantine Museum in Athens: a small carved capital of the period with the inscription 'St Mary Help Irene the Empress'.

For five years she reigned in at least outward splendour, riding through the city in a gold chariot pulled by four white horses, their bridles held by four patricians who were nothing more than ennobled eunuchs. Then in 802 she in her turn was overthrown, and a chamberlain named Nicephorus went to Santa Sophia to be crowned by the patriarch. When confronted with her successor she behaved with remarkable dignity, asking for an honourable exile. Consigned to the island of Mytilene, she eked out a meagre living by spinning wool. After her death her body was taken to the great convent on Prinkipo (Büyük Ada), one of the Princes' Islands, south of the city.

During her reign the Arabs once again erupted into the Empire, and from their new capital Baghdad penetrated to the shores of the Bosphorus itself. At their head was the future

Caliph, Harun al Rashid. But this time they were not destined to cross Europe's moat and besiege the city by land. The Arabs were not the only active enemies: to the north the Bulgarians under Khan Krum were on the march again, drawn towards the city that was the magnet of the barbarians from the east and north. In 811 Nicephorus I was killed in battle, the Khan making a drinking cup of his skull. His son (Stauracius) was so severely injured in the same battle that he survived by only six months, nominating Michael I as his successor. He went nearly as quickly as he came, having been overthrown by army officers who chose a general, Leo (V) the Armenian.

The Bulgarians were back about the walls. Outside the Golden Gate the Khan Krum was making offerings to his gods for the capture of the city—human sacrifices. The two rulers agreed to meet beyond the walls, at the north end in front of the walls of Heraclius. Both parties were to come unarmed, but Leo V had placed three bowmen in an ambush. Something warned Khan Krum all was not well. He jumped on his horse and fled, arrows whistling after him. The wounds in his back were superficial, but he returned to Bulgaria swearing vengeance. However, he died soon after.

Leo V took the opportunity when the enemy left to strengthen the walls at their weakest point, on the long slope down from the top of the Sixth Hill towards the Golden Horn. There, 77 feet in front of the walls of Heraclius he added an outer defence, a second wall 260 feet long with four small towers with loopholes.

Once again treason was in the air, though in the stifling atmosphere of the imperial court it was seldom absent for long. A fellow officer, Michael the Phrygian, who had helped Leo V to the throne, thought he should have received more than he had done, and started plotting. The sequel was dramatic and terrible. On several occasions Leo V warned him to be careful, but Michael took no notice. Finally he was sentenced to death, and condemned to be burnt alive in the furnace which heated the private baths in the imperial palace. Christmas Day was chosen, but to the Empress this seemed unsuitable to say the least of it, and he was respited for a few days. Unable to sleep on Christmas

Eve, Leo V got up and went to the prison. There he found Michael had been freed from his chains, and was sleeping comfortably on the gaoler's bed. Although he went as quietly as he had come, the Emperor was noticed by a slave, who warned Michael. There was no time to lose.

He asked to be allowed to see a confessor, who at once told his friends and fellow-conspirators in the city that the matter was urgent. On Christmas Day, as on other great religious festivals, priests were allowed to enter the palace to sing in the imperial chapel. Among them this Christmas morning (820) were the conspirators, weapons beneath their robes. It was to be Leo V himself who would unwittingly give the signal for his own assassination, by intoning the first psalm. In the uncertain light of dawn in the candle-lit church, dim and glowing with dark colours, they mistook their man, and at first attacked a priest. But for Leo the respite was momentary. His pleas for mercy were met with: 'This is the hour, not of mercy, but of vengeance.' So savage was the murder that there, before the altar, Leo V's right arm—the hand still clutching a cross—was cut right off.

Michael, nicknamed the Stammerer, and quite illiterate, was transferred so quickly from his prison to the throne that for several hours he sat on it still wearing his leg-irons, before a blacksmith could be found. Unfortunately, Michael II was unworthy of such an adventure, and apart from bribing an army of Bulgarians (of all people) to come and drive away 80,000 barbarians who were besieging the city, did little for Constantinople.

'The Unfortunate' was the nickname the Greeks reserved for his son Theophilus. He could be shrewd, but also utterly capricious, as in the sentences he imposed. The story goes that when a poor widow complained about the way his own brother-in-law had heightened his palace, so shutting out the light from her own small home, Theophilus gave her the palace. Another anecdote tells of his engagement. The daughters of patricians from all over the Empire were assembled in the palace, and emulating Paris and the Hesperides, Theophilus walked up and down their lines with an apple in his hand for the one he chose. One girl, called Icaster, caught his eye, but all the gallant swain could think to say was that women had caused much evil in the world. 'And surely sir, they have also been the cause of much good.' Icaster was not going to let that slur pass unchallenged. Theophilus turned away, and gave the apple to Theodora, a girl who kept her opinions to herself.

Married life was to be far from smooth for Theodora, apart from the friction caused by her liking for icons and her husband's detestation of them. Merchants had discovered that by interesting members of the imperial family in their business ventures, their cargoes from abroad were exempt from customs duty. Theophilus found out what was going on, and when he heard an important cargo was due from Syria—in his wife's name, as it were—he was waiting at the top of one of the towers along the city wall at the entrance to the Golden Horn. As he expected, it was flying the Empress's colours. After a few questions when it docked, he ordered the whole ship to be burnt where it was, and returned to the palace to tell Theodora she was descending from an empress into a merchant.

For the most part the Iconoclastic Controversy was as barren and as futile as the destruction of religious art treasures in sixteenth and seventeenth century England. But there was one moment of light relief in the palace. One day the court fool, Denderis, ran into the Empress's apartments, and saw her kissing an icon. He asked what it was. 'My beautiful dolls, that I love,' lied Theodora. Off he went, satisfied with her answer, but when Theophilus asked what was news in the palace, he said: 'When I last visited Mama I saw most beautiful dolls in her room.'

Theophilus realized what the fool had really seen, and literally ran to the Empress's apartments, and in a rage burst into her room—accusing her of idolatry. 'Not at all,' said the self-possessed Theodora: 'that fool of yours saw me and my maidens looking into a mirror, and mistook the faces reflected there for dolls.' Baffled, but still suspicious, Theophilus withdrew. A few days later Denderis was unwise enough to return to the apartments. Theodora's maids fell on the court fool and gave him the thrashing of his life for telling tales. After that whenever Theophilus asked him if he had seen Mama's dolls lately he would merely put one hand over his mouth and the other on his buttocks and whisper miserably: 'Don't speak to me about dolls.'

It is the historian Theophanes who tells the story, and it may well be true. Among the treasures in the church of the Monastery of Vatpodei on Mount Athos is a diptych of Christ and the Virgin—called the Nina or Dolls of Theodora.

Either during or near the reign of Theophilus (823–842) several additions were made to the city's buildings. The Monastery of Manuel St Nicholas (Kefeli Mesçiti) was founded by a general of that name, uncle to Theodora, who more than once saved the Emperor's life in battle. Unable to stand the intrigues and double-crossing of the palace he retired to it himself. Only the refectory remains, a massive and gaunt oblong—it might be a warehouse, with an apse at one end, giving the interior the appearance of a very simple basilica with an open wooden roof. In point of fact this building, about seventy feet by twenty-five, may not date from the time of Manuel himself, but from a later rebuilding in the tenth century. The design resembles closely that of the Refectory of the Great Lavra (founded 963), on Mount Athos, which is still in use and has retained its frescoes.

Not far away in the same district (Fener) in Istanbul are the ruins of the little church of St John in Trullo. Its origins are completely obscure, but with its dome which was raised on a moderately high drum it may well date from this century. Outside, the three apses were unique in Constantinople in that they were semi-circular both inside and out. Even such a large apse as that of St Irene is semi-circular within, but three-sided externally.

Much more important architecturally, and attractive to look at, is the little Kilise-Camii (Church-Mosque) believed to have been dedicated to St Theodore the Tyro, a young Roman army officer martyred for refusing to take part in the persecutions under Maximilianus. It stands at the corner of three narrow and steep alleys in a rather poor quarter on the west side of the Third Hill. Because of the narrowness of the alley it is difficult to see the main front, behind which are three domes in a row over the narthex.

The façade has blind arcades of brick, supported on columns with good capitals, though now very weather-beaten and heavily coated with whitewash. The two on the left of the entrance are of the peculiar melon type, carved to represent the ribs on some varieties of that fruit. Those on the opposite side are Corinthian. Further decoration on the west front comes from panels, about four feet high, set between the columns. They are of marble, carved in shallow relief with abstract designs. The outer narthex, which with five bays is much wider than the church itself, is capped by the three windowless domes already mentioned. In 1937 mosaics of the Virgin and Child were brought to light by archaeologists, and perhaps others will one day be discovered beneath the whitewash which smothers the interior. The doorway into the inner narthex has really fine Corinthian columns on either side, and in the body of the little church, only twenty-nine feet square, the dome is supported on four spindly columns, altered in Turkish times. Here no mosaics remain—or have yet been uncovered in what is still a mosque—and the dome and the vaulting is decorated with typical Islamic abstract painting, flower designs, etc. Whilst not great art it is in its way rather attractive. Of all the Byzantine churches in the city it is one of the best preserved structurally, and one of the most engaging: partly due perhaps to its minuscule proportions.

Theophilus was himself something of a builder. He erected a huge residence on the Asian shore of the Bosphorus, based on descriptions of a new palace seen by the great scholar John the Grammarian when he went on an extremely showy, not to say ostentatious, embassy to Baghdad. Also, he made alterations to the old imperial palace near Santa Sophia, and to the Blachernae Palace just outside the land walls at their north end. It is not always easy to decide which building is being referred to by historians. But it is certain that by the middle of the ninth century the imperial palace reached its zenith. And now, except for some foundations, the beautiful fifth century mosaics sheltered by the Mosaics Museum, it is almost as though it had never existed.

On the south side of the Forum of Augustus was the entrance

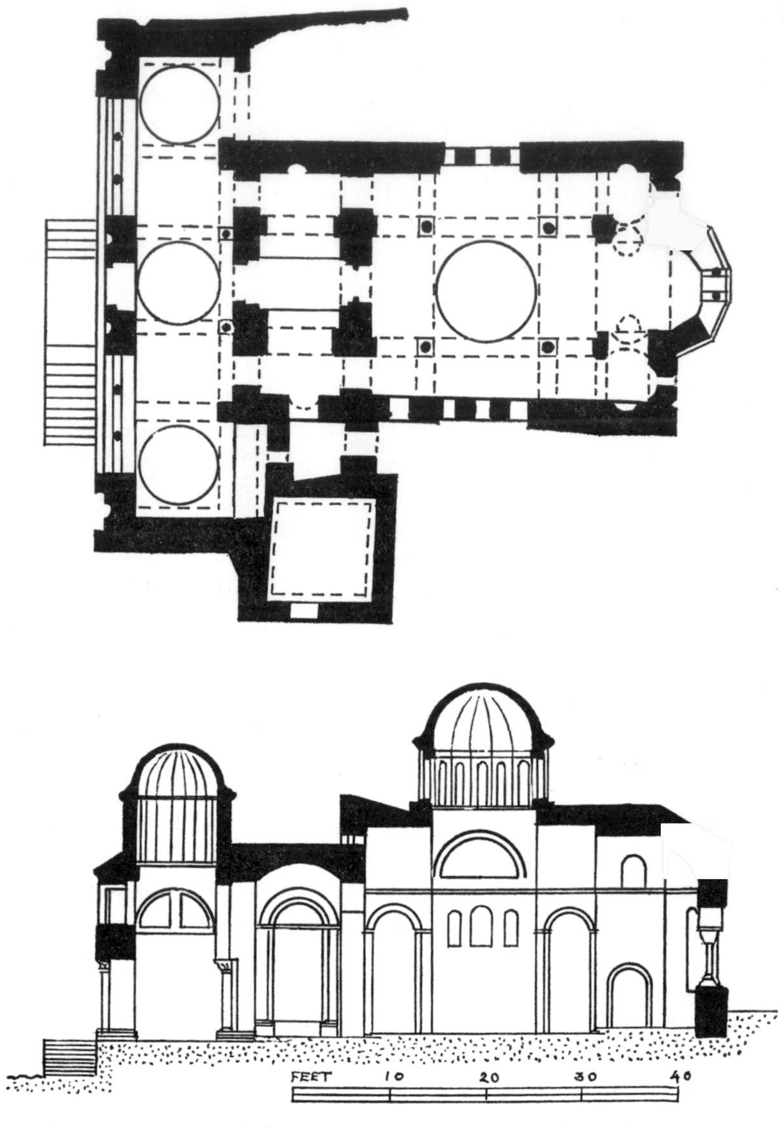

Kilise Mosque, ninth-century church, believed dedicated to St Theodore the Tyro

to the Chalké, that part of the imperial palace with the roof of gilded tiles. Nearby was the Magnaurus, containing the audience chamber, throne room, and banqueting hall of the Nineteen Couches. Directly behind the Chalké stood the Palace of the Daphne—the private part of the imperial residence, which included the Church of St Stephen. Towards the end of the ninth century Basil I added yet another church, with three domes, which must have been magnificently decorated with marble and gold and silver fittings. Today it is as though it had never existed. Lower down the hill, between the Hippodrome and walls stood the sacred or God-guarded palace, containing the private sleeping apartments of the Emperor. Somewhere near the harbour of the Boucleon is the site of the Porphyry Palace (see page 158), where it was the custom for the imperial children to be born.

Theophilus, as has been remarked, was shrewd. He understood the minds and background of many of the men who came to visit his court, and what would impress them. In the throne room stood a full-sized tree of gold, with mechanical birds that sang on its branches: while the throne itself was a masterpiece of showmanship. In the next century, the year was 948, Bishop Liutprand of Cremona, was received in audience by Constantine VII Porphyrogenitus. He left an account of what he saw and what happened. As he approached the throne on which the Emperor was seated the mechanical birds began to sing, and two lifesize lions (also of gold) roared. Three times the bishop had to fall prostrate before the Supreme Being, and touch the ground with his forehead. When he got to his feet again, and looked up it was to discover the Emperor on his throne had been hoisted mechanically nearly to the ceiling, and was now wearing a robe of even greater magnificence. During the interview he never spoke, and when all the wonders had had time to impress themselves on the stranger's mind, he was conducted from the chamber. The dour bishop was not favourably impressed by what he saw, but such theatrical marvels were not primarily intended for a reasonably sophisticated west-European. Such a display must have seemed near-magic to the semi-barbarian and over-awed ambassadors of the Avars, the Bulgarians, the Arabs, and others who normally only saw Constantinople from beyond the Theodosian walls.

On arrival in the city an ambassador stopped at the Golden Gate, where he awaited the court officials who would conduct him to the palace prepared for his reception, where he was quite isolated from contact with anyone in Constantinople. When he went sightseeing he was taken everywhere, so he should only see what was good for the Empire, and not the teeming tenements down narrow alleys just off the Mesé, for example.

At his first audience he offered the presents which he had brought, and was entertained with a banquet at which the other ambassadors were present, graded not in seniority, but according to the Emperor's personal opinion of their country's worth. Byzantium did not herself maintain ambassadors in other countries, but sent numerous envoys to and fro across the civilized world. It was expected as a duty that missionaries and merchants would collect information on their travels which could be of use to the Empire which they passed on to the right authorities on their return.

From time to time the foreign ambassadors came to the Emperor with flowery requests from their own sovereigns to be allowed to marry into the Byzantine ruling house. To escape with some degree of tact from a series of unwanted alliances, the ambassadors were told—with regret—that the founder of their city had proscribed such marriages, and the law was carved on the altar of Santa Sophia itself. This was a downright lie: there was no such law. When they wanted, the emperors and their children contracted marriages with foreigners who were neither orthodox nor, in at least two cases, even Christian.

On January 20, 842, Theophilus died, leaving his five-year-old son Michael as the new Emperor. The date was important, for it marked the end of the Iconoclastic Controversy, and a slow renaissance in the arts in Constantinople.

Michael III grew up into a vicious young man, surprisingly enough encouraged by his own mother, and at the age of eighteen he threw off her regency. Millions were squandered on his male favourites, to the point of almost bankrupting the exchequer. He spent most of his time in the theatre or the Hippodrome. On one occasion he is said to have silenced a messenger bringing news of an invasion, and ordered warning beacons to be extinguished, lest the distraction interrupt an important race.

He treated the charioteers as equals, dined with them and acted as godfather to their children. When in his cups, which was frequently, he gave the most cruel and wanton commands, and then the next morning he would commend his servants for disobeying. To all this he added blasphemy, dressing up as the patriarch and using the altar vessels at most profane banquets, when communion was celebrated with a mixture of vinegar and mustard.

Michael III left a permanent mark on the Serpentine Column in the Hippodrome. In the course of one of his nocturnal orgies he and his companions arranged an incantation during which three muscular men, each with a sledge-hammer, knocked off the heads of the three serpents at a signal given by an unfrocked abbot. All that then remained was one lower jaw, and according to legend this fragment remained until broken off with his iron mace by Mehmet II as he passed through the Hippodrome after the conquest of 1453. But evidently the heads were restored at some unknown date: a sixteenth-century traveller describes them quite fully.

Today the remains of the Column rise up out of a circular stone-lined excavation (the floor of the arena is ten to twelve feet below the present level of the At Meydani), split at the bottom and with the rubble core spilling out of its hollow interior. The once gilded bronze now a deep green in colour, it is a twisted, resentful fragment from a way of life and thought completely alien to the rise and fall of the two glittering civilizations which it has witnessed since it was brought from Delphi to Constantinople.

In its earlier days the city possessed a university with a magnificent library of 36,000 volumes, including an ancient Homer on a roll 120 feet long. Then, in the time of Leo III, the library was burnt, and the university itself abolished. But now, as a result of the efforts made by the Caesar Bardas (Michael III's uncle), a school was opened in part of the imperial palace, under the direction of the learned Bishop of Thessalonika.

When Theodora remonstrated with her son over the way he was ruling—having those murdered who crossed his path, she and his four sisters were confined in the Gastria Convent, which stood near the present Samatya Street on the way to the Golden Gate. The ruins of the chapel (Sancaktar Mesçiti) still stand, though they probably go back no further than the fourteenth century.

But Michael III had nearly run his odious course. When Basil the Macedonian entered the Emperor's life he held an important position in the imperial stables, which he received as a result of his prowess as a horse-trainer. Soon he and his sovereign were close friends, and as a mark of especial favour Michael gave him a discarded mistress to marry. At this time if anyone ruled in Constantinople, it was the Caesar Bardas, and not his nephew. Basil the Macedonian was well aware of Michael's hatred of his relative, and stabbed him to death with his sword. A month later the murderer received the title of Augustus, and was given the ruling of the Empire. Having received so much, Basil decided to take the little that was not yet his, and murdered Michael as he slept.

Chapter 16

867-959

Basil I. His career, ruthless character and reign. The Manganae Palace. Leo VI. His marital difficulties. Mosaic of the Emperor in Santa Sophia. Constantine VII Porphyrogenitus. A man of humanity and creative ability. His book *De Ceremoniis,* a manual of Byzantine court ritual.

From this unpromising background sprang the Macedonian Dynasty, one of the greatest in the long history of Byzantium. Basil I claimed that he was descended from a Roman family which had settled in Adrianople, and come down in the world. Others, who may well have known what they were talking about, said he was a Macedonian peasant of Armenian origin. His son, Leo VI certainly looked Armenian. Also, his wife was suspiciously well equipped with notable ancestors: Constantine the Great and Alexander the Great.

As a child, Basil declared, he had been captured and made a slave by invading Bulgarians but, after being redeemed by the Empire, came to seek his fortune in Constantinople. He entered the city by the civilian gate beside the Golden Gate, and as it was dusk and he had nowhere to sleep, lay down on the step of the church of St Diomed, only a few hundred yards within the walls. There he was found by a monk who not only gave him food, but also helped him find a job, in the service of one of the Emperor's relatives.

With his new master he went to Greece, where his good looks attracted the attention of an ageing well-to-do woman called Danelis, who made her money in the silk business in Patras.

She gave him a number of slaves as a present, whom he promptly sold, investing the money by buying a number of villages in Macedonia. The future Emperor of Byzantium had shrewd business instincts. Fate was on his side. Now his fame as a wrestler and as a horse-tamer had reached imperial ears, and he was given a position of importance in the palace stables. So began the murderous climb to power described in the previous chapter.

As a sop either to his conscience or the Church, Basil dedicated a number of churches to St Michael. He built up the army into a disciplined body, and led it in the field, the first time he had seen active service. But obviously he was Byzantine through and through. Of a troublesome rebel he exclaimed that with God's help he would shoot three arrows through his head. This he did, after the rebel's head had been obtained by treachery, and hung from a tree.

On the credit side Basil I put an end to the squandering of the revenues within the imperial palaces, built roads, aqueducts, hospitals, and—or so it is said—founded or rebuilt one hundred churches. He is also credited with building the Manganae, a palace covering a huge area at the bottom of the hill between Santa Sophia and the Sea of Marmara: even in the hottest weather the palace was moderately cool, catching the breeze coming down the Bosphorus from the Black Sea. In 1871 when the workmen were laying the track for the railway they came across the foundations of a building 322 × 53 feet, and numerous broken columns and capitals. Today, apart from the railway, the region is occupied by the Gülhane Hospital, barracks and their dusty squares, and waste land. At least the view across to Usküdar and Kadiköy is superb.

But above all, in the reign of Basil I, it was the law that needed reforming. On his orders Justinian's Institutes, Pandenects, Code, and Novels were revised—in Greek, a significant change. Slowly the civilization of Greece was winning over that of Rome. The new edition of the laws of the East Roman Empire were called the Basilics, and they remained the basis of civil administration until the final catastrophe of 1453.

In A.D. 886 it was a stag that literally brought Basil I off his throne. During a hunt it turned on the Emperor, caught its horns in his belt and unhorsed him, causing him to fall so violently that he died soon after. There is something reptilian and repellent about the man—which also sums up the whole attitude to imperial majesty and to life: more oriental than western. When one of the Emperor's suite saw what had happened when the stag became entangled in Basil I's harness, he drew his knife to cut the Emperor free. On the spot Basil ordered him to be beheaded. It was forbidden on pain of death to draw a knife near the Emperor.

He left three sons, Leo, Alexander, and Constantine. Leo VI, called 'the Wise' (or 'the Philosopher'), became Emperor on March 1, 886. Certainly the fact that he could read and write was an advance on such rulers as Phocas or Michael II but, in spite of his nickname, his life was one of sensual and gastronomic indulgence. As Gibbon suggests, his academic glory was perhaps a reflection of his teacher, the learned patriarch Photius, a man for long considered one of the principal figures in the breach with the Roman Catholic church.

Like Henry VIII, Leo VI was bedevilled with the question of an heir. His first three marriages were childless, while a fourth would put him outside the Orthodox Church. Remarriage was tolerated, a third was frowned on, while a fourth was positively forbidden. To make matters worse a beautiful black-eyed girl called Zoë had given birth to a son. What was more the birth had taken place in the Porphyry palace of the Boucleon, a building reserved for the legitimate heirs of the emperors of Byzantium. Only after that had Leo VI and Zoë become man and wife.

The Patriarch Nicholas then deposed the priest who had conducted the service, and Zoë was treated as an outcast. At this the Emperor in his turn deposed the patriarch and the schism was not finally ended until 921, when the Synod agreed that a fourth marriage was not allowable. Annually the decision was read from the pulpit of St Irene in the presence of the Emperor—but by that date Leo VI was dead.

Leo VI has his place in the iconography of Santa Sophia, in the great mosaic over the royal door from the inner narthex into the cathedral itself. The mosaic must be the oldest in the city which dates from after the end of the Iconoclastic Controversy and shows figures. On either side the eight identical semi-circular spaces over the other doorways have the simple black crosses on a gold ground, typical of the barren years. In the centre of the mosaic sits Christ, His hand upraised in blessing, and on either side roundels with portraits of the Virgin and the Archangel Gabriel—allusions to the Emperor's homily on the Annunciation—while at the bottom left is Leo VI himself. He is performing the act of homage before Christ which as Emperor he would demand from his subjects: this was proskynesis, touching the ground with the forehead and spreading the hands in supplication. In origin Leo VI was Armenian, and the artist has depicted his curly black beard and pronounced nose with a realism worthy of Goya. Flippantly the Turks say he is pleading with Christ about his illegal fourth marriage. With the remote, austere figure of Christ, the mosaic is one of the glories of Byzantine art, and coming as it does at the end of the Iconoclastic Controversy is of major historical and artistic importance.

After Leo's death the beautiful Zoë was nominally the regent, but there was in fact a succession of self-seekers, who elbowed the retiring Constantine VII out of the picture. For his part the rightful Emperor, his long face accentuated by a beard so that he almost resembled a grandee painted by Velasquez, was really a scholar and an artist, who spent his time writing and making music, eking out a small allowance by selling his own paintings. He only became the rightful ruler because a plot hatched by the two usurping sons of Romanos I misfired. They intended to overthrow their father, banish him to one of the Princes' Islands, and rule in his place. Also, it was part of the plan that Constantine VII should be assassinated at a banquet, but their sister—who was Constantine's wife—warned him in time, and the two schemers found themselves sharing the island with their father.

When news of the happenings in the palace reached the city there was a clamour at one of the gates in the north part of the outside wall (near the present Bab-i-Hamayum Gate leading in the opposite direction into the Seraglio). The people wanted to know what had happened to their well loved Constantine; bareheaded and dishevelled he came and showed himself through the iron bars, and to everyone's relief they could see he was safe and well.

Now at the age of forty Constantine VII really was Emperor in his own palace. Although less memorable than a number of the rulers of Byzantium he was one of the very few for whom morality, charity, justice, and goodness of heart were more than words. Perhaps his best memorial is his writing: a biography of his grandfather Basil I, and that extraordinary book, written for the use of his own son, *De Ceremoniis*. It is a detailed manual of Byzantine court ritual, and gives a deep and comprehensive insight into what went on in that most tradition-bound of imperial palaces. Birth, marriage, death, coronation, anniversaries: all these and a host of other occasions are dealt with in detail. Also, all the greetings that should be chanted at the Emperor are given in full. Constantine wrote in Greek, but so far the book has only been translated into French and German.

In all over ninety occasions are dealt with. By Constantine's time it was customary that the new Emperor should be crowned in Santa Sophia.

'He lights tapers at the silver doors, passes into the nave . . . He prays before the holy gates (in the screen) after lighting more tapers, and ascends the Ambo with the Patriarch. Then, the Patriarch prays over the imperial robe and puts it on the sovereign. Then, the Patriarch prays over the sovereign's crown, and, having finished, the Patriarch himself takes the crown and places it on the sovereign's head. At once the people thrice call out the acclamation "Holy, Holy, Holy, Glory to God on high and peace on earth".'

Then, after the new Emperor has gone to his throne and received the homage of the officers of state there come the acclamations of the well-schooled choruses of the Demes—the leaders of the two great factions: the Greens and the Blues.

First the Chorus:

'This day is the joy and glory of the world . . .'

They pause while the people repeat it three times, as they will repeat everything the chorus declaims.

> '. . . in which the crown of the Empire . . . has been worthily set on your head.
> 'Glory to God, the master of all things.'
> 'Glory to God who made you Emperor.'

And so it continues, repetition upon repetition, and flowery eulogies—typically oriental—in praise of the Emperor, who as like as not is a palace guard who has just bribed his way to the throne, or a nobleman who has come to his present position by way of revolution and murder.

This particular acclamation ends with repetitions of 'Many years to you', and to the Augusta (usually, but not always the Empress), and to both of them, and to the purple-born children, to the whole family, to the parents and so on, and so on. From this system of two choirs answering one another developed the antiphonal music of the church of the Middle Ages. In the west it perhaps culminated in the Venetian school of the sixteenth and seventeenth centuries, where both Gabrieli and Monteverdi (notably in the Vespers, 1610) exploited the architectural possibilities of St Mark's in the placing of divided choirs.

Having crowned the Emperor, Constantine tells how he shall be buried.

'One sets up, in [the chamber] of the Nineteen Couches, the golden bed, and the said mortal remains are exposed there, crown on head, the robe of gold and the purple shoes. . . . Next the Preposite gives a sign to the Master of the Ceremonies and he then says: "Go out, Emperor, here the King of Kings and the Lord of Lords calls you." He says that three times, and at once, the mortal remains are taken up by the officers of the Palace Guard and carried into the Chalké. They place it here and perform the usual rites. When the mortal remains then leave by the Chalké, carried by the Imperial Protospathaires, passing along Mesé [presumably branching off at the Forum of Theodosius, the modern Beyazit Square, to go to the Church of the Apostles]. There the Preposite declaims three times: "Enter, Emperor, the King of Kings and the Lord of Lords calls thee." Then thus, "Take off the crown from thy head." And at once, the Preposite lifts it off and puts a simple headband of purple on him, and then he is placed in the tomb.'

The whole of the palace was bound up with ritual, and 'What must be observed . . .' and 'Acclamations to be chanted' by the chorus and dutiful citizens. 'What must be observed when a purple-born child is born.' 'What must be observed on the promotion of a Caesar', right down the social and bureaucratic scale to 'What must be observed on the promotion of an office chief'. The regulations even laid down 'What must be observed' when a reception had to be held in the private apartments instead of in the grounds because the winter winds were too strong. What went on in the Hippodrome also had its place in *De Ceremoniis*.

'. . . if during a lap a charioteer loses his helmet, even if he is in the lead and his horses are running better than all the [other] chariots, that race shall be counted null and void.'

One of the traditions embodied in *De Ceremoniis* which Byzantium inherited from Rome was the triumph, to celebrate a victory. In the Christian city of Constantine, the victories over the infidels were celebrated most frequently and with the most feeling. One of the bas-reliefs on the pedestal of the Obelisk of Theodosius shows the Emperor attending a triumph in the Hippodrome. There in the front of the imperial box are the prisoners, on their knees bowing their heads and making offerings.

It must never be forgotten that religion permeated every aspect of daily life in Constantinople: even more, if possible, than in western Europe of the Middle Ages. As the triumph unrolled in the Hippodrome the chorus chanted, and the crowd repeated three times:

'"Glory to God, Sovereign of all things. Glory to God who has ravaged the Arab towns. Glory to God who has cast in shame the arrogance of [so and so], the enemy of Christ. Lord, we give thanks to thee for all things because You have great pity for Thy people in making him [the Emperor] rule with such power." Then, when the prisoners fall to the ground, heads in front, the Actuarios make a sign and the Chorus says: "Our enemies have fallen by God's judgement." And the people repeat it thrice.'

Without doubt the oddest ritual described by Constantine Porphyrogenitus is 'What shall be observed at the Banquet of the Nineteen Couches, during the Gothic Games'. These games, more a stylized dance, were performed once a year in the banqueting chamber of the Boucleon Palace. Even then, in the tenth century, their origins were already obscure and the meaning of the gibberish the performers had to declaim lost to the world. Presumably their origins go back to the time of the Gothic invasions at the end of the fourth century.

'On the left side . . . stands the maistor [spokesman] of the Blue Faction with a small number of demotes and lute players with their instruments and behind them the Goths wearing skins turned inside out and different types of masks, holding a shield in the left hand and rods in the right.'

The same order was observed on the right side for the Greens. When the Emperor gave the signal for the evolutions to begin, they were accompanied with declaimed phrases, for the most part completely incomprehensible.

'Striking the shields with the rods as they run forward the Goths exclaim: "Toul, Toul", saying it without stopping, they ascend close to the Imperial table [of gold], and a little distance from it . . . they position themselves in a circular movement like an army. When they have taken up their places: those of the Blues to the left, those of the Greens to the right . . . all together they sing the Gothic songs, the lutes playing the appropriate melodies: "Deumonobuggubele, Gubilous, Gubelares", declaimed the performers, together with phrases like "Ezechias having taken in war the arms of the Assyrians, putting his sole hope in God who loves mankind, has subjugated all the races and the tyranny of the atheists. That the Saviour, good Sovereign, reduces all your enemies to slavery beneath your feet."'

Off they go again: '*Iber, Iberiem, Tou Iggerous, Gergerethro.*' Then the maistores, together with the demotes say the alphabet, declaiming a statement in praise of the Emperor at each letter.

This extraordinary alphabetical game is punctuated throughout with the evolutions of the Goths.

'When the alphabet has been completed, they say "God grant long days to your Holy Empire!" And the Goths striking their shields with their rods, saying without ceasing: "Toul, Toul", leave at a run.'*

The Mad Hatter would surely have been in his element at such a party.

There was even a section headed 'What must be observed when a new fiancée is introduced to the house of her bridegroom', towards the end of which the emotional temperature rises several degrees:

'In the evening the two factions arrive with their own portable organs [two are shown in one of the bas-reliefs on the pedestal of the Obelisk of Theodosius], and the wife-to-be having come down accompanied by tambourines and cymbals, [is] placed on a horse, stops, and the two factions acclaim her. The chorus concludes by singing: "I have gathered the flowers of the field and I have placed them with fervour in the nuptial chamber. I have seen the young married couple like a sun on the precious golden couch. They were embracing each other with amorous desire, joy to contemplate their delightful beauty, and roses for them who are as beautiful as a rose. Joy to the golden couple."'

But perhaps the instructions that best illustrate the cocoon of ritual that surrounded the Emperor concerned his arrival in the Hippodrome before the start of the chariot races. 'Then, after crossing the Augusteus, he enters St Stephen's and from there goes by way of the private staircase into the apartment behind the Kathisma, and there looks on until all is ready.' Down below the charioteers are waiting, and so are the horses. The attendants with their marker flags are in their places, the tiers of seats are all occupied. Now the Emperor is coming down the stone staircase to the shouts of 'Give way!' and simply 'Way!' He goes into his apartment, the dressers are called in and he is robed and crowned. Then he goes into the narrow

* A fresco, depicting the Gothic Games, survives in Santa Sophia, Kiev.

dining-chamber behind the Imperial Box, where he awaits the patricians.

'Having entered, the Patricians with the Strategos fall to the ground, and when they get up again the Emperor makes a sign to the Preposite who says in a loud voice: "If it please you".' Then they form up into a procession, everyone with his allotted place, and when all is ready '. . . the Master of the Ceremonies having taken the extremity of the Emperor's robe, and having folded it, gives it to the Emperor so that when he has reached the throne he can bless the people with this fold according to custom.

'The Emperor . . . goes out and ascends the Kathisma [near where the Kaiser Wilhelm II Fountain now stands on the At Meydani] and standing before the throne blesses the people thrice: first the middle, secondly towards the Blue faction and thirdly towards the Green. Then he sits down on his throne. The Preposite, having come out of the Kathisma, takes his place at the top of the steps and calls the Patricians and the Strategos, who, according to custom, made a deep obeisance to the Emperor, acclaiming him as they leave, they then go and stand at the foot of the steps in front of the great door [or gate]. When all is ready, the Preposite receives a sign from the Emperor, and after coming out, he again goes to the top of the steps and makes a sign of the Cross to these [individuals], who having made a deep obeisance go off to their places on the benches.'

Then, and only then, can the races begin.

Chapter 17

959–1025

Romanos I and the Empress Theophanto. Church of the Myrelaion. Nicephorus II Phocas, murdered by Theophanto's lover, John I Zimisces. Possible scene of the crime. Basil II: Byzantium's last great warrior emperor. His appearance and behaviour. The blinding of the Bulgarian Army. St Mary Diaconissa. St Theodosia.

Whether guilty or not, his son Romanos II (959–963) was damned in the eyes of the city on suspicion of poisoning Constantine VII. But it was understandable to doubt the manner of of any emperor's death if he was not full of years or obviously the victim of an illness recognized as fatal. What was more, in his wife he had an even greater handicap. Theophanto was the daughter of an inn-keeper, ravishingly beautiful, but completely without principles of any kind. Indeed, there were many who thought she and not her husband was responsible for the death of the good Constantine. She was the real ruler in the Boucleon Palace, and on her jealous orders her sister-in-law Agatha was banished from court, and ordered to take the veil in the Myrelaion Monastery. The church remains, now called the Bodrum Camii (Cellar Mosque), a few yards from the busy Ordu Street near the bottom of the hill where it meets the Atatürk Bulvari. The dedication of the church is unknown, but it was in the time of Romanos II that it was restored and the convent re-opened after being closed since the Iconoclastic Controversy. The dome, standing on a drum with windows, is supported on four columns

—the church is the cross-in-square plan with three apses and a narthex—and for a Byzantine building of this date the south side, overlooking the street from the little mound on which the church stands, is quite elaborate. An arcade of three arches and above a cornice formed of bricks set so that they make a small triangular projection. In 1911 the whole district was swept by fire and the Bodrum Camii itself seriously damaged. Today it is still locked up, and reminiscent of a Wren church after the blitz. Close by is the cistern of Mirelaion (the name means Oil-of-Myrrh), another of Constantinople's underground buildings, though not nearly as large as the Yerebatan Serayi or the Binbirdirek Cistern.

For a while Theophanto ruled as regent—after the suspicious death of Romanos II—then chose another husband in the soldier Nicephorus Phocas, brilliant but physically repellent. There was no doubt who was head of the imperial household, and it was not Theophanto. She had numerous lovers, among them John Zimisces, a general who for reasons of personal spite had been reduced in rank and exiled. This Theophanto mitigated to living at Chalcedon, within sight of the palace windows across the mouth of the Bosphorus.

The heavy taxes imposed by Nicephorus II made him exceedingly unpopular in the city. On one occasion, when returning from a visit to the holy spring outside the Pegé Gate (Silivri Kapisi), he was mobbed in the Forum of Constantine, and was lucky to escape down the hill to the palace. After that experience, together with the rumour of an assassination plot, he decided to erect a high wall which completely cut off the Boucleon Palace from the rest of the city. Soon after he added yet another palace in the grounds, overlooking the sea and its façade forming part of the walls.

After six years Theophanto wanted to be rid of her domineering husband, and enlisted the aid of John Zimisces, still across the water at Chalcedon. The coup came on December 10, 969: a bitterly cold night when the north wind had brought snow in its train, and Constantinople was muffled beneath a heavy fall. With difficulty John Zimisces and his party brought their boat across, contending not only with the current, strong at all times, but also the wind, into which they were heading. However, they eventually made it, and came alongside one of the palaces: probably that which has the three big doorways opening onto a large and long vanished balcony (page 149). Perhaps it should be pointed out that the fine road which now encircles the walls along the Sea of Marmara is a recent addition to the city.

Theophanto's women were waiting for the signal—a soft whistle, and lowered a large basket on the end of a rope. One by one the conspirators were hauled up. Last to leave the boat was John Zimisces himself: a handsome but diminutive Armenian. Quietly they made for Nicephorus's apartment, only to find it empty. The Emperor had got wind that all was not as it should be, and chosen to sleep in another room. John Zimisces thought they had been betrayed, and started to retreat. Then a eunuch appeared, and led them to the sleeping Emperor, lying on the floor on a bearskin rug and covered only with a scarlet woollen blanket. He woke to see he was surrounded by thirty daggers and swords. 'Lord have mercy upon me', he exclaimed. Slowly and cruelly the murderers went about their work, and a few minutes later his head was shown at a window to inform the city it had a new Emperor, John I Zimisces.

As the story goes, this all happened the night following the completion of the wall about the land side of the palace. His successors were not blind to the warning, and sentries were always kept posted on the terrace and the quay of the Boucleon harbour.

When John I went in procession to Santa Sophia a few days later for his coronation, he was met at the entrance by the patriarch who demanded that he should dissociate himself from the Empress Theophanto. This John I had no hesitation in doing. Now he had the throne, he could afford to discard the woman who had murdered both her husbands: Romanos II and Nicephorus II. Why should he escape with his life when this terrible creature tired of him? Theophanto was banished to a convent: presumably she left it at some later date as she is supposed to have died during a debauch. But before being dismissed from the palace she literally attacked her own son, the future Basil II, screaming he was illegitimate and that one of her lovers and not Romanos II was his real father.

Contrary to what might have been expected, John Zimisces proved a good ruler: approachable, humane, and brave in battle. In the end he brought about his own downfall with his tongue. When he discovered that much of the newly-conquered lands in the east were being given to the eunuchs who infested the palace he exclaimed: 'And is it for them that we have fought and conquered? Is it for them that we shed our blood, and exhaust the treasures of our people?'

He became the fourth emperor in succession to have his life cut short: possibly by poison (976).

Now Basil II really was Emperor, though he had been so nominally since 959. There is a glimpse of the man behind the magnificent robes, hemmed in by his nobles and soldiers. 'In manner he was abrupt, and rough in character, prone to anger and obstinate, abstemious in his mode of life, and abhorring all delicate living.' (Psellos.) A throw-back to his Macedonian peasant background, perhaps. Undersized, round-faced, with a moderate forehead, bright flashing eyes and a thick beard and whiskers which he twirled incessantly. He spoke in short sentences, more like a peasant than one of imperial rank, and had a habit of sticking out his elbow and resting his fingers on his hips. This man was the last truly great emperor in Byzantium's history.

Beneath his court robes or armour he wore a monk's habit: he never ate meat nor drank wine and led a celibate life. It had not always been like that. When young he enjoyed a riotous time and then, as Henry V of England did after his succession to the throne, changed completely. There was little about Basil II to catch the public fancy, and he did not go out of his way to court popularity. Leading an army was more to his liking than riding in a procession, and his greatest achievement was to break the power of the rapidly growing Bulgarian Empire on Byzantium's northern frontier. To this day he is regarded as a national hero by the Greeks. Perhaps the only thing the Greeks and the Turks really have in common is a mutual dislike of the Bulgarians.

In 1014 he decisively defeated the Bulgarians at Cimbalongus, capturing 15,000 of their soldiers. These Basil II allowed to return home, but when the old Tzar Samuel realized what had happened to his army, he collapsed and died. They came in groups of one hundred, each with his hand on the shoulder of the man in front. The leading man of each group still had one eye, so he could see the way. All the others had been completely blinded. The glittering, brilliant beauty of the dragon-fly belonged to Byzantium, but also the venom of the scorpion.

To his subjects in Constantinople the Emperor was Basil the Bulgar-Slayer (Bulgaroktonos), and the awe and respect they had for him long outlived his death, supporting the Macedonian Dynasty to its tottering close under the raddled and amorous Empress Zoë. Much of importance which concerns the history of the Empire happened during this coldblooded man's reign, such as the conversion to Christianity of Russia (apparently the Grand Duke Vladimir's explanation why he chose Christianity and not Islam was that no Russian could stand a religion which forbade liquor), and Byzantium's dominion over all the Balkans from Constantinople to Belgrade—but all that lies beyond a book concerned with the city and its rulers.

Whilst planning a war against the Saracens in Sicily Basil II died, in 1025, at the age of sixty-eight, leaving the throne to his frivolous and dissipated brother Constantine VIII.

Although Basil II and his circle at court despised the arts, the renaissance which began with the conclusion of the Iconoclastic Controversy had not yet spent itself, and an ever increasing interest was being shown in literature, and new churches were going up in Constantinople—few of which can be dated with absolute certainty—and the illumination of manuscripts had reached new heights.

Two churches are of particular importance: the church of the Monastery of Akataleptos (Kalendar Camii) and Saint Theodosia (Gül Camii). In Arnold van Millingen's magnificent book on the churches of Constantinople the Kalendar Camii is referred to as St Mary Diaconissa, but nothing appears to be known about its history. The only evidence for its date is its similarity to the tenth century Protarton church at Karyes on Mount

Athos. Since the adjoining site has recently been cleared of its old buildings the exterior of this hunched up little church can be seen very well: though, as in the City of London, it is inevitable that before long it will be hemmed in by tall new structures. The oldest part forms a domed cross, with tiny chapels in the angles, and windows of three lights in the transepts. To the east the original apse has been destroyed, though the later double narthex at the west end still remains.

Unfortunately it is kept locked up, as apparently the interior still retains much of its original marble veneers covering the lower part of the walls, set in carved frames, similar to the decoration employed in Santa Sophia and St Saviour in Chora.

If the exterior of Santa Sophia is saved from heaviness by its swelling half-domes rising up to the great cupola, St Theodosia is not. At close quarters the dome, which has no drum nor windows, disappears behind the high walls, which seem to be in good condition and well pointed up. The saint achieved her martyrdom during the Iconoclastic Controversy, in the reign of Leo III. When the Emperor's order for the removal of the huge icon of Christ over the Bronze Gate of the imperial palace was being carried out, Theodosia, at the head of a band of women, toppled the ladder on which the man, an officer, was standing. The fall killed him outright. Theodosia was seized by a soldier and hustled through the city to the Forum of the Ox, where he put her to death by driving a ram's horn through her neck.

If the box-like exterior is frankly disappointing (though the triple apse is handsome, and quite elaborately decorated with blind arches, niches, and above the two side-apses an elaborate cornice), the interior is impressive. No mosaics remain—or have been rediscovered, and walls and vaulting are white-washed. Including the wide narthex, St Theodosia is about eighty feet long inside, with large galleries for women over the west end and the north and south aisles. The arches which support the dome are pointed, which suggests they, like the dome itself, date only from post-Conquest times. Below, the nave is separated from the aisles by an arcade of three openings. So often, when the Turks wished to obtain a large central praying area in a mosque which was a one-time church, they took

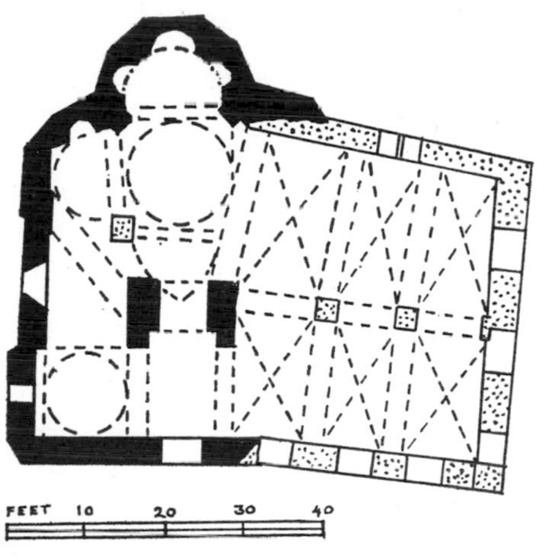

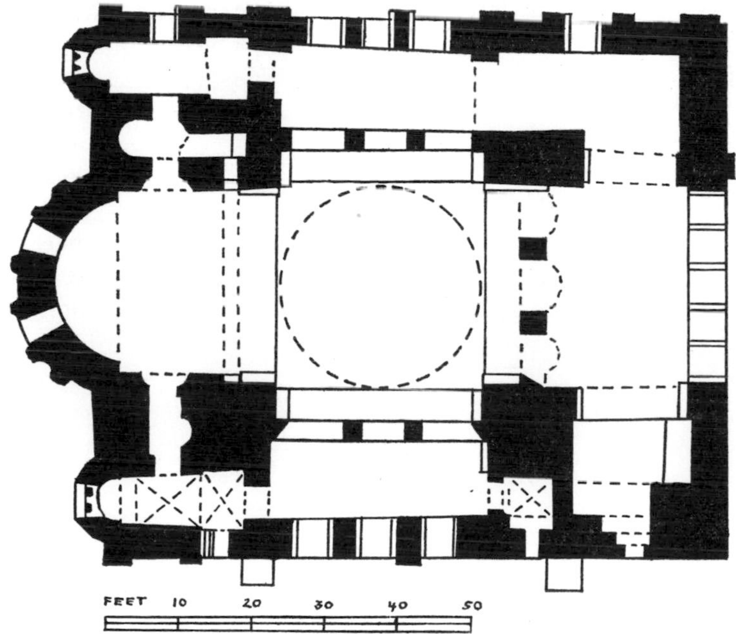

(*Above*) St Mary of the Mongols, Mouchliotissa, 1261, with later additions

(*Below*) St Theodosia, Rose Mosque, a ninth-century church

down the stone or marble arcades between the main arches, and by so doing deprived it of a degree of diversity and mystery. But in St Theodosia they remain: square piers supporting small round-headed arches. Though, of course, on a much smaller scale, the main piers which support the dome are nearly as massive as those in Santa Sophia. The one to the south-east has a small chamber in it, containing a tomb dating from Turkish times. Tradition has it that Constantine XI, Byzantium's last emperor, lies buried there. After his body had been identified—he was killed during the siege of 1453, it was first buried in the Church of the Apostles, and then when that was pulled down to make way for the Fatih Camii—the Conqueror's Mosque—it was moved to St Theodosia. The inscription over the door, in Turkish, reads: 'Tomb of the Apostles, disciples of Jesus. Peace to him.' The Church of the Apostles was demolished in or before 1463, while St Theodosia remained a church until 1506, so at least as far as dating is concerned it is possible. Also, one of the titles of the Byzantine Emperors was Equal of the Apostles, and another The Thirteenth Apostle.

Chapter 18

1025–1056

Palace intrigues. Insurrection in the city. Michael V overthrown. Flees to St John of Studion for refuge. The Empress Zoë (1028–1050). Mosaic portraits of the imperial family in Santa Sophia. St Saviour Pantepopte.

No greater contrast could be found in the imperial palaces than between Basil II and his brother Constantine VIII. He should have worn not a diadem, but a wreath of vine leaves. Little better were his three daughters, perhaps the only human beings towards whom Basil II had ever shown any affection. Eldest was Eudoxia, a retiring woman with a face pitted by smallpox, who chose the life of a nun. Then came Theodora, a miser. At forty-eight Zoë was the youngest: she was the most interesting and least admirable.

In quick succession, when she became ruler, she took two husbands—nonentities—and then the scheming eunuch of a court chamberlain talked her into adopting his nephew as her heir. This was done, and the young man, Michael V Kalaphates (ship's chandler, after his profession), wasted little time in ousting his elderly protectoress. She was expelled so that 'the beast might have the palace to house in all to himself'. (Psellos.) Accused of being a poisoner she was sent with only one maid to wait on her to one of the Princes' Islands: hard outlines in the mid-day sun on the horizon of the Sea of Marmara.

The dutiful Senate approved his actions, and a proclamation was read in the Forum of Constantine justifying the day's events. The people discussed what had happened, the murmuring grew to a roar, and next morning came the explosion. For the first time, according to Psellos, who had an almost Pepysian ability to be on the scene when anything interesting occurred, the women came out from their purdah-like seclusion, bent on seeing Zoë restored to her throne. Michael V was dazed and bewildered by the insurrection he had touched off, and agreed to her return. She came, and showed herself to the crowds from the balcony of the Daphnae overlooking the Hippodrome. That balcony would be roughly on the site of the little pavement cafés on the south side of the At Meydani, opposite the Kaiser Wilhelm II fountain—itself occupying the site of the Kathisma, the imperial box in the Hippodrome.

But the sight of Zoë was not what the crowd now wanted: they wished Theodora to be their Empress. A deputation went to the convent where she was living, but she fled to the chapel for sanctuary, having no desire for the dangerous life of the palace, even if it was God-guarded. With daggers she was literally forced from the altar by the deputation, dressed in royal robes, set on a horse and taken to Santa Sophia where she was acknowledged as Empress.

When Michael V heard of the turn of events he took a boat from the Boucleon harbour, and sailed along the walls until he came to the gate which would bring him to the Monastery of St John of Studion. With him was his uncle, cause of all the trouble.

The mob scented out where they were, and broke into the monastery. Psellos was there, and left an account of what happened. The two fugitives were in the basilica, up by the altar—Michael was clinging to it—while the crowd filled the wide nave: shouting, jeering, and catcalling. Their prey were dressed as monks, and their faces contorted with fear. The situation was stalemate. The mob dare not violate the sanctuary, and Michael V and his uncle would not leave the altar. Towards evening the city prefect came with a warrant for their arrest, and the promise that nothing would happen to them. But the two clung all the harder to the altar, and even when the prefect ordered his men to drag them out, they could not: fear had lent such strength to their hands. Now the crowd was beginning to pity them, and some even went so far as to intercede with the prefect on their behalf. He promised Michael and his uncle they should not be put to death: a slippery promise which he kept—not saying what was really in store for them!

So the crowd allowed them to be dragged from the church by brute force, bundled into mule-carts, and taken a mile or so to the Sigma, that unexplained inward curve in the Theodosian Wall, close to the Third Military Gate. There the two men were blinded. Michael V broke down completely, whilst his uncle—responsible for the whole disaster—showed more courage than might have been expected. Then the two were consigned to the oblivion of a monastery.

Now, on April 21, 1042, Theodora was brought from her convent, Zoë was released from what amounted to house-arrest in the Boucleon Palace, and for two months Constantinople was ruled by two elderly women, each with the title of Empress. After two months of increasing jealousy towards her sister, Zoë decided at the age of sixty-two to marry for a third time. The man she chose was Constantine Monomarchos. To the people of Constantinople he gave a giraffe and an elephant, and to God a church dedicated to St George, which stood near the Manganae Palace, below Santa Sophia.

Two mosaics recently brought to light in the south gallery of Santa Sophia are portraits of this couple. As Zoë changed her husbands, so the faces in the mosaic were altered. Around the edge of the face the mosaic ground is slightly disturbed, showing where the cubes had to be picked out. His features are nondescript and he wears a short beard. More interesting is Zoë. Beneath her crown a little hair shows coming low on either side of the forehead, while her rounded cheeks are quite highly coloured, and together with the considerable amount of jewellery she wears, Zoë looks like nothing so much as a stage clairvoyante.

Theodora indulged her passion for collecting money, while Zoë, painted like a doll—most realistically indicated in the mosaic—though even her enemies had to admit that at over sixty she still had a beautiful unwrinkled skin, made the gynacaeum in the palace reek with the scents she and her attendants spent hours concocting over a huge fire.

Constantine IX Monomarchos (1042–1055) showed no more restraint in his married life than he showed sense in his public one. Now he was in love with the niece of his late second wife, and before long Sklaraina was installed in her own apartments in the palace. The slightly mad atmosphere became even madder when an astonishing document was presented for the approval of the senate, which though called a contract of friendship, was nothing less than a peace treaty between Constantine's wife and mistress. From then on the Emperor invariably appeared in public with his ageing and garishly made-up wife on one side and the beautiful Sklaraina on the other. Neither woman broke the treaty, but in 1044 there was a minor insurrection in the city among those who thought the younger woman was ousting the rightful Empress. 'We will not have Sklaraina to reign over us, nor on her account shall our purple-born mothers Zoë and Theodora die.' As might be expected in this extraordinary *ménage à trois* it was Zoë herself who pacified the mob.

But that was only one side of the times, and an unimportant one, though the folly of these people—not vicious enough to be called decadent—makes welcome light relief among the palace intrigues, assassinations, and blindings that occupy so much of the city's history. In its great days, the time of Justinian, the Empire was one of the largest and most magnificent in history, with a civilization second to none, producing buildings and works of art that take the breath away: now that same civilization was ruled over by a series of elderly bird-brained sovereigns. However, under the Komneni, Constantinople was to recapture something of its former greatness and dignity.

The most important event during the middle of the eleventh century was the final breach between the Roman Catholic and Greek Orthodox Churches, which came about in 1054, when the papal legate placed a bull of excommunication in Santa Sophia. The question of the nature of the Second Person of the Trinity had proved an insuperable barrier. As a result the two halves of Christendom grew further and further apart, until the west completely turned its back on Byzantium, leaving the Empire—by the fifteenth century shrunk to the compass of the walls of

St Irene, after A.D. 740

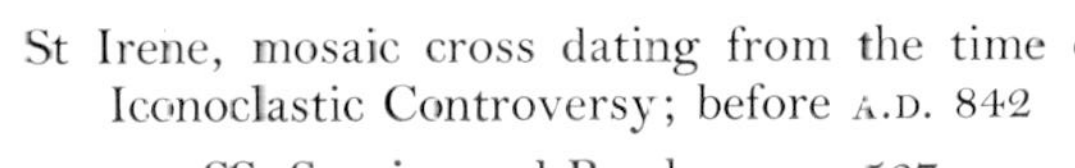

St Irene, mosaic cross dating from the time of Iconoclastic Controversy; before A.D. 842

SS. Sergius and Bacchus A.D. 527

Underground cistern (Yerebatan Sarayi), *c.* A.D. 532

Façade of a Sea Palace, overlooking the Sea of Marmara. Possibly sixth or seventh century A.D.

Constantinople—to its inevitable fate at the hands of the Ottoman Turks.

Five emperors followed the last of the Macedonian Dynasty (the old Empress Theodora ruling alone for two years), and Isaac I Komnenos was no better, but certainly no worse than some that Constantinople had seen in the past, and would see in the future. He may have left little mark on the city, but his niece Anna Dalassena (mother of the future Alexios I Komnenos) built or restored the church of St Saviour Pantepopte (Eskiimaret Camii), which stands on the Fourth Hill, between the Fatih Mosque and the Golden Horn. Belonging to the four column type of church, with a twelve sided dome, three apses, and two narthexes—the outer one a later addition—it is singled out by Professor Arnold van Millingen as being the most carefully built of the later ones in the city. Unfortunately, like so many of the other churches in the city it has no history, or at least none has come down to us.

Chapter 19

The Church

The Greek Orthodox Church in Constantinople. Its origins and differences with Rome. Some of the sects which troubled it. The clergy. The place of art in the decoration of churches. Emphasis in Byzantine art on different religious themes to that in the west. The monasteries. Their origins. St John of Studion in Constantinople. The Stylites living on top of columns.

Now, in the mid-eleventh century, the Orthodox Church stood quite apart at the eastern end of the Mediterranean. The mutual excommunication of pope and patriarch was the culmination of a series of schisms and reunions. In the next four hundred years there would be a series of reunions with Rome, followed quickly by separation; these were not brought about by any change in the beliefs of the Orthodox, but by the need for political alliance with the west against the Turks.

Religion was the strongest factor in the lives of all classes in Constantinople and the Empire: Christianity, strongly tinged with fatalism. If the favourite charioteer in the Hippodrome won, it was the will of God: if a usurping emperor successfully overthrew his predecessor, it was also the will of God. But even so, the Church was not beyond and above the State. Constantine the Great made the relationship between patriarch and emperor quite clear at the famous Council of Nicaea in A.D. 325, which also defined the beliefs of Christians in the Nicene Creed.

Originally there were three Sees of Apostolic Foundation: Rome, Alexandria, and Antioch. But quickly Constantinople was assuming an importance second only to Rome itself. In 381, at the Second Oecumenical Council, held in St Irene, the city assumed a status all but equal to the old capital, while the patriarch's rank and honour was the equal of the western pontiff—to the fury of the patriarch of Alexandria. Then in 451 this ruling was reaffirmed at the Council of Chalcedon, when no dignitaries from Italy were present. The first break with Rome came in 484, followed by reunion in 512. Five and a half centuries later the break was final.

The Orthodox Church, called the Church of the Seven Councils, was in a very real sense missionary: looking towards the pagans of the north—the Slavs—and in the east. Above all, it was the Byzantines who converted the vast expanses of western Russia. The ninth century saints Methodus and Cyril in particular were outstanding for their missionary work, setting out from Constantinople to convert the Slavs. It was the latter who gave them their alphabet, adapted from the Greek, and which is called Cyrillic, which the Russians and Balkan states still use.

Possibly more tolerant of the religious opinions of others than in the west, the Orthodox Church certainly had a great many sects and heresies with which to contend. Gnostics, Docetes, Marcionites, and Manichaens; all denied the Immaculate Conception, declaring that Christ had no existence until he appeared fully grown by the ford across the Jordan when he was baptized by St John. Also, they declared he was a purely spiritual creation with nothing of man about him. Then there was Apollinarianism, a doctrine formulated by a fourth-century bishop who declared Christ's mind was the Logos, or will of God, while his body was that of a man. The Monothelites and Maronites declared the two natures of Christ were controlled by one will, both human and divine. The Nestorians believed that the Logos and the human Jesus were two separate entities. By the denial of the human part of Christ's nature several of these sects thereby made nothing of His crucifixion: if He was a purely spiritual being He would not have suffered on the cross, as a man, for man.

Perhaps the two most important sects to trouble the church in Constantinople were the Arians (taking its name from the fourth century bishop Arius), and the Monophysites. The former declared the Holy Ghost could proceed from the Son as well as from the Father, while the Orthodox Church holds that it can only proceed *through* the Son, as well as from the Father. Of all the sects the Monophysites were probably the strongest in the earlier centuries, believing that there was only one nature, divine, in Christ. They were particularly strong in Syria and Egypt and, after the doctrine's rejection by Constantinople, those two provinces were distinctly hostile to the capital, long before they fell to the Saracens in the seventh century. Several of these sects still survive in out-of-the-way places in the Middle East and North Africa, cut off from the main stream of Christianity: strange remnants, as it were trapped in bubbles of air beneath the flood of Islam. But most curious of all these sects were the Manichaens, heavily and not unnaturally persecuted by the Orthodox Church, who wished to reconcile Christianity with Zoroastrianism—the Persian fire-worshipping religion.

At the head of the Orthodox Church was (and still is) the Patriarch of Constantinople. Below him come the metropolitans (archbishops), then the bishops. In the Empire it was stipulated that bishops must be thirty-five or over, of fair education, and if married they must be separated from their wives. In the later years of the Empire they were usually drawn from among the monks. If those of the clergy below the rank of bishop were married before becoming sub-deacons they could remain so, otherwise they too must separate. In the country the priests were usually very much of the people, as is frequently the case in Greece today, and on large estates their position was little better than that of serfs: they changed hands with the property.

In its art, as in its services, the church expressed the spiritual world. Its walls were painted with a red ochre symbolizing the blood of Christ (St Saviour in Chora has recently been restored thus); and outside, possibly in the centre of an atrium (courtyard or cloister to the west of the building such as those that remain at St John of Studion or St Irene) the congregation would pause to wash their hands and their faces before entering. Penitents and those cut off from the church could go no further than the narthex, whilst those entitled to do so entered, the men going into the nave by the central doors, while the women used those on either side which led up to the gynecaeum, the gallery reserved for their exclusive use. In the early centuries it was not bells that summoned them—the churches, including Santa Sophia itself had no towers even—but the banging of a long wooden board, called a semantron, with a mallet. Still used in some of the monasteries on Mount Athos they can produce a remarkably sonorous sound. Either in the tenth century or else during the Latin Occupation after 1204 a belfry was built between two of the huge buttresses on the west front of Santa Sophia. It has long since vanished.

Around and above the congregation was a representation of the heavenly world. In the dome overhead Christ Pantokrator, the Ruler of the World; in the semi-dome of the apse the Virgin and Child. On the vaults and pendentives the invisible host: the archangels and angels: in the smaller domes such figures as the apostles: on the walls the saints and scenes from the life of Christ. In later centuries it became customary to have the Last Judgement on the west wall, and in the narthex scenes from the life of the Virgin. In Byzantine art the Crucifixion is comparatively rarely depicted. Something of the feeling that it was shameful may have lingered on: a distant remembrance of the early days when the Church was struggling for survival, and contending with such things as the rough scratching on a classroom wall of the school for imperial pages on the Palatine Hill in Rome, by one of the boys, of a man with a horse's head on a cross, in front a figure, and the words 'Alexander, worshipping his God'. In the early years Christ on the cross was represented in art with the elbows almost against the trunk, the hands extended on either side, but no cross—carved on one of the wooden doors of St Sabina, Rome. A far cry from the ghastly realism of such pieces as the Crucifixion in Burgos Cathedral with its real hair. There is not the same dwelling on physical suffering, either for the damned or in the loving care taken to depict in revolting detail the disembowelling, dismembering, burning, boiling, and beheading of saints and martyrs. Two more differing approaches to the same goal, the glorification of the Christian religion through the medium of art, could not be found than at the opposite ends of the Mediterranean: the religious art of Spain and of Byzantium.

Though their influence was not direct, the monasteries played an important part in the life of Constantinople. As has been mentioned it was customary to send the sons of the emperor to be educated at St John of Studion. Certainly their role must have been more important than that of the senate, which could be relied on never to give offence, and never to take it, at least in the presence of the Emperor. Such men as St John Chrysostom and St Theodore the Studite frequently did all three.

Monasticism began to spread in the fourth century in Lower Egypt. One of the first, if not the first, was Pachomius, who formed a colony on the Nile at Tabennisi. By the time of his death there were eleven 'houses', two for women, each grouped about an aesthete who gave spiritual guidance. Far away in Ireland the early Celtic monasteries, rings of turf-roofed huts, were modelled on those in the scorching Egyptian desert: the idea brought to the islands of the west by Coptic missionaries. After Pachomius came Paul of Thebes and St Anthony of Alexandria. The latter shut himself away in an old tomb near Pispir, also on the Nile, where he could meditate in complete isolation. They, together with such as St Jerome near Antioch, were the first hermits. Incidentally, it was this St Anthony who was so tempted by visions of the girls of Alexandria, and not the thirteenth century St Anthony of Padua, whose startling basilica, Il Santo, is modelled on St Mark's in nearby Venice—itself based on the vanished Church of the Apostles in Constantinople: and so by the most devious of ways all the roads would seem to lead to the New Rome!

From these humble origins monasticism grew up in the East Roman Empire: particularly in Egypt, Syria, and what is modern Turkey, as well as in Greece. The sanctity of a hermit living in a cave on a mountainside would attract disciples, who would settle near him, and so the nucleus of a community would be formed. In such a way began monasticism on Mount Athos. In the middle of the fourth century St Basil of Caesarea (in western Turkey, not Israel) formulated the rules by which monks should live and monasteries be run. There is no such thing as 'The

Order of St Basil'; in fact in the Orthodox Church there are no orders such as there are in the west: the Benedictines and the Dominicans, for example.

In Constantinople itself it was not until the reign of Theodosius I (379–395) that monasticism took root. By 536 there were sixty-eight monasteries in the city, of which St John of Studion was the most important. Not all monks entered such establishments for the highest reasons, and both St John Chrysostom and St Theodore found it necessary to curb them and their activities. The weaker brethren were specifically forbidden to wander at will through the city interfering in the affairs of others, encouraged to observe 'a holy silence', stopped from trading for private gain and generally set on the straight and narrow. If a monk decamped twice he was forthwith conscripted into the army. The State might have a use for him if he had no use for the Church.

At first double monasteries were common, as in the west, but at the Council of Trullo in 787 they were suppressed. Something of the life in the Studite Monastery is described in Chapter 6, and that in the Monastery of Christ Pantokrator in Chapter 22. In nunneries ex-royalty were allowed to have a servant, a concession to those imperial women precipitated from the palace to the obscurity of a religious house by revolution or intrigue.

Syrian monasticism was much more rigorous than elsewhere, making a virtue of mortification and physical discomfort in its severest forms. One band, called the Dendrites, took to living in trees, while another lived out a cramped existence on top of columns. Most famous of the latter was St Simon Stylites, who for years made his home on top of a pillar outside Damascus. The principle behind the action was that any unnecessary movement—which would distract the aesthete from his contemplation—would at once be visible to all and sundry. So extreme were some of these Stylites that when they were brought down to the ground they could neither stand nor walk, so atrophied had their legs become from lack of use. Constantinople had its share of these strange people: one perched on top of the Column of the Goths, now among the few relics of pre-Christian

Byzantium which still stand. Fifty feet high, it has a Corinthian capital, and was set up near the citadel of the old Greek city, on the low ground between the Seraglio and the Point. Some believe it commemorates a victory over the Goths by Claudius II, while others that it was surmounted by a statue of Byzas, the sailor-founder of Byzantium in 658 or 657 B.C.

Life on a column was not quite as precarious as it sounds. The Stylite had a rail, sometimes with filled-in sides, round him, not unlike the crow's nest right at the top of the mast of a medieval ship, and in some cases a roof to shelter him from the rain. There is a remarkable illustration of one in the background of a sixteenth century fresco depicting the death of St Athanasios, in the Refectory of the Great Lavra on Mount Athos. There the holy man on the top of his column waits to pull up the rope attached to a basket into which a follower is putting food. In the tenth century the Column of the Goths was occupied by one Daniel. He must have been not unlike a stork nesting on an abandoned minaret. Revered by the public, many people had miniature columns, complete with the figure of their favourite aesthete on its top, to which they gave a place of honour in the home, and kept a lamp burning before it.

Chapter 20

1081–1118

The enlightened Alexios I Komnenos (1081–1118). His remarkable daughter Anna. Her biography of Alexios I. Details of family life. Palace of Porphyrogenitus. Palace of Blachernae enlarged. The First Crusade. Insufferable behaviour of the crusaders. Bohemund's doubts about Byzantine hospitality. Venetian traders settle in Constantinople. Brief siege (1090) by the Patzinaks. St Thekla. Conspiracy of Michael Anemas. He is saved from blinding at the last minute by Anna's pleas. The Anemas Tower. The sect of the Bogomils in Constantinople. Last illness of Alexios I.

With the advent in 1081 of Alexios I Komnenos, the story of Constantinople received a fresh impetus. Not only did it mark an end, at least for the time being, of the incessant palace revolutions, but the period is comparatively well documented, and the principal characters became human beings and not simply rather exasperating puppets manipulated by a horde of scheming eunuchs.

In *Alexiad* the new Emperor's daughter, Anna, recorded her father's life. She herself was a remarkable woman. Intelligent, observant, well read, and with a streak of humanity all too rare in the Byzantine make-up, she produced a book that is still readable today: and of how many books from the Middle Ages can that truly be said? Expressions like 'swollen-headed Latins' are most refreshing.

As might be expected of the daughter of the man who was God's personification on earth, she thought the Komneni little less than perfect, and had a good opinion of herself, but also she had an eye for detail and recorded her father's numerous campaigns very competently. But it is the little glimpses of life in the palace that have the most immediate appeal. The scene at the breakfast table: 'I remember the Empress, my mother, when breakfast was already on the table, carrying a book in her hands and poring over the writings of the didactic Fathers, especially those of the philosopher and martyr Maximus.' Anna admitted this was beyond her grasp, and one day asked her mother how she could 'rise to such sublime heights? . . . the purely abstract and intellectual character of the man makes one's head swim, as the saying goes'. The scene of the ritual-cocooned imperial family actually reading at breakfast, even if it was the work of Holy Fathers, is piquant.

Anna Komnena goes at some length into the origin of the expression Born in the Purple. 'This purple room was a certain building in the palace shaped as a complete square from its base to the spring of the roof, which ended in a pyramid; it looked out upon the sea and the harbour where the stone oxen and lions stand. The floor of this room was paved with marbles and the walls panelled with it, but not the ordinary sorts nor even with the more expensive sorts which are fairly easy to procure but with the marble which the earlier emperors had carried away from Rome. And this marble is, roughly speaking, purple all over except for the spots like white sand sprinkled over it. It is from this marble, I imagine, that our ancestors called the room purple.'

Even its foundations have long since vanished, though from Anna Komnena's description its position can be roughly located among the narrow little streets and the timber houses with their wide eaves, so typical of the old Turkey, that today cover the site. The oxen and lions referred to by Anna stood on the quay of the small imperial harbour, the Boucleon, at the west end of that stretch of walls which enclosed both the city and the palaces —a few hundred yards to the east of SS. Sergius and Bacchus (Küçük Aya Sophia Camii). The hill rises fairly steeply behind the railway line that leads to Edirne and Europe—the eye travelling up to the exquisite outline and soaring minarets of the seventeenth century Sultan Ahmet Mosque. There, somewhere on that slope between the mosque and the line stood the Porphyry Palace, where for centuries so many members of Byzantium's ruling families first saw the light of day.

Various members of the Komneni family did much in the way of building in the city, and most of all the Emperor himself. As the years passed the Imperial Family came to use the huge sprawling palace overlooking the Sea of Marmara less and less, preferring the palace of Blachernae, tucked up against the city walls where the Sixth Hill slopes down towards the Golden Horn. Apart from the fact that the palace had a view across to open country, or rather to a hill as neatly rounded and as steep as the Sussex downs, and that the Emperor could ride straight out through a private gate in the walls (Gyrolymne or Silver Lake Gate), it would seem an odd locale for the imperial residence—were it not for two things: the Sacred Spring and the church of Our Lady of Blachernae. These were the attractions which drew the rulers of the most deeply religious—not to say superstitious—people in Christendom. Every fifteenth of August the Emperor came in procession to purify himself by bathing in the pool, which was sacred long before the time of Christ, and to worship in the church which contained the Robe of the Virgin. So the palace grew. Theophilus was perhaps the first Emperor to make it his permanent residence, completely rebuilding it to please himself, and now it was Alexios I Komnenos who was to make further improvements. But all his work would be swept away by his grandson, Manuel II, when he completely rebuilt Blachernae in the twelfth century.

Much of Alexios I's reign was spent away from Constantinople, campaigning against the Normans and the Seljuk Turks: the one a menace from the west, the other from the east. By the end of the eleventh century those hardy, predatory adventurers from the pleasant Bessin countryside had become a very real danger to Byzantium. Ensconced in Sicily, the Normans were fast making themselves virtual rulers of the east Mediterranean, and giving Constantinople reason for worry. Their leader was Bohemund, a man not unlike William the Conqueror, hard, ruthless, capable, and unscrupulous.

Though they sacked Thessalonika, the second city of the Empire, Alexios managed to hold them at arm's length from Constantinople, and when they did come to his city, it was as crusaders bound for the Holy Land. In 1095 Peter the Hermit preached the First Crusade, directed at the recapture of Jerusalem, which had fallen to Mahomet some twenty years before.

Within a year they reached Byzantium, after a terrible journey across the wilds of Hungary, where two-thirds of their numbers perished. Latin and Orthodox: each regarded the other as the heretic, and while the crusaders looted, the Byzantines cheated. After years of hard-fought campaigns Bohemund could not believe that his old enemy Alexios would not harm him whilst he was in Constantinople. He most certainly did not trust the Greeks when they came bearing gifts in their hands, though it was not horse they were offering him. Wrote Anna: 'That dreadful Bohemund not only refrained from tasting the viands at all, or even touching them with the tips of his fingers, but pushed them all away at once, and though he did not speak of his secret suspicion, he divided them up amongst the attendants, pretending to all appearance to be doing them a kindness.'

Alexios knew how Bohemund's mind worked—it was probably what he would have done had he been in the Norman's shoes—and had sent him food, both cooked and raw. 'The raw meats, however, he ordered his own cooks to prepare in the usual Frankish way. The next day he asked the men who had eaten the supper how they felt. When they replied that they felt exceedingly well and had not suffered the slightest discomfort from it, he discovered his hidden thought, and said: "When I recalled my wars with him (Alexios) and that terrible battle I must own I was afraid that he would perhaps arrange my death by mixing poison with my food."'

Everyone, from the imperial family downwards, loathed the crusaders for their social conceit. To ensure his suitable reception when he reached Constantinople, Hugh, Count of Vermandois, wrote in advance to Alexios so he should have time to make the necessary preparations. 'Know, O Emperor,' wrote the Frenchman, 'that I am the king of kings and the greatest of those under heaven; and it behoves you to meet and treat me on arrival with all pomp and in a manner worthy of my nobility.' No wonder Anna wrote of 'swollen-headed Latins'. Alexios had much to put up with from his unwanted guests suffering from *folie de grandeur*, who were now mustering on the European shores of the Bosphorus.

Then there was that occasion in the Blachernae Palace when a French baron, believed to have been Robert of Paris, attempted to ascend the throne and seat himself beside Alexios. When another of his countrymen attempted to check him he rasped: 'Who is this rustic, that keeps his seat, while so many valiant captains are standing round him?' The remark was translated into Greek by one of the courtiers, but whatever Alexios felt he did not show it, and dismissed the boorish crusaders with some sound advice about tactics when fighting the Turks. Never, he said, let themselves be drawn on by the enemy.

Off they went at last, crossing the Bosphorus at its narrowest point, near where the twin fortresses of Rumeli Hisar and Anadolu Hisar now stand, some six miles from the city. In full cry after the infidel, they forgot the Emperor's warning. The Sultan drew them on, and outside Nicaea (Iznik) they were annihilated beneath a hail of arrows. A huge mound of bones (ten thousand are said to have been killed that day), was piled up outside the little city where over seven and a half centuries before the Nicene Creed had been formulated, and where today storks make their nests on its massive ruined walls.

At about this time the Venetians really obtained a footing in Constantinople, in the form of trading concessions—granted in return for their help in its campaigns. Too lazy or complacent to do its own trading, Byzantium allowed others to do it for her, with the result that her wealth was not renewed—and so began the celebrated decline and fall. Anna described what happened in Constantinople: 'He gave the Venetians all the shops running from the old Hebraic anchorage to that called Bigla and all the anchorages between the two, as well as much real property, not only in the capital and in the town of Dyrrachium (Dubrovnik), but wherever they asked for it. But greatest gift of all, he ordered that their merchandise should not be taxed in any countries under Roman sway, so that they could trade freely where they liked, and not pay any other tax required by the Treasury, but should be exempt from all Roman authority.'

It is a tragic irony that Alexios I, John II, and Manuel I were three of Byzantium's most enlightened rulers, but the fact remains it was in their time that the decline really started.* The old enemies were still at work, whittling away a province here, a few miles there, and in 1090 Constantinople found itself in a state of siege when the Patzinaks swept right up to the walls. Alexios formed an unlikely alliance with the Cumans from South Russia—they were pagans and barbarians, as well as being ruthless fighters, and they all but wiped the Patzinaks off the face of the earth in April, 1091.

In addition to the alterations and improvements which Alexios made to Blachernae, he also rebuilt the little church of St Thekla, between the palace and Golden Horn; just inside the walls of Heraclius. Whilst campaigning in Roumania he sheltered under a tree during a violent storm. Intuition told him to move. He did so, and a moment later it fell across where he had been standing. The day was September 24, St Thekla's day, and he attributed his escape to her intervention; so in appreciation he rebuilt her church below the palace windows. Very simple, with a rectangular plan, an apse and originally a dome over the nave it must have been very different when Anna Komnena knew it. 'In gratitude for his escape he had a very beautiful chapel built in honour of the proto-martyr Thekla, at no little cost, richly furnished and decorated with various works of art.'

Conspiracy against its rulers was the curse of the country, and the reign of Alexios I had its share. The most important concerned several brothers of the Anemas family (pronounced Annanas), and it is interesting in the architectural as well as the political history of the city. Adjoining the Blachernae Palace, and forming part of the city walls, is a massive double tower, which appears to be of different dates. The one to the south, which is the better constructed, consists of alternate courses of stone and several thicknesses of bricks, and it is Anna Komnena who first mentions it by the name of Anemas Tower.

* In 1071 the Byzantine Army sustained its worst defeat ever, at the hands of the Seljuk Turks near Manzikert, in Eastern Turkey.

Michael Anemas was a descendant of the Emir who unsuccessfully defended Crete against Nicephorus Phocas in the tenth century. He and his family were brought to Constantinople to take part in the triumph, but then allowed to live in comfort near the city, and even keep their religion. It was his descendants, three brothers, who were now involved in a treason plot against Alexios I. Their cat's paw was a most unwise senator named Solomon who, when betrayed and brought before Alexios, promptly implicated them. Anna takes up the story: 'Anemas and the others who were the prime authors with him, had their heads closely shaven and their beards cut off, and then the Emperor ordered them to be led through the middle of the Agora and afterwards have their eyes gouged out. So the masters of the ceremonies took them and dressed them in sacks and decorated their heads with the entrails of oxen and sheep, then placed them on oxen, not astride, but sideways, and conducted them through the court of the palace. Lictors gambolled before them, singing a ridiculous song suitable to the procession in a loud voice. So people of every age flocked together to view this spectacle, and even we, the Emperor's daughters, went out to see it secretly. When the people saw Michael looking up to the palace and raising suppliant hands to Heaven, every creature was moved to tears and lamentations, and we, the Emperor's daughters, more than all.' The imperial family must surely have been staying in the old palace by Santa Sophia at this time. If the procession had come from Blachernae it would not have taken the route through the city which Anna Komnena goes on to describe. 'And I in my desire to rescue the man from such misery repeatedly implored the Empress, my mother, to come and see the procession. For the conductors were leading the procession very slowly with the purpose of giving an opportunity for pardon to be granted to the guilty. But as she delayed coming (she was praying with the Emperor), I went down and standing fearfully outside the doors, for I dare not go in, I tried to draw her out by signs. And finally she was persuaded and came out to see the sight. When she saw Michael she pitied him and ran back to the Emperor, shedding bitter tears, and besought him, not once or twice, but repeatedly, to spare Michael's eyes.

He at once dispatched a messenger to stop the executions.' In twelfth century Constantinople he would have run through the Forum of Augustus, and along the Mesé, the principal thoroughfare of the city, which led all the way to the Golden Gate, some four miles away. The names are different, but in twentieth century Istanbul the main streets follow the same course. From the palace the messenger would have run past Santa Sophia, where the plane trees shade the pavements, and taxis and tourist buses wait, past the shattered piece of masonry that is all remaining above ground of the great Forum of Augustus. Up the street called the Divan Yolu, along the Yeniçeriler Street, past the calcined Column of Constantine—corseted in iron: a reminder of that magnificent forum it once dominated. Past the Beyazit Mosque, and down the Ordu Street, which runs through the site of the Forum of Theodosius. The little procession had nearly reached the bottom of the hill, and was nearing the arch across the street which marked the point of no return. Where the present day Ordu Street meets the new Atatürk Bulvari was yet another forum, the Admastrianum, where sentences of death or mutilation were carried out. But about where the little eighteenth century Tulip Mosque overlooks the traffic hurtling down the hill, the messenger caught up with Michael Anemas and his guards. 'By hurrying, the man got there just before they had passed inside the "Hands", as they were called; for he who once had passed them, can no longer be saved from his fate. For the Emperors had fixed up these bronze hands in a very conspicuous place on a lofty stone arch with the fixed intention that if a man, condemned to death by law, should be short of them, and on the way receive a pardon from the hand of the Emperor, he was to be freed from his punishment. The messenger gave the letter granting the pardon to the men leading Michael, and took him back, and on reaching a tower, built close to the palace, confined him there, for such were his orders.'

There he remained, cooped up in the massive tower on the wall, with only one window on its outer face, until he was freed in 1107. Although not the most memorable prisoner to be held there, it is by his name that it is still remembered. Immediately after he left it, the Anemas Tower held another state prisoner:

Edirne Gate, A.D. 413. Entered by Mehmet II after the siege, May 29, 1453

St Mary Diaconissa (Kalendar Mosque) probably tenth century

Anemas and Isaac Angelus Towers. The land walls

Church of the Blessed Virgin: Theotokos Pammakaristos (Fethiye Mosqu
eleventh century. South chapel added *c.* 1315

So-called Palace of Constantine VII Porphyrogenitus (Tekfursarayi) *c.* 115
though possibly later

Georgius, Duke of Trebizond. His crime was attempting to establish his own little empire on the shores of the Black Sea. Two centuries later his dream became a reality when two brothers, offshoots of the reigning house, established the romantic Empire of Trebizond (Trabzon). Defiant, rude, and abusive, Georgius did nothing to help his own cause, but eventually Anna Komnena's husband talked him into a more reasonable frame of mind, and Alexios I set him free, giving him money and honours.

Whether in western Europe or in the Byzantine Empire a political prisoner stood a better chance of receiving mercy than a religious one, and this was even true of the humane Alexios I. About this time, a most curious sect, the Bogomils, had sprung up in Bulgaria, and were even to be found in Constantinople itself. Roughly speaking their beliefs were based on the idea that good and evil were equally balanced in the world. Also they were opposed to authority, work, and the Orthodox church. Later this heresy spread to southern France—the Cathars and the Albigensian Heresy—and among those who helped exterminate it there was Simon de Montfort the Elder.

In Bulgaria the Bogomils were led by a priest named Basil. When questioned by Alexios I himself he refused to recant. A number of the city's inhabitants had been arrested at the same time, because it was rumoured they too were Bogomils, but Alexios was not convinced of their guilt, and hit upon an ingenious way of sorting the orthodox sheep from the Bogomil goats. Two large pyres were built on the ground used by the Imperial Family for polo. One had a cross, for those innocent of the heresy, while the one for the unrepentant Bogomils had nothing. The accused, who thought death inevitable, were given the choice of going to whichever pyre they chose. Those who were orthodox and innocent went to the pyre with the cross, while Basil and his followers went to the one without. To everyone's surprise those about the cross were released on the spot, while the others were taken back to prison. The Orthodox Church went to work on them. A few Bogomils recanted, but the quite unrepentant Basil was ordered to be burnt as a heretic. A huge pyre was lit in the Hippodrome, and the fanatic given one last chance to save himself. Though shaken by the sight of the crackling fire he was confident that like Shadrak and his companions in the fiery furnace he too would be saved, and allowed himself to be thrown headlong into the blaze. 'Then the people looking on clamoured loudly and demanded that all the rest who belonged to Basil's pernicious sect should be thrown into the fire as well, but the Emperor did not allow it.'

Alexios's days were numbered now, and surrounded by his family, he started to succumb to a fatal illness: perhaps cardiac asthma. 'I have often, or rather continuously, seen my mother spending a sleepless night with the Emperor,' wrote Anna Komnena, 'sitting behind him on the bed and supporting him in her arms and relieving his breathing somewhat. But by no means at all was he able to get any relief. For the illness followed, or rather accompanied the Emperor like a noose, and never left off strangling him.' A bed on wheels was constructed so he could be pushed from room to room as the mood took him, or in search of a cool breeze. Then came the day when Anna felt for his pulse but could find nothing. She turned away from the bed. 'The Empress understood what that meant and in absolute despair uttered a sudden loud, far-reaching shriek. She took off her royal veil and caught hold of a knife and cut off all her hair close to the skin and threw off the red shoes from her feet and demanded ordinary black sandals. And when she wanted to change her purple dress for a black garment, no dress could be found at hand. But the third of my sisters had garments suitable for the time and occasion, as she had already experienced the ills of widowhood, so the Empress took them and dressed herself and put on a plain dark veil on her head.'

But family grief soon had to give way to court ritual; that ritual embodied for future generations of Emperors by Constantine VII Porphyrogenitus in his Book of Ceremonies, 'What it is necessary to observe . . .'

Chapter 21

Western Ties

The Varangian Guards. Recruits from England. Their church near Santa Sophia. Henry II of England related by marriage to the Byzantine Imperial Family. His present of a pack of hounds to Manuel I. Game near the city. Russian traders at Constantinople.

In his personal soldiers Alexios I could not have wished for men more keen to defend his interests against the Norman crusaders than his Varangian guards. This *élite* corps was formed in the late tenth century, and at first consisted of soldiers from the north, Russo-Swedes. Swedish Vikings were the first to push into the heart of western Russia, via the rivers, and establish trading posts that later grew into great cities.

These soldiers formed their own little colony within the city, making the district near SS. Sergius and Bacchus their own. They even had their own church: St Mary Varanyistica, which stood to the east of Santa Sophia.

Two thousand miles away, the Norman Conquest took place, and many Anglo-Saxons chose to leave the country rather than submit to the heavy though capable and reforming hand of the Normans. Traversing the whole length of Europe they went to Constantinople to enrol in the palace guards, the fame of which had even reached England. It is a curious, though by no means far-fetched thought that the Varangians from Russia, the Anglo-Saxons from England, and the Normans from France could have had the same great-grandparents. During the Viking raids on the east coast many pledges of lust if not of affection must have been left behind (quite apart from those who chose to settle in the country), while it was from the colonies of Vikings who settled in Normandy that England's conquerors sprang—and the fact that the original settlers of Russia came from Scandinavia has already been mentioned. In Normandy while the inhabitants of Rouen were building its first cathedral, the citizens of Bayeux were still worshipping Odin.

By the time of Manuel I Komnenos the Varangian guard was nearly all Anglo-Saxon, or Danish: great fair-haired 'axe-bearing warriors'. With the change in the composition of the guard, so there was a change in the dedication of their church: to St Nicholas and St Augustine of Canterbury.

If the Varangians were the *élite* of the Byzantine army, they were also just a little arrogant, and not always on the best of terms with the citizens of their adopted country. Then, with the advent of the First Crusade, they found themselves face to face with the hated Normans. How those fingers, grasping the handles of their battle-axes, must have itched as the insufferable crusaders passed to and fro in the Palace of Blachernae.

The guards were not the only ties with England in eleventh and twelfth century Constantinople. The Emperor Manuel I (1143–1180) had for his second wife, Mary of Antioch, cousin of Eleanor of Acquitaine, Henry II's wife. The two sovereigns were on friendly terms, and Manuel I mentioned in a letter the part played by his Varangian guards in defeating the Seljuk Turks in 1176. 'We here felt it a pleasure that it so happened that some of the chief men of your nobility were with us, and we thought we should like to inform you as being our dearly beloved friend and as being so closely united with our imperial majesty by the ties of blood.'

A present that must have been particularly appreciated by Manuel I was a pack of hounds sent by Henry II: all the Komneni were keen sportsmen. To those of the Varangian guard who had known another life, in England, the baying of those hounds as they streamed out of one of the gates in the wall adjoining the Blachernae Palace must have been almost unbearably nostalgic. In those days good hunting could be had within a stone's throw of Constantinople, whilst the Forest of Belgrade (taking its name from a small village in its centre) only a few miles inland in Thrace, must have been a huntsman's paradise. Pheasants, partridges, fat quails, and even boar still abound near Istanbul, and no doubt in Byzantine times bear, deer, and wolves would also have been found: they are still to be encountered elsewhere in modern Turkey.

It was not only as recruits in the tenth century that Russians came to Constantinople, but as traders—aggressively determined to obtain trading rights. From about 860 onwards, years before the worthless Michael III was murdered, they came each summer to the greatest trading city in the world. On one occasion they, in a fleet of large canoes, even attempted to storm the city. Apparently their leader Olaf—with a name like that he must have been a Viking—hung up his shield on the cross in Santa Sophia. The story may be apocryphal, but it symbolizes the attitude of the pagan visitors. Ten years earlier missionaries had visited Kief, with little success, and it was not until 989 that the then Grand Duke Vladimir was converted, together with most of his countrymen, bringing Russia right into the Byzantine sphere of influence. Nearly five hundred years later Russia would act as her heir.

Chapter 22

1118-1143

Anna Komnena hopes to rule in her own right. The reign of John II (1118–1143). His wife Irene. Mosaics of the imperial family in Santa Sophia. The Empress founds the Monastery of St Saviour Pantokrator (*c.* 1120). Her sarcophagus. Imperial tombs in Istanbul. Hospital attached to the monastery.

After her father's death Anna Komnena hoped that with the help of her mother she would be proclaimed Empress, and she showed a most unscholarly annoyance when her brother took the ring from the dead man's hand, becoming John II Komnenos (August 15, 1118). Laying aside her books, she plotted against his life, but was betrayed by her own husband. At this she exclaimed that nature had mistaken the two sexes, and endowed him with the soul of a woman. John II refused to condemn his own sister to death, and only confiscated her personal property, giving it to his friend Axuch. Not only did Axuch refuse to accept the present, but even went so far as to intercede for Anna. John II was prepared to listen to his friend, in origin a Turkish slave, and not only was Anna forgiven, but even received her property back. The last sentence of the *Alexiad* is an oblique reference to her dashed hopes. 'But now my history must be concluded, for if I were to describe sad events any longer I might become bitter.' And with that a most remarkable woman disappears from sight.*

* Like her father Anna was buried in the Church of the Theotokos Pammakaristos (page 222), and though until recently a mosque, the Fethiye Camii, one hopes they still rest undisturbed.

The reign of John II lasted twenty-five years, and were some of the most humane and enlightened that Constantinople and the Empire were to know. Capital punishment was abolished, the stifling court ritual modified, and an attempt was made to pull up the public and private morals of the citizens. Also, John II led his troops into battle against the Seljuk Turks, expelling them from the Asiatic shores of the Bosphorus itself, and even recapturing Antioch (Antakya) down in the south of Turkey.

If his wife the Empress Irene is a shadowy figure in the history of the city—the daughter of King Ladislaw of Hungary, she like her father became a saint—at least we know what she looked like; a pink and white complexion with auburn hair, and we have her memorial in the church that is all that remains of the great Monastery of St Saviour Pantokrator (Mollazeyrek Mosque). Together with her husband, they stand on either side of the Virgin in one of the magnificent mosaics recently brought to light in the women's gallery on the south side of Santa Sophia. She faces the spectator, but the formality of the magnificently dressed Empress is softened by the sideways glance she gives towards her husband, as though to see if everything is as it should be. Just a quick glance that will last as long as the mosaics themselves. With her rather small firmly closed mouth she probably seldom saw or made a joke, but she looks distinctly more alert and intelligent than the Empress Zoë, also portrayed nearby.

St Saviour Pantokrator is a most curious aggregation of buildings. Because of the houses that hem it in, it is difficult to see at close quarters: perhaps the best views are from across the valley up which the Atatürk Bulvari runs from the Golden Horn. From there it looks like three churches with five domes of differing sizes, which in a sense is what it is. Originally the Pantokrator consisted of a comparatively small tenth century church, its origins unknown, with a narthex, three apses and a dome supported on four columns: the typical cross-in-square plan of an unpretentious Byzantine church of the Middle Ages. (The dome was rebuilt in Turkish times.) Beside it on the south side is a large funerary chapel of about the same date, called the Incorporal—nearly as big as the church it adjoins, with two

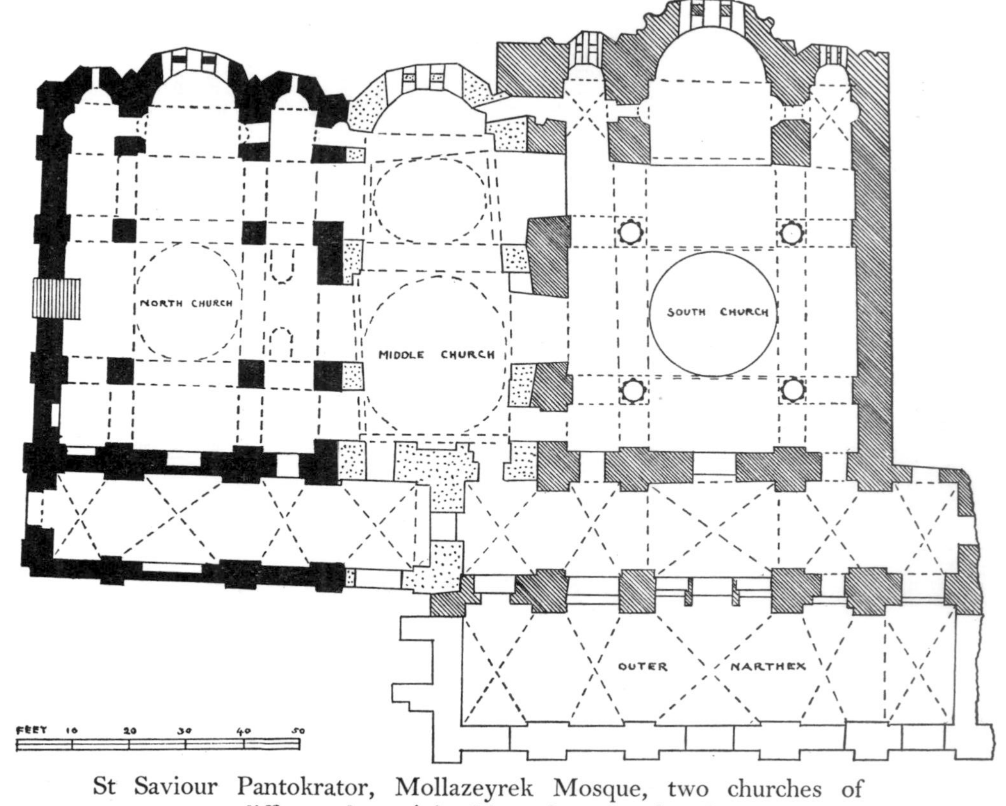

St Saviour Pantokrator, Mollazeyrek Mosque, two churches of different dates, joined by a funerary chapel

domes, one over the nave and the other and smaller one over the bema or choir. They are so close they actually touch, and two of the windows of the drums become as one, looking from one dome into the other.

To this building the Empress Irene added yet another church: the biggest of the three. It has an inner and an outer narthex, which like the one in front of the Kilise-Camii projects on either side of the body of the church. In St Saviour Pantokrator the north end projects half in front of the funerary chapel without regard to its appearance. Over the centre bay of the inner narthex of the south church is a small dome, open from the ground upwards, so the gallery for women above the narthex is in two separate parts. The north gallery connects with the funerary chapel and the north church. At ground level also the three buildings open one into the other (though at present while restoration work is being carried on in the south church it is partitioned off from its companions). The galleries, or gynecaea, where the women were segregated, had openings through which they could see down into the body of the church, and so participate in the services. A human touch in the north church of the Pantokrator is a fireplace, which must have been most welcome when the bitter north winds of winter brought snow from Bulgaria or the steppes of Russia.

A most curious feature, already referred to elsewhere, common to many of the churches in the city, is the irregularity of the plan. At St Saviour Pantokrator it is most marked. Few of the corners of the north church are right angles, while the funerary chapel is not parallel with either of its neighbours, and the smaller of its two bays looks on plan as though it had been drawn by a child. By Byzantine standards the south church is large—though the churches of Constantinople are not quite as unbelievably small as those in Athens: the pocket-sized Metropole Cathedral and the Church of the Apostles for example—but now bare and echoing, its walls whitewashed, though some of the original stone or marble panels remain: in particular, the door-frame from the narthex into the interior.

Details concerning the early years are vague: but Irene probably founded the monastery about 1120, just after her husband's accession to the throne. Many of these religious houses were for men and for women; like Ely in its early years. Soon the Empress discovered the expense was more than she anticipated, and invited John II to come and visit the unfinished monastery —and begged his help. She received it, and there in 1126, shortly after entering as a nun, she died. Today a large tomb of dark green marble stands outside the church—believed to be hers. Throughout Istanbul the explorer will come across these great sarcophagi: a massive porphyry one still in the atrium of St Irene; another fitted with taps and used as a fountain at a corner of the Hocapaşa Caddesi in Sirkeci; a third half buried in the pavement at the north-west corner of the At Meydani—and so on. Apparently there were nine great sarcophagi of porphyry in the Church of the Apostles, including the tombs of Constantine the Great and Justinian I, which were scattered throughout the city after its demolition. Five found their way to St Irene (three now in the magnificent Archaeological Museum), though one, still with its lid, remains in the shade of a fig tree in the atrium. Since only royalty could be buried within the walls of Constantinople all these sarcophagi must have contained members of the ruling houses: of Constantine, of Justin, the Macedonians, the Komneni, the Angeli, and the Palaeologi: dead, turned to clay—and dispossessed.

Though not quite as influential as St John of Studion, the Monastery of St Saviour Pantokrator occupied an important place in the city and its history: the chapel became the burial place of several of the Komneni, and in the last centuries of the Empire's existence, of the house of Palaeologi. In the second half of the thirteenth century the Genoese destroyed the monastery, then occupied by the Venetians, during a spiteful vendetta. They claimed the Venetians had damaged a church and a tower of theirs at Acre and this was their small-minded revenge. They even shipped the stones back to Italy. The church at Acre was St Saba, and the Venetians for their part had transported some of its stones to their city. Two square piers with capitals still stand where they were first erected just south of San Marco—not to be confused with the two big columns at the other end of the Piazzetta.

In its heyday the monastery included a home for old people, a hospice for travellers, and a hospital. The last sounds remarkably up to date. There were five wards: for the surgical cases ten patients to a ward, but only eight for the gravely ill. Each ward had two physicians, three medical assistants, and four orderlies; while in the women's section there were twelve patients together, supervised by a woman doctor, six women medical assistants, and two nurses. There was even a house doctor.

Chapter 23

1143-1185

Manuel I and the Second Crusade. Unflattering eye-witness account of the city. Blachernae Palace rebuilt. Its lavishness. The site today. Basements of Alexios I. Palace of Constantine Porphyrogenitus. The career of Andronikos Komnenos. Usurps the throne and murders his nephew, Alexios II. Andronikos overthrown (1185), and lynched in the Hippodrome.

Death came to John II in 1143 while struggling with a boar he had just wounded. He ran his hand onto a poisoned arrow from his quiver, and nothing could save him. His wish was that he should be succeeded by the younger of his two surviving sons. (Another, called Alexios, has his portrait in mosaic in Santa Sophia near his parents.) Manuel was more fitted to wear the diadem than his elder brother Isaac, so their father's old friend Axuch discreetly confined the elder in the Monastery of the Pantokrator until the formalities of the coronation were over. By then the risk of Isaac becoming involved—willingly or unwillingly—in a treason plot would have dwindled. Exactly forty years later Isaac's son, Andronikos, had his revenge when he murdered Manuel's own son, and for two bloodstained years was Emperor.

Like his father Manuel I was an enlightened ruler, though like Richard I of England he spent much of his reign far from home fighting the growing menace of Islam. However, life was not all marching and campaigning. In times of peace he spent idle, and so the rumour-mongers declared, vicious days in silken dalliance with his niece Theodora on the Princes' Islands in the Sea of Marmara.

Then came the Second Crusade, which was a failure for the west. At this time Byzantium itself was going through a bad phase: her plans to check the Normans in Sicily and southern Italy had come to nothing, and because of arrests of ships belonging to Venice she found herself at war with the Republic in 1171. The war had a lasting result on Constantinople. The Empire formed an alliance with Genoa; the Genoese merchants established their own quarter in Galata, and remained to the very end. With their own churches, factories, warehouses, and quays it was a little piece of Italy beyond the Dardanelles.

A Frenchman, Odon de Deuil, who came to Constantinople in 1146, at the time of the Second Crusade, left descriptions of what he saw. Not all were favourable. '. . . the town is nevertheless stinking and filthy, and condemned in many places to perpetual shade. In fact the rich cover the public ways with their constructions and leave the sewers and dark places to the poor and strangers. There are committed murders, robberies, and all the crimes which haunt obscurity.' Many of the little streets and alleys are still in perpetual shade, but they are certainly not stinking and filthy. There is more litter to be found in the principal streets of London than in Istanbul.

Odon de Deuil also saw the Blachernae Palace, completely rebuilt by Manuel I. 'Its exterior beauty is almost incomparable; and that of the interior surpasses anything I could say of it. In all parts one sees nothing but gilding and painting of various colours. The court paved with marble of exquisite design, and I know not which contributes most to its value, whether it be the great beauty of this palace and the marvellous art it displays, or the precious materials one finds in it.'

The area covered by the Blachernae Palace—if the ruins known as the Tekfursarayi are included, stretches for nearly half a mile down the north slope of the Sixth Hill. From the Karsios Gate (Eğrikapi), halfway along the walls, the hill drops sharply towards the Anemas Tower, and then flattens towards the Golden Horn: overlooked by the walls of Heraclius and Leo V. It was in this area near the bottom of the hill that Manuel I

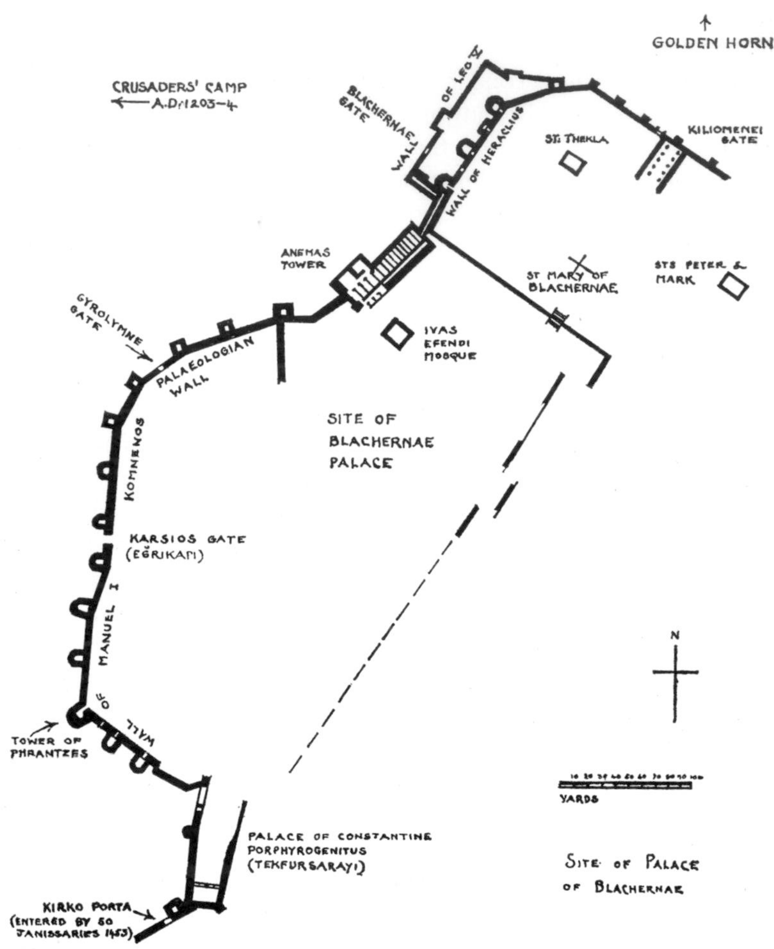

Site of Palace of Blachernae

chose to build his palace, close to the Aghiasma of St Mary, and into which the Imperial Family moved about 1150, abandoning the old Boucleon Palace near Santa Sophia as their official residence. Of this fairy-tale structure, called the Great Palace, nothing now remains above ground. Directly behind the Anemas Tower, on the inside of the wall, is a crypt-like basement, part of the older palace, which may have been one of Alexios I's additions. Apart from the fact that it looks like a prison, an underground hall about two hundred feet long, divided by massive cross-buttresses into fourteen gloomy vaulted compartments—there seems no justification for the name once given it of the prison of the Anemas. That is all that remains of the Great Palace where for just over three hundred years the rulers of Byzantium were to direct their shrinking Empire in ever dwindling splendour. Today the site is covered with backyards, vegetable gardens, waste plots, and houses that if not actually squalid, come close to that category.

Not content with rebuilding the palace, Manuel I added a great wall to enclose the whole of the Blachernae district, until then still in part at any rate outside the city. Starting from just beyond the so-called Palace of Constantine Porphyrogenitus it curves outward and then runs down the hill towards the Golden Horn, rejoining the old wall near the Anemas Tower. Of its fourteen towers the five semi-circular or polygonal bastions are indistinguishable from those of an English or French castle of the same date. Because of the fall in the ground there could be no moat at this point, but standing on the sentry-walk some fifty or sixty feet above the countryside beyond, with massive towers rising even higher on either side, it is easy to understand the confidence the people of Constantinople had in their walls—before the days of gunpowder. With the building of this wall Constantinople had expanded to its furthest point. Even under the Turks there would be no enlargement on the land side of the city.

If the Blachernae Palace of Manuel I is a matter for the imagination, the so-called Palace of Constantine Porphyrogenitus is the most complete piece of secular architecture in the whole Empire (page 165). Standing at the top of the hill; tall, gaunt, and roofless, one side which has no windows formed by the Theodosian Wall itself, while its beautiful arcaded façade looks north, towards the Golden Horn and the hills beyond. Two balconies on the outer walls overlook backyards and rather mean houses, but if the setting is unpromising, the building itself is magnificent. Like so much else in the city, the palace—called the Tekfursarayi by the Turks—is of uncertain date. Once experts thought it was the work of Theophilus (829–842); then the credit was given to Constantine VII Porphyrogenitus, but now the general opinion is that Manuel I Komnenos built it at the same time as the rest of the great Palace of Blachernae. Even so, over eight centuries of existence is not to be dismissed lightly, even in this city of almost incredibly ancient buildings.

Today the upper floor and roof have vanished, and rubble several feet deep chokes the interior. Weeds grow and dust blows about in the courtyard: its level must be much higher than in the days when the Komneni came and went in glittering cavalcades, and the wind blows through the empty windows at first floor level. Those windows, constructed of alternate layers of reddish brick and white stone, the spaces between decorated with mosaic-like designs, are really beautiful and somehow reminiscent of the bays of a French Romanesque cloister. The sentry-walk along the city wall passes through the end one to the right: the vigilance to which the city owed its very existence intruded even into the private apartments of the imperial palace.

Looking down from a narrow ledge high up in the interior the Tekfursarayi is as hollow as the keep of a ruined castle. Only the pigeons suddenly launching themselves into flight from their roosts in niches and cracks on the great walls break the silence, and something of the sombreness—the long farewell—of Byzantium's last centuries still seems to hang about the great ruin.

The new Emperor who succeeded Manuel I in 1180 was only a boy, Alexios II. Like the English Henry VI he too was surrounded by scheming relatives. Isaac, the elder brother of Manuel I, who had been passed over in the succession, had two sons, John and Andronikos. The elder imagined that he had been slighted by his uncle during a military campaign, went over to the Turks, abjured his religion, married the Sultan's daughter, and by so doing became an ancestor of Mehmet II—the man who in 1453 was to capture Constantinople.

But of the two brothers it was Andronikos who was the more dangerous. The fact that his uncle and not his father had been made Emperor had evidently burned deep, but he was prepared to bide his time. When his revenge came, it was complete and horrible.

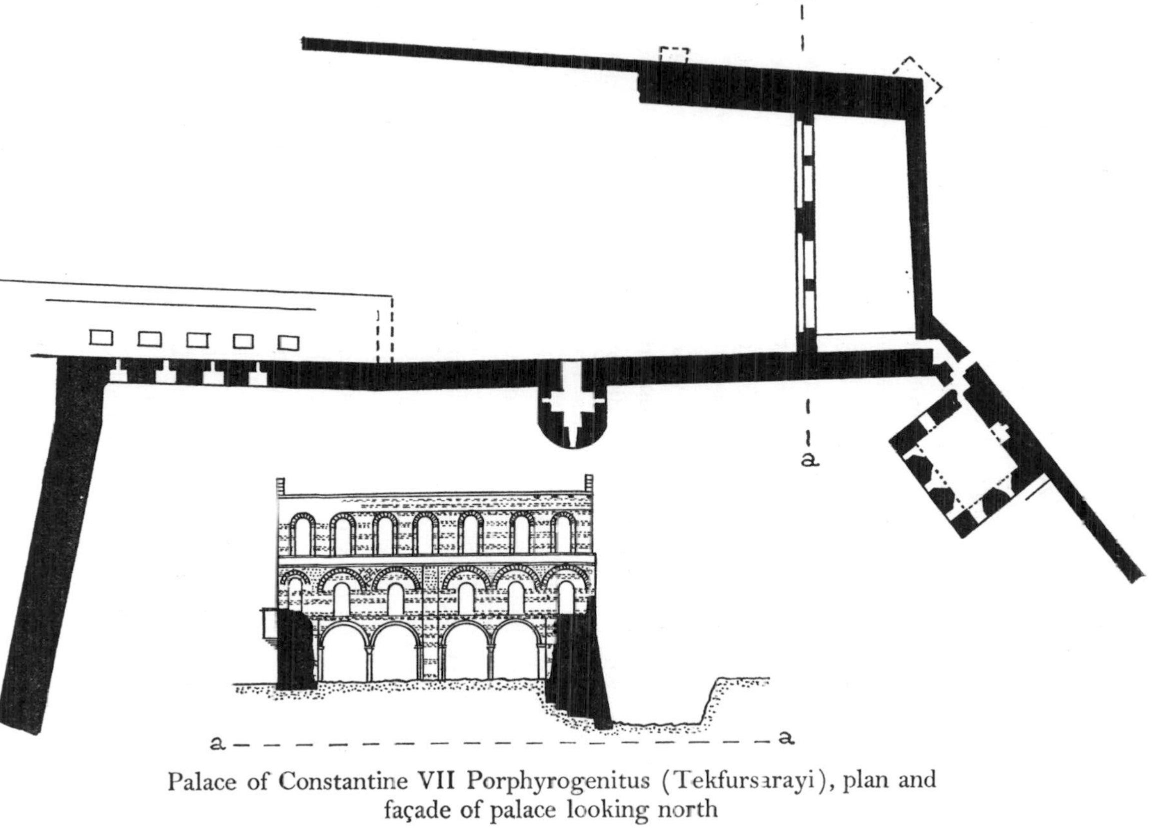

Palace of Constantine VII Porphyrogenitus (Tekfursarayı), plan and façade of palace looking north

Good-looking, muscular, and a keen huntsman, Andronikos had taken as his mistress his cousin Eudoxia, whose sister Theodora had scandalized the worthy citizens by becoming mistress to her Emperor-uncle Manuel I. At least Andronikos was open about the affair: '. . . and both the palace and the camp could witness that she slept, or watched, in the arms of her lover.' However, Eudoxia's brothers attempted to assassinate Andronikos one night, and the scheme only failed because she got wind of the plot just in time. In an attempt to level the score Andronikos started a highly treasonable correspondence with the rulers of Germany and Hungary. When Manuel I heard what his young nephew was doing he ordered him back to Constantinople under arrest.

For twelve years Andronikos was imprisoned in the tower of the Blachernae palace. Then one day he noticed some loose bricks, which he pulled away, discovering a quite large cavity. Taking some food he hid in the hole in the wall, carefully replacing the bricks behind him. The guards, on their rounds, were astonished to find him gone. At once the palace gates were closed, and orders given for his recapture. Suspicion fell on his wife, so she was placed in his cell. In the dead of night she awoke to find him standing by her side. During the day he remained hidden, living on her rations which they divided between them. Love had found a way, but by the time she gave birth to a baby, Andronikos really had escaped from the palace.

This came about when the guards grew careless, but he did not get far, and was brought back in chains. He waited for the right moment, and then the boy who was his personal servant made the guards drunk and got hold of a wax imprint of the key of the cell door which he passed to friends outside. A new key, together with a rope was smuggled in in a hogshead of wine. Andronikos let himself out, descended the tower, hid all day among the bushes in the grounds and the next night scaled the palace wall. On the other side his friends were waiting with a boat; presumably where the Avansaray landing stage is just across the street from the Kiliomeni Gate.

Off he went to his house in the city, where he saw his children and rid himself of his chains, and then set off on horseback:

north across Thrace towards the Balkans. In Wallachia he was recaptured. However, as he and his captors rode through the night he said he was not well and must dismount. Off he went among the bushes. There he thrust his staff into the ground and hung his jacket and cap upon it. Then he made off as fast as he could into the depths of the forest, leaving the considerate Wallachians patiently awaiting his return. Eventually, after many adventures, he reached Kief and the court of the Grand Duke.

Manuel I forgave him after Andronikos had induced the Grand Duke to join them in a war against Hungary. However, he soon spoilt the picture by criticizing the plans Manuel was now making to marry his daughter to Bela, the Hungarian leader, and so draw that country right into his sphere of influence. For this unsolicited opinion Andronikos was 'kicked upstairs' by being given command of the army in Cilicia. But there were complications in his own private life: he had fallen in love with Philippa of Antioch, Manuel's sister-in-law. Love seemed infinitely more desirable than the role of commanding officer, hundreds of miles away to the south-east of Constantinople, and without a qualm he deprived Philippa of her virtue and the possibility of a good marriage. The Emperor was furious with his nephew—so Andronikos kissed her farewell and set off on a pilgrimage to Jerusalem. On the way he met Theodora, the widowed Queen of Jerusalem, and forgot about his journey towards salvation.

The scandal coursed from one end of the Empire to the other. In the capital Manuel gave orders that his philandering nephew was to be captured and blinded. That was easier said than done. Warned by Theodora, he fled with her and their two illegitimate children first to Damascus, then Baghdad, as far north as the Caspian Sea, and finally settled among the Turks of Colonia. From there he and his followers raided the adjacent province of Trebizond, returning home with loot and captive Christians. At this point the church excommunicated Andronikos, who, however, did not turn Turk. Then one day the Governor of Trebizond captured Queen Theodora and their two children, and sent them to Constantinople. Andronikos showed he could be faithful, implored his uncle's forgiveness, and came of his own accord to the city.

When brought before Manuel in the Blachernae Palace he threw himself on the ground, groaned, and wept, and declared he would not get up until some faithful subject had dragged him to the foot of the throne by an iron chain which he himself had fitted round his neck and kept hidden until that moment. The vulgar exhibitionism deceived the court, and not only was he forgiven, but even received back into communion by the Church. However, Manuel decided Constantinople was no place for him, and ordered Andronikos to go and live in the province of Pontius, on the Black Sea coast.

There he remained until Manuel I's death in 1180. Now the Emperor was his cousin, the twelve-year-old Alexios II, for whom his mother, the Empress Mary, acted as regent. She was a Latin, disliked by the people, and let the reins of government pass into the hands of a relative. This led to a small-scale civil war, fought in the Forum beside Santa Sophia, which ended with the rebels running for sanctuary in the cathedral. This, felt Andronikos, was the moment for his return. From Pontius he marched westwards with an ever-growing train of followers, and when he reached the Bosphorus the Navy—such as it was—was waiting to conduct him in triumph down to Constantinople.

He moved into the palace, acknowledged the boy-Emperor, and shut the lad's mother and her coterie out of harm's way. Then he went to the Monastery of St Saviour Pantokrator, to the grave of his uncle Manuel. The Emperor's sarcophagus of black marble, with a representation of the seven hills of Constantinople carved on its top, lay in the funerary chapel which links the twin churches of the monastery. Close by was one of the most sacred objects in this city of relics: the porphyry slab on which Christ's body was reputed to have lain after the Deposition. Brought from Ephesus, it was unloaded at the harbour of the Boucleon, and Manuel himself carried it on his own back up the steep hill to the imperial chapel of the old palace.

Now Andronikos was standing beside the great sarcophagus, shedding crocodile tears for the benefit of the onlookers, but saying: 'I no longer fear thee, my old enemy, who hast driven me a vagabond to every climate of the earth. Thou art safely deposited under a sevenfold dome, from whence thou can never again arise till the signal of the last trumpet. It is now my turn, and speedily will I trample on thy ashes and thy posterity.' All the bitterness he had felt for years that his father had been passed over in favour of a younger brother, his own uncle Manuel, would now spill over.

At his young cousin's coronation Andronikos took the Elements in his hands and swore to protect the youth. But with insidious propaganda he led the people to think that only someone such as himself could save the Empire from decline. He was elevated to the rank of co-Emperor, promptly degraded Alexios, arrested and calumniated his mother the Empress Mary, and accused her of a treasonable correspondence with the king of Hungary (the very charge he had been accused of as a young man). The Empress was tried—three judges refused to have anything to do with the proceedings—and her own son was forced to sign her death-warrant. Then she was strangled and her body thrown into the sea.

Soon it was the turn of the fifteen-year-old Alexios. He too was strangled with a bow-string, and Andronikos completed his insane revenge by kicking the boy's body, exclaiming: 'Thy father was a knave, thy mother a whore, and thyself a fool.' According to the historian Nicetas, who is reliable, Andronikos ordered his nephew's body to be thrown into the Sea of Marmara—to the accompaniment of music. A debonair adventurer had turned into a horrifying tyrant.

In 1184 Andronikos I Komnenos murdered his way to the throne, and for over a year of mounting oppression he remained there. And yet there were good features about his reign. He forbade the practice of pillaging ships wrecked on the shores of the Empire, gave new life to the long-neglected provinces, rewarded good service with worthwhile appointments, and said of the bureaucracy: 'If you do not cease from maladministration, you can cease from living.'

For years the Empire, or at least Constantinople, had become increasingly westernized. Now tournaments were held in the Hippodrome—and more important, in the provinces a feudal system of land-owning families of military background were altering, and unwittingly undermining the whole social structure of the Empire. Instead of men holding land direct from the state, in return for their service in time of war, these military smallholdings had passed as gifts from the government into the hands of private individuals more interested in their own aggrandizement than the country's welfare. From being smallholders with military obligations, the peasants were sinking into a state of semi-serfdom. This was one of the evils that Andronikos tried to correct. But he went about it the wrong way. The great families resented the confiscations, and wholesale executions followed in which almost all the officer class in the Empire was wiped out, with fatal results for Byzantium's future independence. Executions were the order of the day, and Constantinople was prostrate beneath the foot of a tyrant.

Eventually a candidate for the throne was found who was willing to risk his eyes or his life in an attempt to supplant the terrible Andronikos. He was Isaac Angelus, a descendant of Alexios I Komnenos. Word reached the Emperor that there was a plot to overthrow him, and he ordered Isaac's arrest and execution. The latter killed the hired assassin, and escaped to Santa Sophia. There a large crowd gathered to stare and speculate on his fate and determined once and for all to put an end to this reign of terror. This spirit swept out of the vast cathedral into the city itself. Dawn next day saw the prisons being broken open and, while the sun was still low in the sky, Isaac was taken from sanctuary in Santa Sophia to the palace.

While all this was happening, Andronikos was on one of the Princes' Islands, some twelve miles from the city, with both his wife and mistress for company. His wife, even now only fifteen years old, had previously been married to Alexios II, murdered the year before by the man who was now her husband. As fast as he could Andronikos returned to a Constantinople tense and waiting for the next move. The palace was dangerously quiet. Fearfully, he offered the rebels a free pardon. This was rejected out of hand. Then he offered to make his own son, Manuel, Emperor in his place. This too was rejected. There was only one thing the citizens wanted. His life. From the palace gardens he fled from the city in the imperial galley (these events must have taken place in the old palace near Santa Sophia), but soon he was overhauled by a faster and lighter vessel, put in chains and brought back to a people whose blood-lust really was up.

His captors took him to the Tower of the Anemas, on the wall adjoining the Blachernae Palace where so recently he had lived as Emperor. Expert escaper that he was, this was one prison he could not expect to leave, except at the bidding of his gaolers. That same evening he was loaded with more chains, about his neck and feet, and taken before the new Emperor, Isaac II Angelus, in the adjoining palace.

Tyrant that he was, Andronikos was treated with a ferocious cruelty. Hit about the head, his beard was pulled off, his teeth knocked out and his right hand struck off. But they had not the humanity to kill him then and there: that would have been too quick. The streak of cruelty in the Byzantines was all too evident, and he was taken back to the Tower of the Anemas, locked in his cell and left completely alone for several days. Then when his time really had come, the mob extracted the last drop of sadism that was possible.

Blinded in one eye, Andronikos was dressed like a slave and taken the whole way across the city mounted on a mangy camel. Now the quondam Emperor, the Thirteenth Apostle, was abused and hooted at in the streets by the crowd enjoying its East Roman holiday to the full. At the end of his journey he was taken into the Hippodrome, and hung upside down by the feet between two columns, a figure of a wolf on one side, a hyena on the other. There he was within reach of the mob. '*Kyrie Eleison*, Why dost thou break the bruised reed?' was all he exclaimed. Finally, according to Nicetas, three men killed him with their swords; not out of any feeling of compassion for his agony, but to show off their sword-play. Their action, whether intentional or not, was the only humane one perpetrated in the city that day in September, 1185.

Chapter 24

1185–1204

Relations with the crusaders in Constantinople. Isaac Angelus Tower (1188). Emperor overthrown. His son escapes and asks the help of the crusaders. The Fourth Crusade. The Latins land at Chalcedon, 1203. The city besieged. The crusaders' camp. Attack by land and water. Its failure. Isaac Angelus restored to the throne. Crusaders received in the Blachernae Palace. Fire in the city. A palace revolution. Isaac and his son murdered. The crusaders attack again (1204) and capture Constantinople. City again burnt. Looting of sacred relics. Relics of St John the Baptist. Disgraceful scenes in Santa Sophia. Destruction of works of art by the crusaders.

Four times in just over a century the unwanted crusaders passed through the Empire, despising and despised. Alexios I Komnenos had stomached his dislike of their high-handed behaviour within his dominions, but his successors Manuel I and Isaac II Angelus allowed them to be harried, pillaged, and even refused admittance to the cities. Byzantium was terrified, rightly as it turned out in the end, of these hordes of militant Catholics who even included a troop of armour-clad female cavalry, led by a gilt-spurred Amazon called the Golden-footed Dame. But by any standards the East Roman Empire behaved badly: chalk was mixed in the flour sold to the crusaders; base coins were specially minted for trading with them, and all the worst aspects of religious bigotry, political apprehension, and racial dislike were openly displayed.

In the palace of Blachernae King Louis of France had been made to sit on a low stool at the side of the Emperor's throne and, to avoid such a situation, Frederick Barbarossa went so far as by-passing Constantinople altogether. He crossed into Asia via the Dardanelles. The Byzantines really preferred the infidel Turks and Saracens to the heretics from the west. Though divided by religion from the Turks, the rulers of this semi-oriental civilization had more in common with their outlook on life and way of thinking than with men from France, England, Germany, or the Italian republics. Not only did the Komneni maintain a secret treaty with Saracens, but even allowed a mosque to be built in Constantinople. There the orthodox patriarch went so far as to say that forgiveness for sins could be obtained by killing off the heretic Latins. The Greeks were not slow to obtain this spiritual indulgence. Naturally, in the west the dislike of Constantinople was only rivalled by envy for its magnificence and wealth.

The feeling against the Latins reached boiling point in the city soon after Andronikos I came to the throne in 1184. With the active help of the imperial troops men, women, and children —all Franks—were cut down in the streets. Urged on by the orthodox priests the Latin churches, hospitals, and the whole quarter was burnt to the ground, and four thousand survivors sold into slavery with the Turks. Among those caught by the mob was an Italian cardinal. His head was tied to the tail of a dog and paraded through the streets of the city. Many Franks managed to escape by boat, and retaliated by pillaging the towns and villages along the shores of the Sea of Marmara as they fled for the west with accounts of what had happened in the City of Felicity.

Isaac II Angelus, the Emperor who succeeded Andronikos I, was not worthy of his position. Once again, when the Empire needed a good emperor, she was to be disappointed. If there were troubles within the walls of the city, there were also headaches beyond. In 1187 Bulgaria proclaimed its own emperor, while away to the south Jerusalem fell to Saladin. The latter event was the more important for Constantinople itself. As a result the Fourth Crusade of 1203 was mounted, which culminated not with the recapture of Jerusalem from Islam, but with the sacking of Christian Constantinople.

Isaac II lived in the utmost luxury and laziness in the Palace of Blachernae, despised even by his own court jesters. Surrounding him was an enormous staff of eunuchs and servants, no less than twenty thousand of them. Out of sight, and therefore out of mind, the Bulgarians had renounced orthodoxy, and been received most warmly into communion with Rome. Cyprus had been captured by Richard I, who gave it to the French Lusignan family. But Isaac Angelus did not care, and the city and Empire stagnated until he was deposed in 1195 by his own brother, Alexios III Angelus.

At the time the Emperor was out of Constantinople, on a hunting expedition in Thrace. Realizing what lay behind the hostile glances of the imperial guards he fled for fifty miles into Macedonia, but was captured and brought back to Constantinople. There he was blinded and imprisoned in the tower, the twin of the Anemas Tower, on the wall beside the Blachernae Palace where for ten years he had lived in splendid uselessness.

Here at least is a tower whose date is beyond question. It has the carved inscription: 'Tower, by command of the Emperor Isaac Angelus, under the superintendence of Basil . . . in the year 1188.' From the rough workmanship and odd-sized stones it seems the Angelus Tower (to the right, when looking at the wall from outside the city), was built in a hurry. Two-thirds of the way up round stone pillars have been used as building material: they project from the wall like petrified cannon.

Disguised as a sailor, the twelve-year-old son of Isaac Angelus escaped from Constantinople in an Italian ship. Finally he reached his sister Irene, Queen of the Romans. There he heard that a plan was afoot at Venice to organize another attack on the Saracens—the Fourth Crusade.

For Byzantium the Fourth Crusade would be the first intimation of extinction.

The young Alexios—he shared the same Christian name as his usurping uncle—saw in the crusaders a heaven-sent chance to restore his father to the throne. From them he begged money. With no one of mature years to advise or check his rash promises the boy agreed to term after term that would be difficult if not impossible to fulfil when the time came. As soon as the restoration had taken place the Orthodox Church was to be reunited with Rome; the crusaders were to receive 200,000 silver marks; Alexios himself was to accompany them to Egypt—or maintain ten thousand men for their use for one year while, for as long as he lived, he would maintain five hundred knights for service in Palestine.

In the west, the Pope envisaged the return of the East Roman Empire to the Catholic fold; the Doge of Venice envisaged enormous trading rights; the French envisaged the restoration of the Emperor to his rightful throne—and all saw the opportunity to loot the richest city on earth.

First Zara, on the Dalmatian coast, which had sought the aid of Hungary, was besieged and captured. Then on April 7, 1203 one hundred and twenty flat-bottomed horse transports, two hundred and forty troop and weapon transports, seventy provision ships and forty escorting galleys set sail, for Constantinople. On board were the knights and their squires, with the shields arranged along the bulwarks on either side. Overhead their banners fluttered, and as they cast off—the sound of music.

Down the Adriatic, round Greece, and up among the islands of the Archipelago. Through the Dardanelles, and on across the Sea of Marmara to the Princes' Islands. There they intended to land and replenish their supplies and stocks of corn, but a gale blew them across the intervening twelve miles, almost to the walls. 'So near did they run to the shore and the city, that some volleys of stones were exchanged between the ship and the rampart. As they passed along, they gazed with admiration on the capital of the East, rising from her seven hills, and towering over the continents of Europe and Asia. The swelling domes and lofty spires of five hundred palaces and churches were gilded by the sun and reflected in the waters; the walls were crowded with soldiers and spectators; and each heart was chilled by the reflection, that since the beginning of the world, such an enterprise had never been undertaken by such a handful of warriors.' (Gibbon.)

Seven and a half centuries later the approach by sea is still one of the most impressive and beautiful sights imaginable. The walls are there from which the Greeks attacked the crusader's ships; the swelling domes of Santa Sophia, and the empty façades of the Sea Palaces; though now the 'lofty spires' (which, anyway, were a figment of Gibbon's imagination) are the pencil-thin minarets of innumerable mosques.

At Chalcedon (Kadiköy) the army of forty thousand was landed: the crusaders stepping straight onto Asiatic soil, and three days later while moving a mile or two up the coast towards Chrysopolis (Scutari, now called Üsküdar) eighty French knights routed five hundred Byzantine horsemen. An inauspicious beginning for the defenders.

The navy was at its lowest ebb: the grand admiral had even sold off the sails and spars, and the usurping Alexios could not raise himself from his apathy, in spite of the reports which had preceded the crusaders. He sent an embassy across from the city to the crusaders' camp. They returned with a blunt reply from the Doge of Venice. 'In the cause of honour and justice, we despise the usurper of Greece, his threats, and his offers. Our friendship and his allegiance are due to the lawful heir, to the young prince, who is seated among us, and to his father, the Emperor Isaac, who has been deprived of his sceptre, his freedom, and his eyes, by the crime of an ungrateful brother . . . Let him not insult us by a second message: our reply will be made in arms, in the Palace of Constantinople.'

Then, on a beautiful day, June 6, 1203, the crusaders crossed the Bosphorus. Their six divisions were led by the Count of Flanders. Ahead, drawn up on the shore, 70,000 Byzantines on horse and on foot awaited them. When the water was still waist-deep, the knights jumped from the ships and their men followed; with a rattle the drawbridges of the horse-transports dropped down—and the defenders vanished like dew in the sun. Where they actually crossed is uncertain, but five miles up the coast from Üsküdar, where the stream—the Fresh Waters of Asia, enters the Bosphorus, is about the narrowest point: there, centuries later, the Turks built the twin fortresses of Anadolu and Rumeli Hisar.

Now the French knights and infantry were marching south

again, along the European side of the Bosphorus, towards Constantinople and its suburb of Galata. They stormed the Galata Tower, the predecessor of the present structure, while the Venetian ships attempted to break the boom across the mouth of the Golden Horn. Twenty warships, the pathetic remnants of the Byzantine navy, were captured or sunk, and the weight of the crusaders' galleys broke the massive chain. The military side of the operation was conducted by the French, and the naval by those first-rate sailors, the Venetians.

From Galata the French marched along the north shore of the Golden Horn until they came to the bridge (there had been one on the site since the days of Justinian), just beyond the present day Ayvansaray landing-stage where the little water-buses that ply up and down the Golden Horn make a call. The Greeks had cut down the bridge, and it took Count Baldwin's men twenty-four hours to repair it so the French could cross over.

They actually sited their camp on the hill which overlooks the north-west corner of the city. Below them, as they stood on its summit, were the walls of Heraclius and those added not a century before by Manuel I Komnenos, to protect the Palace of Blachernae from whose windows the usurping Alexios III was watching the preparations for attack. According to the historian Nicetas, the crusaders and the people on the walls were within speaking distance of each other. It is perfectly possible. Inside the city Alexios III was bolstered up by his son-in-law, Theodore Lascaris. It was one thing to blind and imprison a defenceless and rather foolish brother, but another when a huge crusader army was camped outside the walls, bent—among other things—on restoring him to his throne. For his personal defence Alexios III relied on his Varangian guards, those great fair-haired men with massive battle-axes who were for the most part Danish or English.

After ten days of preparation, during which time the Venetians managed to break the boom across the entrance to the Golden Horn, and the French brought up two hundred and fifty siege-engines against the land walls, the attack came, on the seventeenth of July. At one point the French scaled the walls of Leo V, and fifteen knights and sergeants were engaged in bitter hand-to-hand fighting with the Varangian guards. Finally they were forced to retreat, leaving two of their number as prisoners.

Meanwhile a mile or so away down the Golden Horn the Venetians—fighting under the doughty eighty-year-old Doge Dandolo, who was quite blind—had been more successful with their waterborne attack. In the succeeding centuries the shore has built up, with the dumping of rubbish and the building of houses on piles, and so the water has been pushed further and further back from the city walls. Today the Aptülezel Paşa Street, as well as a motley collection of buildings separates the walls from the Golden Horn. The actual point where the Venetians chose to make their attack was near the Petri Kapisi. An odd choice, for at that point, in fact, the wall is double, the Petrion. But the attack was successful. Their galleys, full of soldiers, and the ships with catapults mounted aft, had swept in towards the quays, with the Doge in their midst, the Standard of St Mark before him. Now the Republic's banner was floating over one of the towers. But when the storming of the city was not only possible, but probable, the Venetians heard that their French comrades had been surrounded by sixty squadrons of Byzantine cavalry. Abandoning their foothold they withdrew and went to the aid of the French. At this unexpected turn of events the cavalry drew off, back into Constantinople, probably re-entering through the Karsios Gate (Eğrikapi) half-way along the walls of Manuel I.

But the usurping Alexios III had had enough. In the dead of night he gathered together 10,000 lbs. of gold, abandoned his wife, and slipped away in a small boat to the safety of an obscure harbour down the Thracian coast.

On the nineteenth of July the rightful Emperor, Isaac I Angelus, was brought out of his prison and restored to the throne he could no longer see. The next day he sent word to the crusaders that he was once again Emperor, and could his young son come to him? Thinking of the reward promised by the boy the crusaders sent only four ambassadors to the palace. Through the Gyrolymne Gate, near the Anemas Tower, they went straight into the Blachernae Palace, where surrounded by his

English and Danish guards the old Emperor, his Hungarian wife, and the senators awaited their coming.

Isaac I, the Empress, the chamberlain, and an interpreter went with the ambassadors into a private room. He knew nothing of the terms to which his son had agreed, and when they explained he did not say yes, and he did not say no. Alexios was allowed to enter Constantinople, still virtually in a state of siege, and together with his father he went to Santa Sophia to be crowned. For a while the citizens and the crusaders rubbed shoulders in suspicious amity. The whole of Galata was allotted to the French and the Venetians, who spent much of their time sightseeing. With their wonder grew their avarice, but for the moment all was uneasy peace.

The time was approaching when the crusaders must move on to the Holy Land. The young Alexios was afraid of being left alone to face both his people and his treasonable relatives. For 1,600 lbs. of gold the Marquis of Montferrat agreed to accompany Alexios on a progress through the European parts of the Empire, so he could show himself to his subjects—with the comfortable thought that he had French swords to protect him. But in Constantinople itself the tide of sentiment was turning against the father and son. Age and blindness had not diminished Isaac's appetite for vice, while the church was busy stirring up feeling against his son for abandoning orthodoxy.

While Alexios and Montferrat were absent the situation in the city was exacerbated by a number of Flemish pilgrims who set fire to the Saracen Mosque, situated somewhere near the modern Sirkeci Station. That was in August, 1203. For two days and nights that part of the city blazed; the flames reached right across to the walls along the Sea of Marmara, near the church of SS. Sergius and Bacchus (Küçük Aya Sophia Camii), doing thousands of pounds' worth of damage. For their own safety the crusaders stayed in Galata, and disowned responsibility for the disaster.

The hostility of the Greeks grew, and when the young Alexios returned from his progress, there was an ultimatum. The two factions drifted towards open war, and the day soon came when three Venetian senators and three French knights rode into the palace of Blachernae and bluntly told him that unless he fulfilled the promises made for his father's restoration when he first sought their help they would no longer hold him as a sovereign or a friend.

Alexios was between two fires: his own people despised him as an apostate, while the crusaders despised him for breaking his promises. In an attempt to find a successor to the throne the purple was offered to every senator in turn, but all refused. Another palace revolution was in the making. Alexios Ducas, called Mourzoufle (beetlebrows) because of his heavy black eyebrows, was the man at the centre. First he stirred up the citizens against the crusaders, then he gained the confidence of Alexios IV, becoming his great chamberlain. The trap was ready for springing. In the middle of the night, February 8, 1204, he rushed into the imperial bedchamber and woke the Emperor, telling him there was a riot and that the palace was being attacked.

More asleep than awake Alexios was hurried down a secret staircase by Mourzoufle, as he thought to safety, but in fact into a cellar or underground dungeon. The basements of the palace of Alexios I Komnenos behind the Anemas Tower perhaps? There the youth was chained up, left for a few days, and finally either strangled or poisoned. After that it was the turn of his father, the blind Isaac, and he too was murdered.

The Venetians and French were scandalized, and demanded 50,000 lbs. of gold—presumably as a fine (though was it their affair to interfere in the admittedly sordid internal politics of the Byzantine Empire?). Mourzoufle refused to pay, and the second siege of Constantinople began. Whatever his faults, the new Emperor was a fighter, of a kind. He made an attempt to destroy the Venetian galleys with fire-ships, but it failed. During one sally towards the crusader's camp Mourzoufle, now called Alexios V Ducas, lost not only his shield, but even the imperial standard with its picture of the Virgin. The great walls, which had defeated so many enemies in the past, now kept out the French, and the offensive was launched against the harbour area.

The attack, when it came on April 9, 1204, was in the same area as the year before. The defenders raised the walls with wooden mantlets, and watched the galleys and smaller ships coming towards them. They sailed right up to the walls. Gangways were dropped—flying bridges—from the crows' nests of the ships onto the top of the walls, and in a hail of stones and arrows soldiers swarmed across. The hand-to-hand fighting was bitter, but the engagement was indecisive and in the evening the crusaders drew off. Then on April 12, they lashed two ships together, the *Pilgrim* and the *Paradise*, which the strong north wind blew against the walls. On board were the Bishops of Troyes and Soissons. Soon four towers and three gates had fallen to the attackers, urged on by Doge Dandolo. Alexios V had his tent close to the church of St Theodosia (Gül Camii) just behind the walls by the Aykapi. If his reserves, billeted in the Monastery of St Saviour Pantepopte (Eskiimaret Camii) about half a mile away on the top of the Fourth Hill, rallied to him they might be able to dislodge the crusaders from their foothold as they had done the year before. But they did not come. The reserves made off as fast as their legs would carry them, across the city to the palace of the Boucleon.

Now the crusaders were quite established inside the city, fighting their way towards the palace of Blachernae. When they reached it they had captured the headquarters of the resistance by the Greeks. The siege was over, and for the first time in its history Constantinople had been taken by storm.

Fire, the enemy all through the centuries of Constantinople, broke out; but this time it was no accident. It was done deliberately by the crusaders to stop the Greeks fighting a rearguard action from house to house. All night the French and the Venetians were on the alert for any emergency, but with the morning came a procession of citizens, crosses at their head, offering their submission. Their Emperor had abandoned them, escaping via the Golden Gate; and now the defenceless city awaited its inevitable rape.

The Byzantines appealed to the Marquis of Montferrat to protect them, and whilst he forbade the violation of women, there were no restrictions on looting. It was not every man for himself—officially. The stolen property had to be deposited in one of three appointed places; churches as it so happened. When all that was either valuable or moveable had been gathered together, its worth was estimated, and then divided. The smallest share went to the footsoldiers, a double portion to the equivalent of sergeants; a share four times as large as the footsoldier's to the knights, and so on up the scale. One French knight was hanged, with his shield about his neck, for trying to keep back part of his pilferings. This warned the others to be more careful.

The plundering was not confined to the soldiers and sailors. Among the crusaders were many such as Martin, Abbot of Parisis in Alsace. Together with his chaplain he went to the Monastery of St Saviour Pantokrator. There he stormed at a white-haired old priest who, when he realized what was wanted, took them to an iron safe which he unlocked. Without a qualm the two Latins rifled it, taking all that was of value, including some of Constantinople's most sacred relics. Among the sixty-two items the abbot stole was a reputed fragment of the Cross and some drops of Christ's blood.

As might be expected in a city that had been looted by crusaders and torn by civil war, that went bankrupt and was finally captured by the Ottoman Turks, there remain singularly few of the reliquaries which were once in every church of any standing or importance. But even so two magnificent reliquaries are still in Istanbul: in the treasury of the Seraglio. One is the hand of John the Baptist, sheathed in a gold arm, the fingers bent in benediction, with a small part of the back of the hand left open to expose a few mummified tendons. On the case is the inscription in Greek: 'This hand baptised Jesus the Lamb of God.' Its date, like that of the second reliquary, is uncertain. In a container resembling a lantern with crystal windows in a frame of gold heavily set with stones is a reputed fragment of the Baptist's skull. The actual relic is contained in a gold cover; also with an inscription in Greek on it.

Looting went on all over the city: not even Santa Sophia escaped. In fact, it fared worst of all, and the scenes which went on in there are an eternal disgrace to the crusaders and all they were supposed to stand for. The victors, drunk not only with bigotry, caroused in the great nave with the women of the town, used the chalices as wine cups, destroyed icons, mosaics, and vestments, and generally behaved like barbarians. The huge veil which hung before the altar, of silk sewn with half a million pearls, was torn down and ripped to pieces. A naked prostitute was set on the Patriarch's throne, and she also burlesqued the rites of the Orthodox Church, celebrating Communion with wine in which blood and filth had been mixed. Horses and mules were driven right into the sanctuary to load them with stolen treasure: the silver doors torn off the pulpit, for example. When Mehmet II, a Moslem, entered Santa Sophia after the capture of the city in 1453, he stopped to rebuke one of his soldiers who was merely damaging the floor.

All but one of the great bronze doors was destroyed, the sole survivor being the one from the courtyard into the south porch. Unfortunately, it today has a heavy grille in front, which makes it difficult to see really well. Though not as old as Santa Sophia itself, it is thought to date from the time of Theophilus, died 842, though there is a defaced inscription referring to his son Michael III, murdered 867.

The story of the crusaders' behaviour was little better at the Church of the Apostles—the Westminster Abbey of Constantinople. There the illustrious dead, including Justinian himself, were ripped from their tombs, presumably in the search for jewellery and valuables.

One who left a description of the sack of the city was the well-to-do senator and historian, Nicetas. His palace was burnt, and he and his family had to hide away in a house he owned near Santa Sophia. Of all people, it was a Venetian merchant who played the good samaritan. He dressed up as a Latin soldier, and guarded the door of the house, keeping his fellow countrymen from entering and looting. On one occasion it was Nicetas himself who came to the rescue of a young girl who was being carried off. He ran shouting through the streets after the crusader would-be rapist, and it was at least to the credit of some of the Latins that they rescued her unharmed.

When it was safe for Nicetas and his family to make their escape from the city, it was on foot and wearing their oldest clothes—so as not to draw attention to themselves, and with their faces dirtied. One of the women was fairly far advanced in pregnancy. The little group had to walk the whole length of the Mesé, quitting Constantinople by the public gate beside the Golden Gate. On their way into the country they fell in with the patriarch, almost naked and riding alone on a donkey.

Had it been done by the Avars or the Bulgarians who had captured the city, the wanton destruction that was done by the crusaders could not have been worse. Nicetas recorded some of the magnificent statues they destroyed for the metal. A she-wolf suckling Romulus and Remus; an eagle tearing at a serpent in its talons; an ass with its driver—of great historical interest too: it was set up by Augustus after defeating Mark Anthony and Cleopatra's Egyptian fleet at Actium; an equestrian statue of Bellerophon and Pegasus; Paris presenting Aphrodite with the apple of discord; a statue of Helen; a huge statue of Hercules, and a similar one of Juno. Then there was a brass obelisk with rural scenes on its sides: could this have been the Walled Obelisk or Column of Constantine Porphyrogenitus which stands on the site of the Hippodrome, and is known to have been covered with metal plates? The holes still remain on the weather-beaten obelisk for the metal clamps which held the plates in position. The four bronze horses which stood on either side of the Kathisma—the Emperor's box in the Hippodrome—were taken to Venice. Today they must be the most famous horses in the world: prancing upon the façade of St Mark's Cathedral: dedicated to a saint whose body the Venetians stole from Alexandria.

Chapter 25

Art Treasures

Art treasures taken to the west by the crusaders. Destruction of Phidias' statue of Athena. Bronze statue taken to Barletta. Icons. The difficulty of seeing a comprehensive survey of Byzantine art in any one place.

Whilst condemning the crusaders for their wholesale looting in Constantinople there is at the back of the mind the realization that at least as far as future generations were concerned there was a credit side. Had not such treasures as the bronze horses of Lysippus been taken to Venice they would undoubtedly have been melted down by the Turks after the conquest of 1453. Indeed, whilst Istanbul is unrivalled for studying the architecture of Byzantium, civil and military as well as ecclesiastical (*pace* Ravenna), it is elsewhere that one must look for its art: other than mosaics and late Roman sculpture.

In their agony, as Constantinople burnt, the inhabitants turned on one of their finest treasures: the statue of Athena, which about 449 the great Pericles ordered Phidias to cast in bronze, which was set up on a tall plinth half-way between the Propylaea and the Parthenon on the Acropolis in Athens. Twenty-nine feet six inches high, it was huge, set high above the city that bore her name. She stood armed, leaning on the spear she held in her right hand, and on her left arm a shield. Then, in the time of Justinian, the bronze colossus was taken to Constantinople, and set up in the Forum of Augustus. She faced the west, and it was from the west that the barbarian crusaders had come. Now, in 1204, the superstitious inhabitants thought it was she who had beckoned them to come, and in their rage and futile grief they destroyed that which Phidias had created.

A bronze taken to the west by the crusaders is the huge statue now outside a church in Barletta, in southern Italy. Apparently the arms and legs are early Renaissance restorations: one hand holds an orb while the other grasps a cross. The figure is that of a Roman warrior. The face, with glaring eyes and a rather small bad-tempered mouth seems to have some affinity with the profile of Valentinian I on the coins. It has been attributed to Heraclius (died 641), but his face was long and surely he was never without a beard. One of his nervous mannerisms was that he was always running his fingers through it.

The most wonderful collection of icons in the world must be that in the Byzantine Museum in Athens, of which a remarkable number really are Byzantine; if the term is taken to include only those painted before the extinction of all parts of the Empire by the mid 1460s. What with the Iconoclastic Controversy which resulted in the all but total destruction of icons before A.D. 842—one suspects that almost anything pre-eleventh century, now aged almost to the darkest monochrome, is attributed to St Luke—and the superimposition of an alien religion and civilization, their rarity can be well understood. Though it would be fair to mention that after the fall of the part of the Empire that was Greece (as the modern geographical term is understood) the monks of Athos were allowed a remarkable amount of independence and toleration on their peninsula.

Only once in a lifetime can exhibits be gathered together from the whole of Europe, including the U.S.S.R., as was done for the Exhibition of Byzantine Art, first at the Edinburgh Festival and then at the Victoria and Albert Museum in 1958. Then it was possible to see, under one roof, a comprehensive survey of this most remote and elusive art-form: from the ivory diptychs of late Roman times right through to the small portable mosaics which came into favour when the well-to-do could no longer afford to have their houses or chapels decorated with full-scale ones. At such a time it was also possible to see magnificent jewel-studded reliquaries, Bible covers of the tenth and eleventh centuries, as well as such pieces as the silver-gilt and enamelled icon (the face and hands of gold) of the Archangel Gabriel, from the treasury of St Mark's, Venice: a treasury in every sense of the word, including onyx chalices set with enamel miniatures of saints, while in the cathedral itself there is Pala d'Oro behind the altar. That was legitimately acquired, commissioned by a tenth century Doge when in Constantinople.

It is to Budapest that one must go to see regalia: an eleventh century diadem for a princess, with full-length figures in enamel on the gold panels, and a crown, quite squat with four bands supporting the cross, given before 1077 by Michael VII Dukas (an unmemorable ruler otherwise), set with huge roughly cut stones and pearls. It was a present to Gèza I of Hungary from Michael VII, and includes portraits of the two sovereigns, the implication being that the Hungarian was Michael's vassal.

London, Paris, Florence, Berlin, Venice, Athens, and Leningrad: it is in such cities that the art of Byzantium is to be found, scattered to the four corners of Europe, far from the Constantinople of their origin on the shores of the Sea of Marmara.

Chapter 26

1204-1261

The Latin Empire with Constantinople as its capital. Usurping Emperor Alexios V thrown from Theodosian Column. Baldwin II (1237–1261) tries to raise funds in west Europe. Crown jewels pawned to the Venetians. Sacred relics sold. Michael VIII Palaeologus recaptures Constantinople from the Latins.

On May 9, 1204, six French and six Venetian electors met in the palace of Blachernae to choose a new and Catholic emperor for Byzantium. After Doge Dandolo had refused the office, it was accepted by Baldwin, Count of Flanders. In a ritual going back to pre-history and the Norse sagas he was raised on a shield. Then he was carried shoulder high to Santa Sophia, and there invested with the scarlet shoes of his imperial dignity. Three weeks later he was crowned by the Latin Legate, and the Venetian clergy installed themselves in the offices left vacant by their orthodox brethren. As spoils of war the new Emperor sent the city gates and the chain which closed the harbour to Palestine: visible proof to the crusaders there of what had happened at Constantinople.

Next they set about dismembering the Empire as though it was a carcass in a butcher's shop. In Greece independent states were set up: the Despotate of Achaia, the Duchy of Athens, and the Kingdom of Thessalonika. In the Archipelago the Venetians acquired Crete, Euboea, Naxos, and Zante. Constantinople itself received the same treatment by partitioning. There the Venetians settled in three of its eight quarters, occupying those most useful to them as traders, along the Golden Horn.

Two of Byzantium's former rulers still lived: Alexios III and Alexios V Mourzoufle. The latter made his way to the older man's camp. After a friendly welcome he was seized while having a bath, blinded, and turned loose as a beggar—and a warning. Alexios V attempted to cross over into Asia, but was captured by the Latins, tried and sentenced to death. A lengthy debate followed among his judges who were trying to make up their minds just how he should die. Finally they agreed he should be thrown from the top of the Theodosian Column, 147 feet high, which had a spiral staircase leading to the top. Today Beyazit Square occupies the site of the forum in which it stood. A huge crowd came to watch the sentence being carried out, the sixth emperor to die violently in twenty years: a terrible record reminiscent of the convulsions of the earlier Roman Empire.

Just before Constantinople fell to the crusaders, Alexios V's sister married the Greek Theodore Lascaris, who during the days of turmoil before the end had offered himself as Emperor, and had been refused by the apathetic citizens. With a number of followers he slipped across the water into Asia, to Nicaea, where he proclaimed himself first Despot and then Emperor. An orthodox Emperor in exile, and a rival Catholic usurper in the capital. Meanwhile another Alexios, son of Andronikos I, went to Trebizond (Trabzon) with his brother, where in that remote little city on the Black Sea they founded the diminutive Empire of Trebizond. There, until it too was overwhelmed by the Ottoman Turks in 1461, the descendants of Alexios Komnenos reigned in civilized and educated splendour. In the west Michael, an illegitimate offshoot of the house of Angeli, established himself as Despot of Epirus on the west coast of Greece.

The following years saw six Latin rulers in Constantinople, and four Byzantine ones in exile, at Nicaea; years which concern the history of the Empire rather than the great city itself. During those years there must have been occasions when the crusaders wondered whether it had been such a good idea to come and dismember the East Roman Empire. There was more life in it still than they had anticipated.

At Nicaea the exiled ruler, John Vatatzes, had found an ally in the powerful ruler of Bulgaria, Ivan II Asen. Together they besieged Constantinople with an army of a hundred thousand men and a fleet of three hundred ships. There were only one hundred and sixty knights in the Latin army, but when they made a sortie beyond the city walls the Byzantine and Bulgarian besiegers turned tail and fled. That was in the open country outside the Theodosian Walls. On the other side the inhabitants and a number of foot soldiers attacked the enemy ships, bringing twenty-five of them into the harbour. In the following year the Latins again beat off another attack on the city.

In 1237 the last Latin Emperor, Baldwin II, came to the throne in Constantinople—and spent as much of his reign as he could as far from the place as was possible. On three separate occasions he journeyed round the west trying to solicit arms for his soldiers and gold for his coffers. But the prestige of Byzantium had sunk low, and when he came to England he received a reprimand from Henry III for entering the country without permission. As for the Papacy—that was ready to bestow a fortune of spiritual wealth on Baldwin II, but the hand raised in blessing held nothing tangible to help his immediate needs.

What forces and money he could muster Baldwin wasted on an unsuccessful campaign in Thrace, and he was forced to make an alliance with the Turks and the Comans. The latter were pagans, and to cement the treaty a dog was sacrificed outside the land walls of Constantinople, between the two armies. In the palace the day-to-day expenses were covered by stripping lead from the roofs, which was sold, and demolishing buildings to get at the timber for fuel. The Emperor was so out-at-elbow that he literally pawned his son to the Venetians, leaving the boy Philip in their city as a pledge for a loan. That was not all: what had been the greatest and richest city in the world was now forced to sell its remaining relics, which had been gathered together from all over the Middle East since the time of Constantinople's inauguration in A.D. 330. To a deeply religious people their dispersal must have been heartbreaking.

Whether or not the true relics of Christ and the Virgin Mary, the fathers of the church, and the saints, they were objects of sincere veneration to thousands of Greeks, and now they were being sold. Most precious of all was the Crown of Thorns, which the city pawned for 13,134 pieces of gold to the Venetians when Baldwin happened to be abroad. The Byzantines were unable to redeem it, and the relic passed into the hands of a Venetian merchant named Nicholas Querini. When Baldwin II heard what had happened he contacted his relative Louis IX (Saint Louis), who sent two ambassadors to take charge of the situation. 'On opening a wooden box, they recognized the seals of the Doge and the barons, which were applied on a shrine of silver; and within this shrine the monument of the Passion was enclosed in a golden vase.' Paris was to receive the treasure now.

In France the whole court advanced as far as Troyes to meet the relic, and the king himself, wearing only a shirt and barefoot, carried it into the capital. Before long other treasures of the imperial chapel in Constantinople made the same journey westwards. A portion of the Cross; baby linen worn by Christ; the lance; the sponge; the chain of his passion; the rod of Moses and a part of the skull of John the Baptist. To house all these relics Louis built the Sainte Chapelle—imposing a tax on the Jews to help raise the necessary funds.*

One relic still in Istanbul which has an honoured place in the patriarchal church of St George (eighteenth century) is the column of the Flagellation.

Year by year John Vatatzes was encroaching on the Latin Empire, and the Kingdom of Thessalonika linked up with the Empire of Nicaea. But in 1254 the able man died, to be succeeded by his son Theodore II Lascaris. Since he was still young the real ruler was someone else: Michael Palaeologus. This man was descended from an old and important family in the capital—whose emblem was that of the two-headed eagle, later adopted by the Russia of Ivan III, and until the revolution of 1917 a living link with the Empire of which it was the religious, political, and artistic heir.

Michael Palaeologus was determined to recapture Constantinople, and of all men alive at that time he was the most suitable for the job. Bland, charming, courteous, and capable; he was

* Though broken in three during the Revolution, it is now in the Treasury of Notre Dame, Paris, and exhibited each Friday during Lent.

also false, scheming, ruthless, cruel—in short a typical Byzantine of the ruling class.

By now the maritime cities of Genoa and Venice had fallen out over trading rights, having waxed fat on the prostrate body of the Empire. Since Venice was all for defending Constantinople for the Latins, Michael Palaeologus enlisted the help of the Genoese. In 1260 he crossed the Bosphorus into Thrace, and from there directed the operations for the expulsion of the Latins. An attempt to get into the city with the help of a treacherous baron proved a failure, and it was not until 1261 that Michael Palaeologus's general lay with his army to the north of the city, between it and the Black Sea. There he enlisted the support of the local peasants, and soon the army had grown to 25,000 men. Then came the moment the exiles had been waiting for: off sailed the Venetians with thirty galleys, carrying French soldiers to attack a small town on the Black Sea coast.

An aged Greek drugged the guards on duty at the Pegé Gate (Silivri Kapisi), about half a mile from the southern end of the Theodosian walls. The attackers climbed over the built-up fortifications, killed the sleepy and bewildered Latin guards, broke down the barricaded entrance and opened the gates. As the exiles marched in, the inhabitants rose up to welcome them.

When Baldwin II was awakened by the din, and told the cause, he only too willingly slipped away to the sea shore. His luck was in. The Venetian galleys had just returned. As fast as he could he went on board, and set sail first for the island of Euboea, and then on to Italy. For the remaining thirteen years of his life he led a semi-mendicant life round the courts of Europe, trying to raise funds to help regain the throne from which he had fled with such alacrity. But no one in the west would listen, or perhaps even cared. From beginning to end the Latin domination of Constantinople had been a discredit to all concerned.

Chapter 27

1261-1282

Michael VIII returns to Constantinople. State of the city. Genoese settle in Galata. Character of the Emperor. Union with Rome. Mount Athos. Emperor's daughter married to a Mongol ruler. Returns in 1281 to Constantinople and founds a convent. St Mary of the Mongols. Literature in the city. St Saviour in Chora. The church and its mosaics.

A messenger came to Michael Palaeologus's bedside in the small hours of July 25, 1261, woke the sleeping man and told him he was no longer an Emperor in exile, but that Constantinople was his. As proof he showed the sword, sceptre, headgear, and scarlet shoes abandoned by Baldwin II as he fled from the palace. Twenty days later, on August 14, Michael VIII Palaeologus appeared before the Golden Gate, to make his solemn and triumphal entry into the city, where only the old could remember the days when their Emperor had been a Greek like themselves, and a member of the Orthodox Church.

Preceded by the icon of the Virgin, the palladium of Constantinople, Michael entered the city on foot, going in solemn procession to the Monastery of St John of Studion. There after giving thanks to God in the basilica he continued his way through the city, on horseback now, to the old palace of the Boucleon. Of the infinite number of icons in Constantinople none was more revered or sacred than the one now temporarily resting in the Studite Monastery. St Luke was reputed to have painted it (in all over seventy icons are attributed to the author of the third Gospel), which came to Constantinople as a present to Pulcheria, the sister of Theodosius II. For centuries it was kept in the church of St Mary—the Gülhane Hospital at the bottom of the hill just inside the main gateway in the Seraglio wall occupies the site—where it remained until the Venetians stole it in 1207. But now over fifty years later it had returned.

Constantinople was in a depressing state: huge areas had been burnt in the two fires in 1203 and 1204: little rebuilding would have been done in the poverty-stricken years which followed. Nearly everything moveable of any worth had been carried off by the crusaders, the palaces were dilapidated—stripped of their roofs and in a state bordering on ruin. When Michael VIII reached the palace of Blachernae he found that the court of Baldwin II had left it in such a filthy condition that a thorough cleaning up was necessary before he could move in.

By degrees the depopulated and wrecked city was brought back to life. Many of the Latin workmen who were not able to pack up and return to the west at the same time as their better-off compatriots were allowed to remain in the districts originally allotted to them. This was the time when the Genoese, who helped the Byzantines get their city back, were given the exclusive use of the suburb of Galata: a right they retained up to the Turkish conquest. From early times the suburb with its picturesque houses climbing up the steep hill had been dominated by a tower; but now, in accordance with the Treaty of Nymphaion (the palace near Izmir in which Michael VIII was staying when he heard of the recapture of Constantinople) it and the walls about Galata were to be demolished. This was one of the terms the Emperor demanded if the Genoese were to be allowed to settle in the city again.

Michael VIII forced his way to the throne, and like a score of predecessors and successors he did not hesitate to use cruelty to make his power absolute. The youthful John IV Lascaris, the rightful Emperor, was hardly a menace, but Michael ordered his blinding. After this had been done and John IV banished to Nicaea, Michael Palaeologus issued a statement that for nauseating hypocrisy must be without equal. In all seriousness he declared that because of his nobility of soul he had ordered the most humane of six methods of blinding to be used on the boy.

In November, 1273 Michael VIII made his own son, later Andronikos II, his co-Emperor. Danger from the west was not entirely a thing of the past, and in the following year he approached the Pope with a view to reuniting the two churches. If Byzantium became Catholic, there would be no excuse for repeating the events of 1204.

The Greek clergy was naturally anxious, but by diplomatic figure-skating the question of the Filioque—which caused the rupture between the two churches—was not made an insuperable issue. The two opposing views, the procession of the Holy Ghost from the Father *by* the Son (Orthodox), and the procession of the Holy Ghost from the Father and also from the Son (Roman Catholic) were to be equally acceptable. The pressure to bring the Orthodox clergy into line with Rome could come later, after the union had been effected. To the Orthodox, daily growing more uneasy, Michael said blandly that they should regard the Pope as no more than the first patriarch, and that anyway—Rome was a long way off.

An embassy laden with presents set off for Rome, and at the Council of Lyon Gregory X received the erring portion of his eastern flock back into communion. For a start the Filioque was added to the Nicene Creed, which was chanted in Latin and Greek (1275).

In Constantinople the Romanization of the Orthodox Church began with the absolution of the priests, and continued with the torture and execution of the recalcitrant. The future patriarch, Veccus (or Bekkos), was one of those to suffer imprisonment in the Anemas Tower. To this day the name of Michael VIII Palaeologus is held in detestation in monastic circles. On Mount Athos, where history and legend are as one, he is well remembered. At the Monastery of Zographou twenty-seven monks who refused to accept the union fled up the defence tower, where all were burnt to death by Michael's henchmen. It is not recalled with pride that at the Great Lavra several of the monks celebrated Mass in the church. In due course the apostates died, but when disinterred after three years, they showed no sign of decay. This the monks took as a memorial of the monastery's lapse from Orthodox grace, and placed them in a cave, high up on the tip of the peninsula. There they still are, in the Cave of the Wicked Dead.

When the Papal Nuncio asked Michael VIII how the work was going, the Emperor showed him four of his own relatives, chained in the corners of a cell. One of them died, one was released, and two were blinded, but much good did it do him. When the Pope realized his conversion to Rome was merely a political expedient against a possible enemy—Baldwin II, still hoping to win back his throne—he excommunicated him at once, and the two churches went their separate ways once again.

In his own family circle Michael VIII could be as ruthless. To secure an alliance with the Mongols he gave two of his natural daughters as brides to their chiefs. One was sent to Nogaya, who ruled a principality on the Black Sea; while the other, Maria, was sent to Holagu, who in 1258 had destroyed the Caliphate of Baghdad. But he died before her arrival, so instead she married his son Abaga, after he became Christian. Then in 1281 he was poisoned by his brother, and she was able to return to Constantinople. There she founded the Convent of St Mary, attached to a church first built in 1261, which she had acquired immediately after her return. It still stands, in a narrow street in the Fener District: St Mary of the Mongols (Mouchliotissa). Unlike most of its kind it was not converted into a mosque after the Conquest. The story behind this is both attractive and true. Such was the satisfaction of the Sultan, Mehmet II, with the mosque (Fatih Camii) designed for him by the Greek architect Christoboulos, that he allowed St Mary of the Mongols to remain in their hands. The grant was later confirmed by Beyazit II to the architect's nephew in gratitude for *his* work on the latter's own mosque. On plan the little church is a domed quatrafoil, the only one in the city, with a central dome supported on four semi-domes. In front is the customary narthex, but at some uncertain date very extensive alterations were carried out when one of the semi-domes was cut away and replaced by a quite large aisle.

A mosaic of Maria Palaeologina remains in the city: dressed as a nun, on the east wall of the south dome in the outer narthex of St Saviour in Chora.

St Saviour in Chora (Kahriye Mosque). Thirteenth–fourteenth century south chapel showing contemporary frescoes

St Saviour in Chora (Kahriye Mosque). Inner narthex. Mosaic of scene from the life of the Virgin, *c.* 1400

Now, as the net tightened about the shrinking Byzantine Empire, and revolution, civil war, and disorder rocked it almost without stopping, the intellectual flame seemed to burn all the brighter. Literature had never been a major glory, in the way it was in classical Greece: Byzantium's role in that field was not so much creative, as the custodian of its classic heritage. A heritage that would only be revealed to the world—ironically enough—when Christian Constantinople itself was dead, and its scholars had migrated to the west where they quickened the flowering of the Renaissance.

In the earliest times, after the official recognition of Christianity, literature was a continuation of the pagan Greek tradition. Slowly the stream died, and the fifth century Zosimus can be called the last of the pagan historians, while the contemporary Athanasius with his *Life of St Anthony* was the first Christian one. The number of writers who left records of their own times and life in Constantinople are all too few: Procopius wrote fully about the reign of Justinian the Great, including a biography of the general Belisarius, and when feeling embittered followed it up with his *Secret History,* in which he left little muck unraked or names untarnished. In the eighth century St John of Damascus restated the faith of the Orthodox Church in good classical prose. By then Greek had quite superseded Latin as the language of scholars as well as of the man-in-the-street. In the ninth and tenth centuries there came a flowering of literature in Constantinople, reflected in the writings of the learned Patriarch Photius and of Constantine VII, with his biography of his grandfather Basil I, and his manual on Court Ritual. The eleventh century saw a rise in popular songs and epic stories, such as that of Digenes Akritas, the Robin Hood of the East Roman Empire—though the parallel is not very close. Slowly interest in Constantinople was awakening in Classic literature. That such interest had been stifled by the early church, struggling against paganism, was natural enough, but now it was safe for scholars to dip deeply into Plato, Thucydides, or Homer. Two of the most readable books in Byzantine literature date from the eleventh century: Psellus's *History,* and Anna Komnena's *Alexiad.* The latter is full of quotations from

Homer, much as educated English writers might quote Shakespeare.

All through Byzantine history the thirst for religious knowledge is most marked, but today it is perhaps the incidental details about domestic life in the empire that form the most interesting parts of the lives of popular saints and church dignitaries. As a result of this outlook, only one novel emerged in over a thousand years of literary activity, and that has a religious theme: *Barlaam and Ioasaph,* a Greek variation on an Indian life of the Buddha, written about the year 750. Lyric poetry is as badly served. Much in the visual arts came from Persia, but nothing (it would seem) from her poetry, and the sole representative of that field is a fifteenth century manuscript of Rhodian love-poems. Epigrams, usually on religious themes, were fashionable, but hardly compensation for the total absence of anything for the stage in the tradition of Euripides.

Under the Palaeologi came the age of the encyclopaedists, and the expenditure of much time and thought on religious controversy: polemics seldom enrich literature, and Byzantium was no exception. In the visual arts the fact that patrons were not as well off as before the Latin conquest is marked: no longer could they afford to have their mansions decorated with mosaics. Instead they bought portable mosaics: icons—in some cases diptychs—made up of tiny cubes of coloured glass or marble. A few survive in the museums of western Europe, but they are exceedingly rare. A most notable exception, in a church, are the exquisite decorations added to the two narthexes of St Saviour in Chora (Kahriye Mosque) by the well-to-do Theodore Metochites, a most intelligent man with a vast fund of knowledge on many subjects, including astronomy. At court he held the office of the Grand Logothete of the Treasury to Andronikos II, a most inept Emperor as obsessed with religion as the English Henry VI, and about as incapable of directing his country's affairs. It was at this time, the beginning of the fourteenth century, that the church of St Saviour in Chora assumed the appearance which, with the exception of the Turkish minaret, it still has to this day.

If Santa Sophia is the most magnificent and impressive church in the city (and, when the spell it can cast has had time to work, one might add—in the world), the little church of St Saviour in Chora is the most beautiful. It was originally outside the walls of Constantine, hence its name of St Saviour in the Fields, but when the Theodosian walls were added in A.D. 413 it then stood about two hundred yards behind them, near the Edirne Gate, at the bottom of a steep little hill. From the top, looking beyond the domes and roofs of St Saviour in Chora, is a wonderful panorama of present-day Istanbul (frontispiece): the Galata Tower away to the left, and most prominent the huge dome and two minarets of the Fatih Camii (Conqueror's Mosque), standing on the site of the Church of the Holy Apostles.

The second church, probably built in the time of Justinian I, still stands, forming the core of the present building. A cross in square (the arms do not project beyond the sides) with a dome, a large apse and two lateral ones forming separate chapels make up this part. The dimensions are small, the interior being not more than forty feet square. Ruined and neglected during the Iconoclastic Controversy it was not until the end of the eleventh century that it was restored by Maria Dukas, niece of Isaac I Komnenos and mother-in-law of Alexios I Komnenos. How much she was responsible for in the way of new building is uncertain, but after the Latin occupation it was once again in ruins—when Theodore Metochites came to its rescue. To him it owes its two narthexes, possibly the central dome (or does this date from Maria Dukas' time?), the chapel occupying the full length along the south side and the exquisite mosaics and marble fittings in the church itself.

The outer narthex consists of five bays, the vaults and lunettes decorated with scenes from the life of Christ. At this late date in Byzantium's history mosaics had taken on a softer, more supple, more human, and less remote appearance. You have only to compare them with the tenth century Christ Enthroned, over the royal door in Santa Sophia, for the change to be strikingly apparent. One of the reasons was that the artists were no longer shackled by rules and regulations concerning what they could and could not depict, and how it should be done. Instead of a plain gold background (if a background of gold can be so

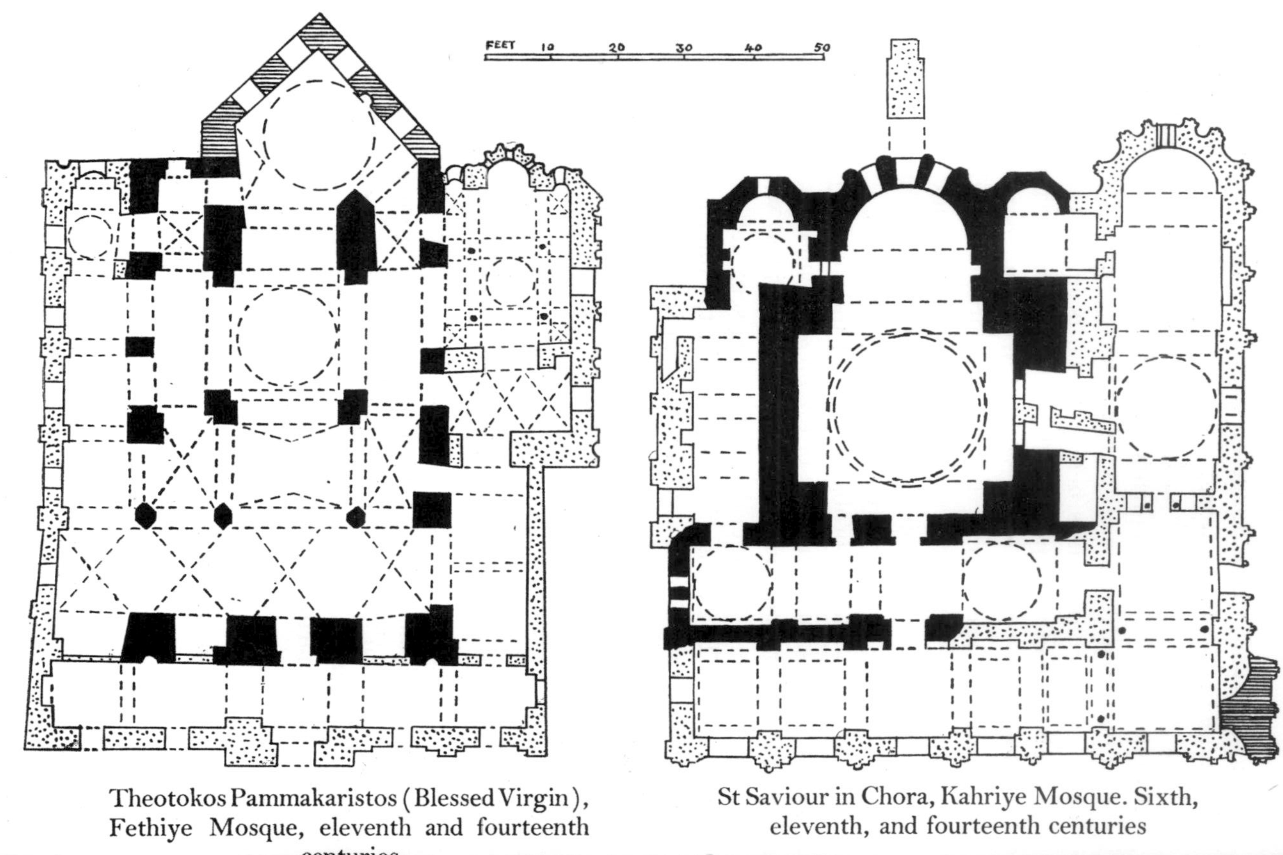

Theotokos Pammakaristos (Blessed Virgin), Fethiye Mosque, eleventh and fourteenth centuries

St Saviour in Chora, Kahriye Mosque. Sixth, eleventh, and fourteenth centuries

described) there are now houses, interiors of rooms, and distant views of towns. Only the sky is golden. It is the artist himself who speaks, expressing his own personal vision of these scenes from the lives of Christ and the Virgin Mary. A figure with a bundle on his shoulder trudges towards Bethlehem for the numbering; behind comes Mary, riding an ass with pricked-up ears. She turns back to look towards Joseph, old and a little inclined to stoop. In the background a town climbs up the slope of a craggy hill. That is in the north bay of the outer narthex. At the other end, in the sixth bay to the south, there is the same humanity: the disciples stand erect and tranquil, while Christ leans over to cure a paralytic man seated on the ground, and others with various afflictions crowd forward, their faces expressing anguish and awakening hope. The iconography of the Church now shows the love of man as well as the love of God. There is something almost of the art of the miniaturist in these mosaics in St Saviour in Chora: the work of the manuscript illuminators of Les Belles Heures du Duc de Berry (after 1410) come to mind. There is the same glowing quality about the colours, one of pigments on parchment, and the other of tiny cubes of mosaic, some only three sixteenths of an inch square, on walls and vaults.

The scenes from the life of Christ are in the outer narthex: they are not chronological; in the sixth bay from the north Christ healing the paralytic is next to Herod ordering the Massacre of the Innocents. Because of the parecclesion—the chapel on the south side of the church—the inner narthex has only four bays, two of them with domes, which show from the outside. Their positions seem quite random, one is over the north bay, and while the other is over the corresponding bay to the south: from outside it appears half in front of the central dome. Over the main doorway into the church itself there is a mosaic of Theodore Metochites offering his church to Christ, reminiscent of the famous one of Justinian offering *his* church to the Virgin in Santa Sophia. Theodore wears an enormous turban, which by the fourteenth century had become a common sight in the streets of the city, worn by the well-to-do.

In this narthex the mosaics are of the life of the Virgin, and mostly unfamiliar: Mary receiving wool to weave the veil of the Temple for example. The Annunciation is in the north dome. While the church itself has the thin sheets of marble which decorate the walls still in position, most of the mosaics have vanished; but over the inside of the main door is a beautiful Dormition of the Virgin.

The parecclesion, the last part to be built, is in fact a complete church in itself. An arcade of three openings leads from the narthex into the chapel which consists of two bays, the west one with a dome on a drum, and the second much shallower and springing directly from the vaulting. Here the decorations are not mosaic, but painted on tempera and seem to show Florentine influence. They include the Saints Sergius and Bacchus, who had their own church, built in the time of Justinian, near the harbour of the Boucleon; while in the dome are figures of twelve archangels.

But it is the mosaics in the two narthexes that spring to mind whenever one is thinking of St Saviour in Chora. Heavenly may be an affected and overworked word, but it is the only one to describe their softly glowing colours and the other-worldly figures that people them. The restoration of the whole church has only been completed recently, and the painstaking work on the mosaics in particular is superb. Now, after centuries under plaster when the church was the Kahriye Mosque—the neglect in the nineteenth century was such that the central cupola had fallen and parts were quite open to the weather—they are as clean and as fresh-looking as when Theodore Metochites saw them (though where the mosaics have vanished altogether there has mercifully been no attempt to replace them with something quite new). Today it is no longer a place of worship, being in the care of the Director of the Aya Sophia Museum, and of all the one-time Byzantine churches in the city it is the loveliest.

Chapter 28

1282–1348

The behaviour of the Patriarch Anastasius. The family troubles of Andronikos II. Monastery and church of the Blessed Virgin. The Parecclesion Chapel. Last important building erected in Constantinople before the Turkish Conquest. Mosaics now undergoing restoration. Low state of the administration. Civil war during the minority of John V (1341–1347). Riot in part of the Palace of Constantine VII Porphyrogenitus converted into a prison. Extraordinary situation (1347) of two emperors and three empresses. Empire bankrupt. Eye-witness account of a banquet. The Black Death. Religious arguments. John V recaptures Constantinople by a daring trick. Turks allowed to sell Christian slaves in the city market. The Galata Tower built. Genoese practically running the city. Fight with the Venetians.

In Constantinople the Emperor Andronikos II was completely subservient to the patriarch, a domineering old man named Athanasius. Eventually popular feeling against the latter was such that he was removed from office; whereupon he behaved most oddly. Having written and signed a statement in which he excommunicated all those who engineered his downfall—and in that he included the Emperor—he placed it in a sealed earthenware pot, which was left in one of the galleries high up in Santa Sophia. His intention was that in the distant future it should be found (presumably after his own death when no retribution could overtake him) and with it the anathemas he dare not breathe openly in the faces of his enemies. However, after only four years some youths who were searching for pigeons' nests came across it, broke the seal—and Athanasius's secret was out. Once out, the curse (like an obstreperous djinn) could not be got back in again. But since Athanasius had been deprived of the rank of patriarch he could not take the curse off his superstitious sovereign, who now felt himself cut off from his Church by the hole-in-the-corner excommunication.

There was only one thing to do: restore the old man to his former office. One night a monk woke Andronikos II telling him of death and destruction in the shape of plague and earthquake. For the Emperor the rest of the night was spent in prayer, fright, and repentance. Then in the morning off he went on foot to the patriarch's cell, and begged him most humbly to take up his old appointment. Athanasius made a show of offended dignity, but soon enough was back on his throne in Santa Sophia. This was too much for those who had hoped they had seen the last of their high-handed shepherd. His footstool was spirited away, and in its place a libellous drawing of Andronikos II with a bridle in his mouth being led to the feet of Christ by Athanasius, appeared in its place.

The point was not lost on the Emperor: his vanity had been touched, and without compunction he ordered the patriarch's instant removal.

When Michael, the Emperor's son, was eighteen, he was made co-Emperor. The young man had the sense not to dispute with his father's supremacy, and was well liked by both his family and the people. But if his son was no trial to the Emperor, his grandson certainly was.

The future Andronikos III was the apple of the old man's eye. The more he had, the more he wanted. Heavily in debt to the Genoese, he was a most riotous individual, and did little to uphold the prestige of the crown. The fact that his mistress was a 'matron of rank, and a prostitute in manners', aroused his suspicions about her fidelity. One night he posted archers about her doorway with instructions to shoot down whoever passed.

They carried out their orders, to discover they had just killed

Andronikos's own brother, Manuel. The grief was too much for Michael, and he soon followed his son to the grave. Far from being broken by the double tragedy he had caused, Andronikos was delighted, as everyone could see. At this his grandfather decided to change the succession, and nominated another of his grandsons as the future Emperor. The young Andronikos was brought to trial, but before the sentence could be announced the old ruler was warned that the palace of Blachernae was full of his hateful grandson's followers. A treaty of reconciliation between the two followed almost at once.

During the last fifteen or twenty years of his reign Andronikos II had considerable contact, some of it friction, with the Monastery of the Blessed Virgin (in Greek the Theotokos Pammakaristos). Today only the church remains, the Fethiye Camii, standing on the Fifth Hill overlooking the teeming narrow streets that run down through the Fener district towards the Golden Horn. The actual church was built in the reign of John II Komnenos, which pins it down to the first half of the twelfth century, but it was only with the addition of the parecclesion chapel, similar in size and position to the one at St Saviour in Chora, that the church took on the appearance we see today.

As was the case at St Saviour in Chora, the church of the Theotokos was embellished by a man who was also an official at the court of Andronikos II. Michael Tarchaniotes was a counsellor, and it was his wife who added the chapel, complete with three miniature domes (page 165). The abbot of the monastery, who later became patriarch, was prepared to stand out against his Emperor, and such was his spiritual power that when summoned before a church court Andronikos II at once obeyed, going there late at night. The charges against him included arranging a marriage between the thrice married, forty-six year old King of Serbia and his own six-year-old daughter, and imposing heavy taxes on such essential items as salt—while he himself was a spendthrift. The Emperor acquitted himself, but the terms which he and the patriarch were on after the episode can be imagined. Time and again the cleric withdrew to the monastery, only to re-emerge shortly after, but finally he admitted defeat and left Constantinople for good.

The parecclesion must be the last important piece of architecture built in the city before the Turkish conquest. From now on there would be no money for such things: indeed there would be precious little money for anything. As Constantinople waned, so the little hill-city of Mistra in southern Greece waxed, and it is there that the last phase of true Byzantine architecture can be seen: before it too was swallowed up in the Ottoman Empire.

The twelfth century church was about fifty feet wide by seventy-five feet long: without the apse which was destroyed in Turkish times and replaced with a triangular one, covered with a dome, with the mirhab correctly orientated towards Mecca. The central dome raised on a tall drum, with twelve windows alternating with twelve buttresses, each window surmounted with a rounded pediment, is typical of these later churches. Aisles with barrel-vaulting are on three sides of the dome: the fourth being occupied by the apse, while to the west is a narthex of three bays running across the front of the church. Then about the year 1315 the additions were made which included an extra aisle on the north side, an outer narthex on the west, and the beautiful little chapel on the south.

The parecclesion is complete in every detail. Outside it has a south front elaborately decorated in brick, with a transept which does not project beyond the main building line, three apses, also elaborately decorated, and three domes. Inside it has a tiny narthex with a gynecaeum above, which is surmounted by the two smaller domes, side by side; while the main part consists of the four-column type (though two were removed after the Conquest) which supports the central dome—about eight feet in diameter. Like the St Saviour in Chora the church of the Theotokos is no longer used for worship, and at the present time the mosaics in the chapel are being restored. Though not as complete as those in the other church, they should be a beautiful addition to the city's treasures. In the dome is Christ Pantokrator, surrounded by the Twelve Apostles: most lovely, while figures of saints have been brought to light on the walls and the soffits of the arches. All are receiving the painstaking restoration lavished on those in St Saviour in Chora.

Like many before him, Andronikos III had stopped at nothing

to obtain the throne, but when it was his he showed himself quite incapable of ruling. All around the Empire the Turks were forever encroaching: it would not be very long before the Empire and the city of Constantinople were one and the same thing. The army was entirely composed of foreign mercenaries, the navy was dependent on foreign ships, and the currency was in an equally bad way. The Nomisma, once respected by all nations, was now called the hyperpyron and contained only fourteen carats gold.

From the very beginning Byzantium had been ruled by a very highly organized bureaucracy, and now in Constantinople it had reached an all-time low in corruption: appointments went by favour or wire pulling, and little or nothing could be achieved without encouraging officials with bribes. At this point Andronikos III died, leaving his nine year old son John V Palaeologus as Emperor.

Naturally there was a regent, in the person of John Cantecuzenos, but before long he had a rival in the powerful and arrogant Admiral Apocacus. The almost inevitable happened—and Byzantium was plunged into a full-scale civil war, which lasted six years, from 1341 to 1347.

As much as anyone John Cantecuzenos regretted the struggle, remarking of the difference between foreign and civil war: 'The former is the external warmth of summer, always tolerable, and often beneficial; the latter is the deadly heat of a fever, which consumes without remedy the vitals of the constitution.' What this man looked like we can see from two manuscript illustrations in a book of homilies written by him, and now in the Bibliothèque Nationale in Paris. Tall, aesthetic, with penetrating eyes, and a long grey beard, divided in two. His character was not flawless, though: his conceit is difficult to stomach. When he refused to release a number of his friends from their oath to the Palaeologi, with whom he was warring, he could record his own wisdom in the words: that he did it 'by my sublime, almost incredible virtue'.

When victory finally came to him it was through the wholly unexpected death of Admiral Apocacus. On the admiral's orders a large number of citizens of all classes in Constantinople had been arrested on suspicion of disloyalty and imprisoned—possibly in the so-called palace of Constantine VII (Tekfur-sarayi). The walls were being raised and part of the building subdivided into cells, and each day Apocacus came to see how the work was going, and to hurry on the labourers. So confident was he that he never bothered with an escort. Suddenly one morning two members of the Palaeologi family, among the prisoners, set on him and clubbed him to death. All the prisoners broke loose inside the building, the admiral's head was hacked off and shown from the battlements to the crowd outside. The district was in uproar. While the Empress, Anne of Savoy, hesitated, the sailors from the Arsenal on the Golden Horn decided to revenge their admiral. By then the prisoners had broken out of the palace and taken refuge in a nearby church, possibly St Mary of Blachernae. There the sailors found them and literally butchered the escaped prisoners before the altar.

But after that the tide turned in favour of John Cantecuzenos, and on January 8, 1347, he once again set foot in Constantinople, where he made most satisfactory terms. His daughter Helena would marry the young John V Palaeologus, while he himself remained ruler for ten years.

Now Byzantium saw the odd spectacle of two emperors and three empresses in the poverty-stricken Blachernae Palace. John VI Cantecuzenos, John V Palaeologus, Anne of Savoy (John V's mother), Irene (wife of John VI), and Helena (wife of John V and daughter of John VI). However, the magnificence of the surroundings was in an inverse ratio to the number of emperors and empresses. At the end of the civil war the imperial palace in Constantinople was in about as threadbare a condition as Charles I's Whitehall Palace at the beginning of his war. Wrote Nicephorus Gregoras: 'The jewels in the crowns were glass, the robes not real cloth-of-gold but tinsel, the dishes copper, while all that appeared to be rich brocade was only painted leather.' At the start of the civil war the Empress Anne of Savoy had pawned the crown jewels to the Venetians for 30,000 ducats, and they were never redeemed.

In 1317 Irene, a daughter of Andronikos II had left money to pay for the buttresses, as massive as cliffs, added to support the north and east sides of Santa Sophia. Earthquake was an ever-present menace in the area, and in 1347 part of the great cupola was brought down by a tremor. Among those who very kindly sent funds for its repair was the Grand Duke of Moscow. His share was used to enlist Turkish mercenaries in the Byzantine army.

Now Constantinople had to face a terrifying invader: one which its walls could not keep out—the Black Death. In 1348 it started in the Crimea, quickly reached the city, and swept on towards the west. In its wake it is said that only one-ninth of the citizens remained alive.

During the years just passed the civil war was not the only talking point in the city. Controversy raged round a most extraordinary religious issue, and a great deal of heat was generated on the subject of light, the divine light which transfigured Christ on Mount Tabor. The contemplative had always played a considerable part in Greek Orthodox monasticism, and from 1341 to 1351 the Church was bedevilled by the opinion—originating among the monks of Mount Athos—that by entering into a trance-like state engendered by fasting and staring fixedly at the navel, the mind could transcend all wordly physical and mental awareness, achieving a state which was nothing less than the pure and perfect essence of God himself. The fact that a complete vacuum engendered by staring at an empty stomach would surely have been rather at variance with the will of God never seems to have entered anyone's head. The light to which the monks of Athos were trying to attain was that which surrounded Christ during the Transfiguration: the uncreated and eternal light of God. To this day the doctrine, called Hesychasm, from time to time gives trouble to the Orthodox Church.

During the civil war John Cantecuzenos supported the Hesychasts on Mount Athos. There was a political motive for this: the inhabitants on the Holy Mountain were the strongest moral force in the Empire, and by backing them in the controversy he was sure of their support.

When he grew up John V Palaeologus showed he was more keen to campaign with Venus than with Mars, and in an attempt to get him away from his debauched companions in Constantinople, John Cantecuzenos took him on an expedition to Serbia. This resulted in friction when the regent tried to leave John V in Thessalonika, and himself returned to the city on the Bosphorus. Back came the young Emperor, and recaptured Constantinople with a ruse worthy of the wily Odysseus himself. Two galleys and two thousand men were not enough to storm the capital. So, with the help of the Genoese, one dark and stormy night John V Palaeologus sailed under the walls along the Sea of Marmara right up to the gate near the present lighthouse, and hurled empty oil jars at the walls. What with the sound of smashing pottery and agonized cries for help from the crews and the soldiers, the guards on shore thought a merchant ship was being wrecked. Voices called up that the soldiers could have a share of the oil which they claimed was on board, if only they would help. The gate opened, out came the guards, and were promptly killed. Within minutes John V Palaeologus was inside the city, and joining up with his followers.

Rather than cause yet another civil war John Cantecuzenos gave up his right to the throne, and became a monk, first in Constantinople and then in the Vatpodei Monastery on Mount Athos, where his tomb is still in the church. Devout he may have been, but he was directly responsible for the most shameful episodes in the last century of Constantinople's existence as a Christian city. This was when he allowed the Turks to sell Christian slaves in the market in the city, where they would fetch a better price than elsewhere. There, for all to see, the young people were made to stand in rows on the cobbles, so they could be thoroughly inspected by prospective buyers. The girls were naked.

As the Empire grew weaker and smaller, so the insolence of the Genoese in Constantinople grew. In 1349 they rebuilt the Galata Tower, demolished in 1261, and also the walls about their suburb between the Golden Horn and the Bosphorus. The tower still stands, a familiar and useful landmark visible from many parts of the city. It is circular, 223 feet high, and reminiscent of the round bell-towers to be found along the shores of the Ligurian Sea south of Genoa (and for that matter on the other side of Italy, on the shores of the Venetian Lagoon), the most famous of which is no less than the Leaning Tower of Pisa. Twice burnt down, in 1791 and 1824, the Galata Tower has been used all through the centuries by fire-watchers, though at the speed with which the old timber houses are being torn down in present day Istanbul, the tower will soon be redundant.

The Genoese certainly had the upper hand, and knew it. Since Byzantine merchant ships hardly existed, the city was dependent on the Italians for bringing in supplies of grain and fish. First the Genoese took over the Customs, then the fisheries, and finally the toll from ships passing through the Bosphorus. From these revenues, amounting to 200,000 pieces of gold, they graciously allowed the Emperor an allowance of 30,000.

Events came to a head in 1348 when a small boat from the city dared to fish in the mouth of the Golden Horn. The Genoese attacked and sank it, and murdered the crew. To this the interlopers added insult to injury by telling the citizens they should give up navigation altogether, and underlined the point by burning two galleys. In the following spring the Greeks made an attempt to assert themselves, and sent an army and seven galleys against Galata. The army was routed and the galleys captured. Back and forth went the victorious Genoese ships, garlanded with flowers, towing the galleys up and down in front of the Sea Palaces, under the humiliated gaze of the Emperor. While John VI Cantecuzenos considered the pros and cons of signing a peace treaty with the Venetians and their allies the Catalans from Spain, the Genoese made up his mind by catapulting stones into the heart of the city.

The alliance was signed, and the two maritime republics fought out a savage naval battle among the Princes' Islands. Both gave and received a terrible mauling, which in the long run only succeeded in uniting them against the cause of their misfortunes: Constantinople.

Chapter 29

1341-1451

The Turks closing in on Constantinople. The janissaries. Four emperors quarrelling over the Empire, now fifty miles by thirty. Beyazit I demands Constantinople. Moslem pilgrimage centre at Eyüp. Turks defeated by Timur (1402). The Mongols reach the Bosphorus, but do not cross. The Empire reduced to the city itself (1425). Eye-witness account of the Empress leaving Santa Sophia. A further attempt at union with Rome (1438). Constantine XI, the last Emperor, crowned at Mistra. Plan to marry a Georgian princess (1452).

From 1341 to 1391 John V Palaeologus reigned at Constantinople, while his adversary Sultan Murat I could boast two capitals: one on either side of the Christian city. In Europe he held court in Adrianople (Edirne), and in Turkey itself at Bursa: each only about one hundred and fifty miles away by road. Perhaps the most important of Murat's actions, so far as it concerns Constantinople, was the formation of the janissaries (Yengi cheri, the new soldiers). Forcibly recruited as boys from among his Christian subjects, they were brainwashed until by the time they were adult the Sultan had no more fiercely loyal men in his army. For centuries the janissaries were the terror of Europe, and it was they who actually stormed the walls of Constantinople in 1453. Later they became the bane of everyone's life in Turkey, from the Sultan downwards, and in 1826 they were exterminated on the orders of the enlightened Mahmud II, to the relief of all.

stanbul from the Sea of Marmara. Site of the imperial palaces between the Ahmet I Mosque (left) and Santa Sophia

The Golden Horn. Galata and the Galata Tower, 1349

Rumeli Hisar, built by Mehmet II, 1452

The Bosphorus. *Foreground:* Europe. *Background:* Asia. *Left:* entrance to the Black Sea. *Right:* towards Istanbul

It was not the ruling of his shrunken Empire that occupied John V's time, but other men's wives. The situation was not made easier by his eldest son, Andronikos, who went to the Sultan's court at Edirne, and there formed an attachment to Sauzes, one of Murat's sons. They shared an imagined grudge against their respective parents—because they were not the favourite sons, so they set about planning the overthrow of their fathers. It was discovered almost at once: Sauzes was blinded, dying soon after from his sufferings, while the all-powerful Sultan ordered the Emperor to blind his own son Andronikos, and demolish the fortifications which he had built behind the Golden Gate, the Castle of the Seven Towers, on the site of an early Byzantine fortification.

Andronikos, his wife, and their five-year-old son were imprisoned in the Anemas Tower, and it was given out that the males had been blinded in accordance with the Sultan's demands. In fact it was so done that Andronikos lost the sight of only one eye, while his small son escaped with a slight squint. After two years they were released. Andronikos made a treaty with both the Genoese and the Turks, seized his father and elder brother, Manuel, when they were all staying at the palace of the Pegé, not far outside the walls, and after a siege of thirty-two days took the city. Now it was John V and Manuel who saw the inside of the Anemas Tower, where they also remained for a similar period of two years, eventually escaping to Chrysopolis (Scutari, now Üsküdar) with the help of a monk. Off they went to the new Sultan, Beyazit I, to seek his help.

The scene was little short of contemptible: four emperors—John V and his son Manuel II versus Andronikos IV and his son John VII, quarrelling over the division of an Empire fifty miles long by thirty miles wide: like the Norwegians and the Poles in *Hamlet*, to fight for a plot whereon the numbers cannot try the cause. John V and Manuel II were to have the city, and Andronikos IV and John VII the countryside beyond the Theodosian walls. At the time of the death of Theodosius the Great, nearly a thousand years before (A.D. 395) one emperor had been sufficient to rule the Empire stretching from the Tweed to the Euphrates. Now four were incapable of ruling an area the size of Suffolk.

After a dotage in which all passion was not spent, John V died, leaving the loveliest of cities to his son Manuel II, who at the time was at the court of Beyazit I. In 1389 the blackbirds flew from the field of carnage of the Battle of Kossovo to tell the Serbian queen that her husband, the Czar Lazarus, and her nine sons-in-law were all dead and that the Turks had overthrown the Serbian Empire. The Sultan determined to take for himself the city of Constantinople: in Turkish then sometimes called Kizil Elma, the Scarlet Apple.

One day Manuel II received a letter from the Sultan. 'By the divine clemency, our invincible scimitar has reduced to our obedience almost all Asia, with many large countries in Europe, excepting only Constantinople; for beyond the walls thou hast nothing left. Resign that city: stipulate thy reward: or tremble, for thyself and thy unhappy people, at the consequences of a rash refusal.' But the Emperor was able to buy ten years' grace, at a price of 30,000 pieces of gold to be paid annually. Also a royal mosque was to be built inside the city itself: the Davut Paşa Camii (1397), which was rebuilt in 1485. It stands in the street leading to the Silivri Kapisi. As far back as the twelfth century a Moslem traveller who came to Constantinople could write: 'Outside of the City there is the tomb of one of the companions of the Prophet. The big mosque erected by Maslamah, son of Abdel-Melik, is within the city. One can see the tomb of a descendant of Hussein, son of Ali, son of Abu-Thalib.' The reference to a tomb of one of the Prophet's companions must be to Eyüp, who died during the protracted siege of the city by the Arabs in A.D. 668. Today the tomb of Eyüp, in the courtyard of a large mosque, is one of the most sacred spots in the Islamic world: the courtyard at all times crowded with pilgrims, and walking among them with solemn indifference, several storks.

Before long Beyazit I broke the treaty when he took up the cause of John VII (who had received the countryside just beyond the city walls), and Manuel II turned to the French for help. Marshal Boucicault set sail from Aigues Mortes with four ships. Forcing his way past seventeen Turkish galleys stationed at the entrance to the Dardanelles he brought six hundred tough men-at-arms and 1,600 archers to reinforce the garrison. But after a year's campaigning, with nothing gained, the Marshal decided to return home. What was more his troops had not been paid—there was nothing in the coffers—and they were short of provisions. In fact, in Constantinople there was not even the money to pay for the candles and oil for Santa Sophia.

With him on the journey back to France went Manuel II, on a fund-raising expedition round the courts of western Europe. In his absence John VII, little more than a Turkish puppet, was to occupy the throne. Once again Beyazit I demanded the city, and it seemed nothing could stop him picking the Scarlet Apple. But there was someone more powerful than himself, and more terrible.

From out of the east, across the deserts of Persia, came Timur the grandson of Genghis Khan, fresh from his capture of Delhi. Word had reached him that Beyazit was growing too powerful for his own good. On November 11, 1400, the Tartar sacked Aleppo. Next year the inhabitants of Damascus were massacred: eight hundred years before they had murdered a grandson of the Prophet, and now they were being made to pay for it. Baghdad fared no better. Behind him Timur left a terrible trophy piled up on the site of the city: ninety thousand human heads. Then in 1402 he turned north-west towards Anatolia, where on the 28th of July he defeated Beyazit at the Battle of Ankara. In Marlowe's play *Tamburlane* he made the conqueror keep the Sultan in a cage: in reality Beyazit travelled in the wake of Timur in a litter with steel shutters. But after only eight months death ended his humiliation.

Nothing, or so it seemed, could save Constantinople from being reduced to a heap of blood-soaked rubble like the great cities of the south. The Mongol horde swept on, to the shores of the Sea of Marmara. In the face of this terrifying threat the Turks, who controlled the Dardanelles, and the Christians, who controlled the Bosphorus, sank their differences, and refused to lend transport vessels to Timur. Both Prince Süleyman (Beyazit's son) and the Byzantine Emperor paid him tribute, and waited to see what would happen next.

Capriciously, Timur changed his mind when he had the city almost within his grasp, and the way was open into Europe.

Instead he decided to conquer China, and withdrew to his fabled capital of Samarkand. On the route from the golden city to Pekin he died, at the age of seventy, in 1405, having brought death and destruction to more people than anyone before the advent of Nazi Germany.

Now that the danger from Timur had passed it was not long before Christians and Turks flew at one another's throats. In June, 1422, Murat II (1421–1451) besieged Constantinople with 200,000 soldiers; but once again the walls were too strong for an enemy, and after two months he was forced to call off the siege, and return to Bursa to stamp out domestic treachery.

Now the Empire was in truth encompassed by the city walls. After Manuel II's death in 1425 he was succeeded by his son John VIII Palaeologus, and allowed to rule the city on payment of annual tribute to the Sultan. The west had turned its back on the New Rome, surrounded on three sides by water and on all sides by the Turks. In 1369 John V had visited Venice, the Republic that had done so much to destroy Byzantium's greatness, to raise loans; while in Rome he had abjured orthodoxy in the hope not so much of spiritual reward as desperately needed tangible support. He even sought the help of John Hawkswood, the condottiere who in Italy had sold his lance to the highest bidder in the wars between such city-states as Pisa and Florence. But Giovanni Acuto, as the Italians called him, only fought for cash, and the bankrupt Empire could not pay his price. Without help and with very little money John V returned to Constantinople. Thirty years later his son Manuel II was making the same mendicant round. In 1400 he came to London, but England was too preoccupied to do more than listen politely. The situation would have been all too familiar in Byzantium: Richard II had just been murdered, and now the usurping Henry IV sat uneasily on the throne.

How much the glory had departed since the days of Justinian and Theodora; glittering, magnificent, remote, and awe-inspiring, is caught up in one little episode played out in the shadow of Santa Sophia: the building that is the distillation of Byzantium itself.

A French traveller watched the Empress preparing to return

to the palace of Blachernae from the Cathedral of the Divine Wisdom. 'She left, accompanied only by three ladies, three ladies-in-waiting and three eunuchs. One carried a stool and when she mounted, one of the old ladies-in-waiting took her cloak, went round to the other side of the horse and held the cloak up as high as she could. She (the Empress) put her foot in the stirrup and bestrode the horse like a man. The old lady-in-waiting then covered her with the cloak and put on her head the tall pointed hat decorated with three golden plumes. The little group then set off towards Blachernae.'

The summer of 1438 saw John VIII at Venice, Ferrara, and Florence. In the last-named city yet another attempt was made to end the schism of the two churches. The vexed question of the Filioque was weighed in favour of Rome—that the Holy Ghost proceeded from the Father and the Son. In return for this concession on the part of the Orthodox Church the Pope promised military and naval support, and in 1440 the union was read in Florence Cathedral.

Eight years later John VIII died, and was succeeded by his brother, Constantine XI Palaeologus (or Drageses). In the little hill city of Mistra, near the site of the ancient Sparta, he was crowned in the Metropolitan church. A double-headed eagle, emblem of the family of the Palaeologi and of Constantinople itself, is carved on a white flagstone, marking the spot.

Unwisely, he rejected the idea of marrying a daughter of the Doge of Venice. That city, he felt, was too far away to be of any real help. So instead he sent Phranza, his great chamberlain, on a showy mission to Georgia and Trebizond. There they heard Murat II had died, and for a while it was on the cards that Constantine would marry his widow, the Christian daughter of the Despot of Serbia. In Constantinople the whole court was against the idea, and the Sultana herself decided the issue—by taking the veil. Then the plan went forward that he should marry a Georgian princess. So pleased was the girl's father that instead of asking the customary price for his daughter he considered it a privilege to offer the near-penniless Emperor 56,000 ducats, and a yearly allowance of a further 5,000 ducats.

In the spring of 1453 the Byzantine galleys were to sail up the Bosphorus and across the Black Sea to bring the Georgian princess to Constantinople for her wedding to the Emperor.

They never set sail.

Chapter 30

1451-1453

Mehmet II becomes Sultan. He builds the fortress of *Rumeli Hisar*. Its appearance on the Bosphorus. Ultimatum to Constantinople. Mehmet II prepares for the siege. April, 1453, the siege begins. Attacks on the land walls. Mehmet's treatment of one of his admirals. The Turks drag their ships overland to the top end of the Golden Horn. Mehmet's last offer to the Emperor. The scene the night before the final attack. The assault on the land walls and from the harbour. The scene in St Theodosia. Mehmet II enters Constantinople. The inhabitants barricade themselves in Santa Sophia. The city falls, and Constantine XI is found dead, killed alongside his soldiers.

On February 9, 1451, an event took place which was of the utmost importance for Constantinople. At the age of twenty-one Mehmet II ascended the throne of his fathers in Edirne. His attitude to Islam was orthodox (though some doubted his sincerity), he was a good linguist, a poet, interested in the arts—he invited Bellini to his court—was politically mature at an early age, and a real soldier. But on the debit side he could be cruel and treacherous. In the west his type was familiar in the Renaissance princes of Italy.

Before many months had passed Mehmet II decided to build a fortress on the European shore of the Bosphorus, opposite Anadolu Hisar, built by Beyazit I in 1390–1393. Ambassadors sent by the Emperor to protest received short shrift: 'I form no enterprise against the city,' said the Sultan, 'but the Empire of Constantinople is measured by her walls. Have you forgotten the distress to which it was reduced, when you formed a league with the Hungarians; when they invaded our country by land, and the Hellespont was occupied by French galleys? Murat was compelled to force the passage of the Bosphorus; and your strength was not equal to your malevolence. But when my father had triumphed in the field of Varna, he vowed to erect a fort on the western shore, and that vow it is my duty to accomplish. Have you the right, have you the power, to control my actions on my own ground? For that ground is my own: as far as the shores of the Bosphorus, Asia is inhabited by Turks, and Europe is deserted by the Romans. Return, and inform your king, that the present Ottoman is far different from his predecessors; that his resolutions surpass their wishes; and that he performs more than they resolve. Return in safety—but the next who delivers a similar message may expect to be flayed alive.'

By land or by water Rumeli Hisar is a most impressive sight: roughly triangular in shape the fortress has one massive tower at the bottom of the hillside, separated from the water by the roadway, while the other two stand quite far apart about halfway up the slope (page 229). Massive curtain walls with battlements and intermediate towers link the great circular drums, the tallest (the north tower) being ninety-two feet high and seventy-eight feet in circumference. Inside, because of the steepness of the site, most of the area is taken up with steps and terraces: the ruins of a little mosque used by the janissaries being all that remains of buildings erected for the garrison in the time of Mehmet II.

That so massive a fortress as Rumeli Hisar could be built in three months seems impossible; but it was so. Two thousand men laboured and sweated at the Sultan's command, and any building materials that came to hand were used, including churches. Christians rash enough to attempt to protect their property were killed without a moment's hesitation. Byzantium could expect no mercy from Mehmet II.

Just inside the main entrance from the road a low terrace looks across the Bosphorus towards the towers and battlements of Anadolu Hisar rising above the trees. Between the two, they completely covered the waterway, for on the terrace were twenty cannon. The knowledge that hardly out of sight from Constantinople, round a bend in the Bosphorus, the Turks were building a great castle must have struck chill to the inhabitants. By the autumn of 1452, as the leaves turned russet and started to drop, they realized that only their own walls stood between them and extinction. The west seemed to have forgotten them, and now that Rumeli Hisar was complete they were cut off from the Black Sea and the little Christian states of Georgia and Trebizond.

A warning of what was to come happened on the 26th of November when a Venetian ship tried to slip between the fortresses—so reminiscent of the Rhine. It was sunk by the cannon, the captain impaled, and his crew of thirty beheaded. For garrison Rumeli Hisar had four hundred janissaries, and its other name of 'Cut Throat' (Bogaz Kesen) was more than apt. Before then forty reapers had been butchered when they attempted to drive out Turkish cavalry-horses which had been turned loose in the corn fields—literally within sight of the walls of Constantinople.

The point of no return had been reached. For the last time as a Christian city Constantinople closed its gates. A message was taken from the Emperor to the Sultan: 'Since neither oaths, nor treaty, nor submission, can secure peace, pursue your impious warfare. My trust is in God alone: if it should please Him to mollify your heart, I shall rejoice in the happy change; if He deliver the city into your hands, I submit without a murmur to His holy will. But until the Judge of earth shall pronounce between us, it is my duty to live and die in the defence of my people.'

A brave statement, and a forlorn one.

All through the winter of 1452–1453 Mehmet II planned the overthrow of Constantinople; this foreign body lodged in the heart of his ever-expanding Empire. Where mines were to be placed, where scaling parties were to attack: everything was considered. For a thousand years the walls of Constantine, of Theodosius, and of Heraclius had kept out an enemy using conventional weapons; but now warfare had entered the gunpowder age. No longer were castles and whole cities impregnable behind their keeps and curtain walls, and the Sultan was one who had kept abreast the latest developments. At Edirne an enormous cannon was cast by Urban, a renegade Hungarian. At its first trial it fired a fifteen-pound cannon-ball more than a mile.

Next came the task of transporting it towards Constantinople. The journey of one hundred and fifty miles took two months, the cannon mounted on thirty linked waggons drawn by sixty oxen. Before the monster went an army of two hundred and fifty workmen, smoothing the way.

With the return of spring the Turks closed in about the city. On April 6, 1453, their army advanced towards the great walls on the land side, and before the gate of St Romanus (Top Kapisi) the Sultan set up his standard and his tent. The siege by the Ottoman Turks of what had once been the greatest and perhaps was still the most beautiful city in the world had begun.

Of the regular troops in the Turkish army their number may have been 80,000, reinforced with many semi-trained soldiers. Phranza, the Greek great chamberlain, estimated that in all they were surrounded by more than a quarter of a million men, all with a fanatical desire to see the banners of Islam floating over the city of Constantine.

Within the walls there were about 50,000 inhabitants, but when the call went out for defenders only 4,970 had the pride and the courage to call themselves Romaioi: inhabitants of the 'New Rome which is Constantinople'. It looked as though the backbone of the defence would lie with two thousand foreigners under the command of the Genoese soldier Giovanni Justinani. The prospect at sea was equally black: beyond the chain stretching across the Golden Horn floated eighteen galleys and two hundred ships of other descriptions.

Despairingly, and now too late, yet another union with Rome had been made in Santa Sophia on December 12, 1452. Its predecessor had been dissolved by John VIII Palaeologus. Like all the others, this latest one had been brought about by necessity, and not sincere desire for a union of the two churches. The real

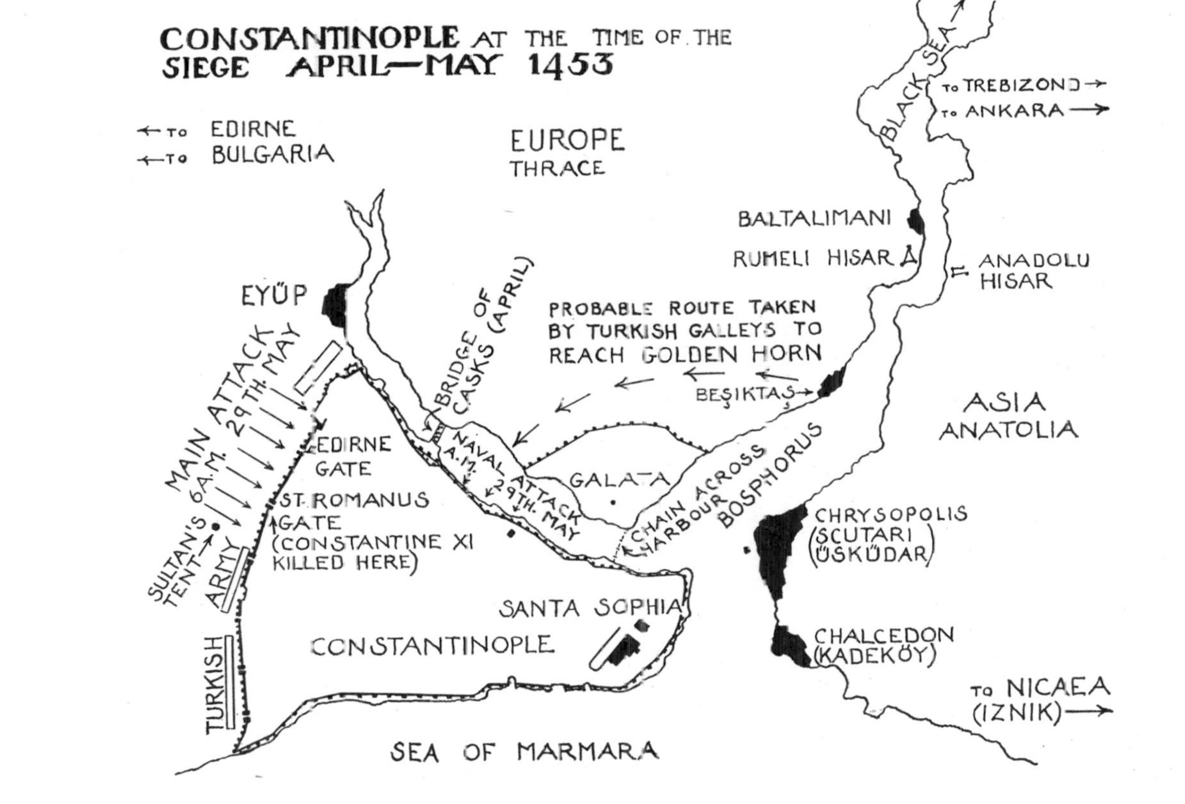
CONSTANTINOPLE AT THE TIME OF THE SIEGE APRIL—MAY 1453
← TO EDIRNE
← TO BULGARIA
EUROPE
THRACE
BLACK SEA
TO TREBIZOND →
TO ANKARA →
BALTALIMANI
RUMELI HISAR
ANADOLU HISAR
EYÜP
BRIDGE OF CASKS (APRIL)
PROBABLE ROUTE TAKEN BY TURKISH GALLEYS TO REACH GOLDEN HORN
BEŞIKTAŞ
ASIA
ANATOLIA
MAIN ATTACK 6 A.M. 29TH. MAY
EDIRNE GATE
NAVAL ATTACK A.M. 29TH. MAY
GALATA
CHAIN ACROSS HARBOUR
BOSPHORUS
ST. ROMANUS GATE (CONSTANTINE XI KILLED HERE)
SULTAN'S TENT
ARMY
TURKISH
CHRYSOPOLIS (SCUTARI) (ÜSKÜDAR)
SANTA SOPHIA
CONSTANTINOPLE
CHALCEDON (KADEKÖY)
TO NICAEA (IZNIK) →
SEA OF MARMARA

feelings of the Byzantines were summed up in the remark that they would rather see Constantinople wearing the turban of Mahomet than a cardinal's hat. Indeed, the general attitude was that extinction was better than union with the Latins, who to their disgust had used unleavened bread during the Consecration of the Elements in Santa Sophia.

The siege began in earnest on the 7th of April. Built—and strengthened—in the time of Theodosius II, when the fear of Attila had made men's blood run cold, the land walls had withstood the assaults of the Avars, the Arabs, the Bulgarians, and a host of other enemies. Now the whole strength of the Turkish was ranged against them: 70,000 foot soldiers, 20,000 cavalry, and 1,200 janissaries. For centuries to come the Turkish cannon were the finest in the world: now they were being set in position opposite a number of the gates. Three were trained on the Karsios Gate (Eğrikapi), in the middle of the walls of Manuel I, while the monster from Edirne had been mounted in front of the Gate of St Romanus (a fact that is still remembered in its Turkish name, Top Kapisi, which means Cannon Gate). Because of the risk of overheating, and consequent explosion, it could only be fired seven times in one day.

First of all attempts were made to fill in the great ditch in front of the outer wall with barrels, trees, and anything that came to hand. Such was the crush and turmoil that from time to time those on the edge were pushed over the brink by those bringing up more materials, and buried alive beneath the causeway the attackers were trying to build. In addition to the cannon, catapults were raining stones into the city, while now it was the Turks who were using Greek fire against the Byzantines.

With the help of an enormous siege tower, covered with three thicknesses of hides, a scaling ladder was fixed onto the Gate of St Romanus, over one hundred feet high, but as night was coming on the Turks could not push home the attack. When it was pitch dark a number of citizens, encouraged by the Emperor and the Genoese general Justianani, came out, burnt the siege tower and cleared the half-completed causeway out of the ditch.

Mehmet II was baffled. He had expected Constantinople to

fall at the first assault, but like the crusaders of two and a half centuries earlier he found there was unexpected life still in the city-Empire. It even reached the ears of the Greeks that he was planning to withdraw. Perhaps they would be saved yet. Had not five ships with provisions and reinforcements from Kos thrust through the Turkish fleet of 320 vessels and reached the city?

From the Galata shore Mehmet II watched the engagement, and almost unable to control himself with rage at the way it was going rode out into the sea, right alongside his admiral's ship. With his sceptre he rained blow after blow on the man, a turncoat Bulgarian, and ordered him to be impaled then and there. The janissaries would not allow it, and the Sultan had to give way, an indication of who one day would be the real rulers of Turkey.

The land walls remained unstormed, and now the Greeks were counter-attacking: catapulting stones into the Turkish army, while Johann Grant—a German engineer—scotched attempts to lay mines under the walls of Manuel I, where because of the steep slope of the hill down towards the Golden Horn there is no moat.

The great chain, supported on small pontoons, still kept the Turkish galleys out of the Golden Horn (until recently it formed part of the exhibits in the museum in St Irene, which has been undergoing extensive restoration). Then he, or one of his advisers, had a really bold idea. Transport a fleet of galleys behind the hill on which Galata stands, and launch them in the Golden Horn, behind the boom. Which was exactly what they did.

Over seventy light galleys were built on the orders of Mehmet's admiral, at Baltalimani, a hamlet adjoining Rumeli Hisar. When they were ready they were brought down to Beşiktaş, in Byzantine times called Diplokionion, now almost a suburb of Istanbul, separated from it, one might say, by the huge nineteenth century Dolmabahçe Palace. From there they took to the land: the actual route used is uncertain, but the roadway of greased sleepers up which the galleys were dragged on the night of the 22nd of April must have crossed the modern Cumhuriyet Caddesi somewhere near Taxim Square. From there it was down hill, towards the Golden Horn through the Kasimpaşa district, reaching the water upstream of the present-day graving docks and Atatürk Bridge. In Mehmet II's time a stream ran down the valley into the Golden Horn, called the Bülbül Dere —Nightingale Stream: though today as far as nightingales are concerned the area must have much in common with Berkeley Square. The upper end of the Golden Horn is shallow: now more than a mile shorter than five hundred years ago, and this meant that the Turkish galleys, being of shallow draught, could keep beyond the reach of the Italian and Byzantine boats.

When dawn revealed to the sentries on the city walls what had happened, they must have realized the utter helplessness of their situation. Only a miracle could save them now. Before long Mehmet II constructed a pontoon floating on empty oil and wine casks which projected across the Golden Horn at its narrowest point: opposite Balat. On it was mounted a cannon. Perhaps someone had told him this was the section where the crusaders had breached the walls during their attacks in 1203 and 1204. The inhabitants were not slow to react to this new threat. A small harbour existed inside the city at this point: its entrance onto the Golden Horn being through three arches in the wall which were closed with gates. Suddenly a fire-ship, manned by forty young commandos, shot out, bent on destroying the pontoon and if possible some of the galleys. The attempt failed, and in full view of those on the walls the forty were beheaded, on the Sultan's orders.

In savage but understandable retribution the defenders assembled two hundred and sixty Turkish prisoners on the walls, and beheaded them in sight of their compatriots.

For forty days the siege continued. Each day Constantine XI and his chamberlain Phrantzes used to go up onto the bastion on the walls of Manuel I (the third from the south end of this section) from which they had an extensive view along the walls of Theodosius nearly as far as the Edirne Gate. From this lookout they could watch the Serbian engineers used by the Turks attempting to undermine the defences. Apart from scotching their mines with counter-mines, there was nothing they could do, except watch, and wait.

The end was approaching. Mehmet sent the Emperor one last message, giving him the opportunity to leave the city and go to Mistra. He refused. If the city was going to die, he would die with it. Though the cannon had failed to break down the Karsios Gate, elsewhere the bombardment was having effect. Two towers near the Edirne Gate had been battered down. Justiniani was in charge of the area, defended by his Genoese mercenaries, and it was there that Mehmet II now concentrated his attack. The final assault was to come on the 29th of May, and two days before the religious and military preparations began. They were fighting in a holy cause, and should they be killed, it would be martyrdom. All were to wash seven times, to pray, and to fast until the following evening. 'The city and the buildings are mine,' said the Sultan, 'but I resign to your valour the captives and the spoil, the treasures of gold and beauty; be rich and be happy.'

The night before the attack the whole of the Turkish camp, and even the ships in the Golden Horn, was twinkling with pinpoints of light. Before every tent and from every mast hung a lantern, and there were even fireworks lighting up the sky. Tomorrow the Turkish crescent and not the Cross would be triumphant over the city.

A number of the defenders wanted to come out onto the terrace between the inner and outer walls near the Tekfursarayi, but could not do so because of the Turkish fire, so a small postern, walled up many years before, was reopened. The action achieved little or nothing, and when the defenders returned the doorway was left unblocked.

Within the city Constantine XI and his officers prepared for the great attack, while in the palace of Blachernae the halls and chambers echoed with cries of grief and of fear. In a matter of hours 1,123 years of imperial majesty would be swept away, and a line of emperors reaching back to the days of ancient Rome itself would be overthrown. Debased, pathetic and at times contemptible the Byzantine Empire had become, but as it receded into the shadows it knew a grandeur not seen in its history for centuries. Like the gods in Valhalla awaiting the ravens, the Emperor and the remnants of his court awaited the end. For the last time, at eleven p.m., he went to Santa Sophia, and where the great Justinian had exulted that he had surpassed Solomon's temple, in tears Constantine XI Palaeologus received the Sacrament. Looking down from the semi-dome of the apse was the great mosaic of the Virgin with the infant Jesus. Magnificent, but now in the ill-lit cathedral, remote and shadowy. In the royal porch the torches of his companions would hardly have been strong enough to reveal the mosaic of Justinian offering his church to the Virgin, or the first Constantine offering his city. Beside him the inscription: 'Constantine among the Saints, Great King.'

The last Constantine mounted his horse and rode off into the darkness, on his way to talk with and encourage the guards.

Beyond the walls the Turks brought up their siege engines to the edge of the moat, and the deep ditch near the walls of Manuel. In the harbour their galleys slipped over the water, right up to the wharves and the walls.

There was no sleep for anyone that night. The chamberlain described the scene. 'When, at the first cock-crow, we arrived at the Karsios Gate (Eğrikapi), we dismounted and climbed the tower [the bastion from which they had watched the progress of the siege]. Outside we could hear a great tumult. The sentinels told us it had been like that all night; the Ottomans were in fact bringing up and placing their siege-engines for the assault on the walls: they were already in the ditch.'

The attack began, on the area where the cannon had already breached the walls near the Gate of St Romanus (the gaps had been packed with brushwood by Justiniani's men) and in the harbour in the area between Ayvansaray and Aykapi. After two hours the walls still had not been scaled. Then Giovanni Justinani was shot through the hand, and he turned from the shattered wall. 'Your wound is slight,' implored Constantine XI, 'the danger is pressing; your presence is necessary; and whither will you retire?'

'I will retire by the same road which God has opened to the Turks.' He went, and with him his troops, the backbone of the defence. A few days later he died from the wound on board his ship.

The defence in the middle of the Theodosian wall was crumbling, and now about a mile to the north fifty janissaries had discovered the undefended Kirko Porta, the postern which had been unbricked two days before and not closed up again. Once inside the walls they were soon on the battlements, throwing down rope ladders to their companions. Almost in a matter of minutes the Tekfursarayi and the palace of Blachernae were overrun. Along the Golden Horn the Turks were on the walls, and engaged in bitter hand-to-hand fighting in the maze of narrow streets in the Fener district. To this day the Turks call the little church of St Mary of the Mongols the Kanli Kilise, the Church of Blood, in memory of that morning when the cobblestones were running red.

Nearby, up a few steps from the street along the inside of the walls, they reached the church of St Theodosia, and burst in. That day, the 29th of May, was her feast day, and they found the church full of Greeks, men, women, and children, desperately imploring her aid. In honour of the saint the church had been wreathed with roses, a fact the conquerors noticed, and remembered. St Theodosia became the Rose Mosque: Gül Camii.

Back at the Edirne Gate and the adjoining stretches of wall the fight was nearly over. One Hassan, a huge janissary, was the first to reach the top of the outer wall, together with twelve others. Almost at once he was killed. Had he lived he could have claimed the most beautiful and the richest woman in the city from his Sultan, together with a king's ransom in treasure. But ten, twenty, fifty, then a hundred appeared to take his place. The outer wall had been overrun, and there, before the inner one, Byzantium made its last stand: the Emperor fighting in the midst of his soldiers. No robe or special armour distinguished him from his subjects, and as just another soldier he was killed, and thrown from the battlements, to be lost to sight beneath the growing pile of dead.

At mid-day Mehmet II the Conqueror, mounted on a white horse, entered Constantinople through the Edirne Gate (page 164). He was twenty-three years old.

Some two thousand of the inhabitants were cut down by the blood-drunk victors. Then the city was quiet. In droves the terrified people—prompted by some mass urge—left their houses and made their way towards Santa Sophia. Crowded almost to suffocation they locked themselves in, and waited for the miracle to happen that had been foretold years earlier: that an angel with a sword would deliver them from the Turks. But it was Turkish soldiers who came with axes to break down the doors. Some of the terror and despair of that day still seems to linger in the massive, marble-lined aisles of the vast one-time cathedral.

The young and the old, senators and nuns, matrons and street-porters—all were made prisoner; to be sold as slaves or concubines. Like animals they were driven through the streets. Then, when the human loot had been secured, the Turks turned to the churches and palaces. As the conquerors spread out through the huge city, the Genoese and the Venetians embarked in their ships, taking as many of their countrymen with them as they could, and set sail across the Sea of Marmara, past the Princes' Islands, to tell the west what by its spiteful indifference it had helped to bring about.

From the Edirne Gate Mehmet the Conqueror rode across the whole length of Constantinople, towards Santa Sophia. As he passed the Hippodrome he stopped to look at the mutilated Serpentine Column, which the Turks believed to be the talisman of the city. As a trial of strength he hit what was left with his iron mace, breaking off the projecting fragment. Or so one version of the story runs. Then he rode on, across the Forum of Augustus, to Santa Sophia, now marked out to become the principal mosque of the Ottoman Empire.

Soon a muezzin was calling to the faithful that there was only one God, and his name was Allah. For Santa Sophia a long chapter had ended, and another was beginning.

From there Mehmet the Conqueror crossed to the old imperial palace, long neglected and now almost ruinous. As he passed through it the Sultan murmured: 'The spider has woven his web in the imperial palace; and the owl hath sung her watch-song on the towers of Afrasiab.'

A melancholy and ghastly trophy was brought to him, the head of Constantine XI, whose body had been identified by two janissaries who noticed the imperial eagles embroidered in gold on his slippers.

It was placed for all to see at the foot of the equestrian statue of Justinian the Great in the Forum of Augustus. Imperial Byzantium had been extinguished, but over conqueror and conquered alike there still brooded the massive outline of Santa Sophia.

Istanbul–Pevensey Bay

Principal Dates

B.C.

? Passage through the Bosphorus of Jason and the Argonauts on their way to find the Golden Fleece.

? Fishing village of Lygos (near Seraglio Point).

658 or 657 Byzantium founded by Byzas, leader of a group of Megarian (Greek) colonists.
Occupied by the Persians during fifth century invasions of Europe.

340 City saved from a night attack by Philip of Macedon by the moon. It adopts the crescent as its emblem.

A.D.

193–196 City besieged by Septimus Severus. Fortifications destroyed after its capture. Hippodrome built (203).

324 Constantine the Great decides to transfer his capital from Rome to Byzantium. The city hastily enlarged, and new buildings erected.

330 Now called Constantinople, the city inaugurated as the New Rome on May 11th.

337 Much of the city has to be rebuilt in the reign of Constantius.

361 Julian the Apostate reverts to paganism. Harbour of Julian built.

378 Aqueduct of Valens completed. Emperor killed in battle by the Goths, who threaten the city.

379 Theodosius I, Emperor.

380 Golden Gate built.

390 Obelisk of Theodosius set up in the Hippodrome. Four bronze horses brought to Constantinople from Greece (now in Venice).

404 Riots follow the exile of St John Chrysostom. Santa Sophia burnt.

413 The walls of Theodosius II built.

A.D.	
447	Walls damaged by earthquake. Threat to the city by Attila. Walls repaired in two months.
463	Monastery of St John of Studion founded.
512	Justin I, a Macedonian peasant, becomes Emperor.
527–565	Justinian and Theodora. Constantinople at its zenith. Church of SS. Sergius and Bacchus (527).
532	Much of the city, including Santa Sophia, burnt in the Nika Riots. The present Santa Sophia begun. Underground Cistern and St Saviour in Chora built.
602	Phocas, an illiterate centurion murders his way to the throne.
626	Constantinople besieged by the Avars and Persians.
668	Beginning of a six-year siege by the Arabs.
716	Siege by Arabs and Persians.
c. 725	Beginning of the Iconoclastic Controversy.
?	St Andrew in Crisi built.
797	Constantine VII blinded by his ambitious mother.
820	Leo V murdered in the Imperial Chapel.
?	St Theodore (Kilise-Camii) built.
842	End of the Iconoclastic Controversy. Renaissance of the arts in Constantinople.
867	Basil I, founder of the Macedonian dynasty.
912	Constantine VII Porphyrogenitus, patron of the arts.
?	Church of St Mary of Constantine Lips.
?	Church of the Myrelaion.
976	Basil II, Emperor.
?	Church of St Theodosia. Church of St Mary Diaconissa.
1028	The Empress Zoë (mosaics in gallery of Santa Sophia after this date). St Saviour Pantepopte built.
1054	Final break with Rome.
1081	Alexios I, Emperor. Blachernae Palace enlarged.
1096	The first crusaders at Constantinople (First crusade).
c. 1120	Monastery of St Saviour Pantokrator founded.
?	Church of the Blessed Virgin (Theotokos Pammakaristos) built.

A.D.

c. 1150 Blachernae Palace rebuilt. Walls of Manuel I built to enclose it within the city. Palace of Constantine Porphyrogenitus (Tekfursarayi) built.

1185 Andronikos I lynched in the Hippodrome.

1195 Isaac II Angelus deposed. His son, Alexios III, seeks help from the west.

1203 Crusaders come to Constantinople (Fourth crusade) and demand Isaac's restoration. The city besieged.

1204 Isaac restored. Palace revolution. Isaac and his son murdered. City besieged again, and stormed. Looting and burning. Byzantine Empire divided among the crusaders. Latin Emperor in Constantinople, while the exiles make their capital at Nicaea.

1261 Michael VIII recaptures Constantinople from the Latins. City in a deplorable state. Genoese settle in Galata.

1275 Temporary reunion with Rome.

1281 St Mary of the Mongols founded as a convent.

c. 1290 St Saviour in Chora restored, mosaics added. Parecclesion Chapel added to the Church of the Blessed Virgin (Pammakaristos).

1300 Empire shrinking rapidly due to Ottoman Turkish conquests.

1341–1347 Civil War. Empire almost bankrupt.

1349 Galata Tower built.

1402 Timur defeats the Turks. Mongols reach the Bosphorus.

1448 Constantine XI, the last Emperor, crowned. The Empire reduced to Constantinople itself.

1452 The Turkish fortress of Rumeli Hisar built to close the Bosphorus to the Christians.

1453 April: siege by Mehmet II begins. May 29th. Constantinople captured by the Turks

Emperors of Byzantium

CONSTANTINE DYNASTY

	A.D.
CONSTANTINE I	324–337
CONSTANTIUS II	337–361
JULIAN	361–363

End of Constantine Dynasty

NON-DYNASTIC EMPERORS

JOVIAN	363–364
VALENS	364–378

THEODOSIAN DYNASTY

THEODOSIUS I	379–395
ARCADIUS	395–408
THEODOSIUS II	408–450
PULCHERIA	450–453
MARCIAN (Married Pulcheria)	450–457

End of Theodosian Dynasty

LEONINE DYNASTY

LEO I	457–474
ZENO (Son-in-law, married Empress Ariadne) ..	474–491
LEO II	474
ANASTASIUS I (Second husband of the Empress Ariadne)	491–518

End of Leonine Dynasty

JUSTINIAN DYNASTY

JUSTIN I	518–527
JUSTINIAN I	527–565
JUSTIN II	565–578

TIBERIUS II (adopted son) 578–582
MAURICE (married Tiberius' daughter) 582–602

End of Justinian Dynasty

NON-DYNASTIC EMPEROR

PHOCAS 602–610

HERACLIAN DYNASTY

HERACLIUS.. 610–641
CONSTANTINE II 641
CONSTANTINE III (Constans II) 641–668
CONSTANTINE IV 668–685
JUSTINIAN II .. .. 685–695 and again 705–711

End of Heraclian Dynasty

USURPERS DURING REIGN OF JUSTINIAN II

LEONTIUS 695–698
TIBERIUS 698–705

NON-DYNASTIC EMPERORS

PHILIPPICUS BARDANES 711–713
ANASTASIUS II 713–716
THEODOSIUS III 716–717

SYRIAN DYNASTY

LEO III 717–741
CONSTANTINE V 741–775
LEO IV 775–780
CONSTANTINE VI 780–797
IRENE (As Regent and then as sole ruler) 780–802

NON-DYNASTIC EMPERORS

NICEPHORUS I 802–811
STAURACIUS (Son) 811
MICHAEL I (Son-in-law of Nicephorus) 811–813
LEO V (The Armenian) 813–820

Phrygian Dynasty

MICHAEL II (The Stammerer)	820–829
THEOPHILUS (The Unfortunate)	829–842
MICHAEL III (The Drunkard)	842–867

End of Phrygian Dynasty

Macedonian Dynasty

BASIL I	867–886
LEO VI (The Wise)	886–912
ALEXANDER	886–913
CONSTANTINE VII (Porphyrogenitus)	913–959

Usurpers during and after the reign of Constantine VII

ROMANUS I..	919–944
ROMANUS II	959–963
NICEPHORUS II	963–969
JOHN I ZIMISCES	969–976

Continuation of Macedonian Dynasty

BASIL II (The Bulgar-slayer)	976–1025
CONSTANTINE VIII	976–1028
ZOË (Daughter of Constantine VIII)	1028–1050
ROMANUS III (Zoë's first husband)	1028–1034
MICHAEL IV (Zoë's second husband)	1034–1041
MICHAEL V (Nephew of Michael IV, adopted by Zoë as her heir)	1041–1042
ZOË AND THEODORA (sisters, joint empresses)	1042
CONSTANTINE IX MONOMACHOS (Zoë's third husband) ..	1042–1055
THEODORA (As sole Empress)	1055–1056

End of Macedonian Dynasty

Non-dynastic emperors

MICHAEL VI STRATIOTICUS	1056–1057
ISAAC I KOMNENOS	1057–1059
CONSTANTINE X DUKAS	1059–1067
ROMANUS IV DIOGENES	1067–1071
MICHAEL VII PARAPINAKES	1071–1078
NICEPHORUS III BOTANIATES	1078–1081

Komnenos Dynasty

ALEXIOS I	1081–1118
JOHN II	1118–1143
MANUEL I	1143–1180
ALEXIOS II	1180–1183
ANDRONIKOS I	1182–1185

End of Komnenos Dynasty

Angeli Dynasty

ISAAC II ANGELUS	1185–1195 and 1203–1204
ALEXIOS III (Brother)	1195–1203
ALEXIOS IV (Son of Isaac II)	1203–1204

Usurping Emperor

ALEXIOS V DUKAS (Son-in-law of Alexios III)	1204

Latin emperors installed by the crusaders

BALDWIN OF FLANDERS	1204–1205
HENRY OF FLANDERS	1206–1216
PETER DE COURTNAY (never ruled)	1217
YOLANDE	1217–1219
ROBERT II OF COURTNAY	1221–1228
BALDWIN II	1228–1261
JOHN DE BRIENNE (Regent)	1229–1237

End of Latin Emperors

Byzantine emperors in exile at Nicaea during the Latin occupation of Constantinople

THEODORE I LASCARIS (Son-in-law of Alexios III Angelus)	1204–1222
JOHN III DUKAS VATATZES (Son-in-law of Theodore I)	1222–1254
THEODORE II	1254–1258
JOHN IV	1258–1261

Byzantine emperors restored at Constantinople
Palaeologius Dynasty

MICHAEL VIII	1261–1282
ANDRONIKOS II	1282–1328

MICHAEL IX (Son; co-ruler)	1295–1320
ANDRONIKOS III	1328–1341
JOHN V	1341–1391

Usurping Emperor

JOHN VI CANTACUZENOS	1341–1354

Continuation of Palaeologius Dynasty

ANDRONIKOS IV	1376–1379
JOHN VII	1390
MANUEL II	1391–1425
JOHN VIII	1425–1448
CONSTANTINE XI DRAGASES	1449–1453

Survivals of Christian Constantinople in Istanbul

Santa Sophia. A.D. 532–537. (Aya Sophia Müze.) Intact, with Turkish additions. Since 1935 no longer a mosque, but a museum. Mosaics undergoing restoration.

St John of Studion. A.D. 463. (Imrahor Camii.) Very ruined, remains of atrium, west front, outer walls, apse and north arcade of the nave. In the care of the Aya Sophia Museum.

SS. Sergius and Bacchus. A.D. 527. (Küçük Aya Sophia Camii.) Intact, with Turkish additions. Still in use as a mosque.

St Irene. 6th, 7th, and 8th centuries. Never a mosque. Intact. Until recently an Artillery Museum, now completely restored and empty (1962). In the care of the Aya Sophia Museum.

St Andrew in Crisi. 9th century. (Koca Mustafa Paşa Camii.) Intact, though much altered by the Turks. Still in use as a mosque.

St Theodore the Tyro. (Dedication uncertain.) 9th century? (Kilise-Camii.) Intact, with minor Turkish additions. Still in use as a mosque.

Monastery of Manuel St Nicholas. 10th century? (Kefeli Mesçiti.) Only the refectory remains, now a mosque.

St John in Trullo. Date? Very ruined.

Church of the Myrelaion. 10th century? (Bodrum Camii.) Still standing, though badly damaged in the fire of 1911.

St Mary Diaconissa. (Dedication uncertain.) 10th century? (Kalendar Camii.) Reasonably intact, though apse destroyed. No longer a mosque and closed.

St Theodosia. 9th century. (Gül Camii.) Intact, with Turkish additions. Still in use as a mosque.

SS. Peter and Mark. Date? (Koca Mustafa Camii.) Still in use as a mosque.

St Thekla. Date? Still standing?

St Saviour in Chora. 6th, 11th, and 14th centuries. (Kahriye Camii.) Intact, with Turkish additions. Superbly restored. No longer a mosque. In the care of the Aya Sophia Museum.

St Mary of the Mongols. 1261–1281. Intact, though much altered. Still in use as a church.

St Saviour Pantepopte. 11th century? (Eskiimaret Camii.) Still standing, used as a mosque.

Church of the Monastery of Constantine Lips, together with the church of St John. 10th century. (Feneriisa Camii.) Altered in Turkish times, damaged by fire, particularly in 1917, though still standing. In the care of the Aya Sophia Museum.

St Saviour Pantokrator. 10th–12th centuries. (Mollazeyrek Camii.) Intact, with Turkish additions. In part rather dilapidated, but now the South Church is undergoing restoration. In the care of the Aya Sophia Museum.

Theotokos Pammakaristos (Blessed Virgin). 11th–14th centuries. (Fetihye Camii.) Intact, with Turkish additions. Parecclesion and its mosaics undergoing restoration. No longer a mosque. In the care of the Aya Sophia Museum.

Gastria Convent. Date? (Sancaktar Mesciti.) Very ruined.

Bogdan Sarayi. Date? A ruined chapel over a crypt. Now only the crypt remains.

Underground Cistern. A.D. 532. (Yerebatan Sarayi.) Intact and unaltered. Still with water in it.

Cistern of One-Thousand-and-One Columns. 4th or 6th century. (Binbirdrek.) Intact.

Cisterns of Aspar, Mocius, and Aetius. Open air water tanks. Now used as gardens or playing fields.

Blachernae Palace. Hardly a vestige remains, except the so-called basement of Alexios I. (Difficult to get into.) The site now covered with gardens and dilapidated wooden houses.

Imperial palaces. Vanished with the exception of a staircase and some foundations, and also the fine mosaic floors now preserved in the Mosaics Museum.

Sea palaces. 6th–7th centuries. Completely ruined with the exception of a fine façade overlooking the Sea of Marmara.

Manganae Palace. 9th century. Foundations discovered during the laying of the railway in the 1870s.

Palace of Constantine VII Porphyrogenitus. c. 1150. (Tekfursarayi.) The walls intact to the roof level. Floors vanished, interior very ruined, though minor restorations recently carried out.

Towers of Anemas (11th century?) *and Isaac Angelus* (1188.) Ruined, in particular the Anemas.

Golden Gate. A.D. 380. (Part of the Yedikule.) Intact, with Turkish alterations. Undergoing restoration.

Walls of Constantine. A.D. 330, with later restorations. Much ruined, but stretches still standing along the Sea of Marmara. Along the Golden Horn only a few stretches remain, the towers surrounded by houses.

Walls of Theodosius II. A.D. 413 and 447. In places much ruined by war and earthquake, but magnificent.

Walls of Heraclius and Leo V. 7th and 9th centuries. Still largely intact.

Hippodrome. 2nd century B.C. and 4th century A.D. All but vanished, with the exception of the Obelisks of Constantine Porphyrogenitus and Theodosius, and the remains of the Serpentine Column. A number of columns from the Hippodrome re-used in the türbe of Süleyman the Magnificent.

Column of Constantine. A.D. 330. The Burnt Column. Very calcined by the numerous fires in the city. No statue.

Column of Marcian. 5th century. Intact, with capital.

Column of Arcadius. 5th century. Only the plinth remains.

Forum of Theodosius. A few vestiges on the south side of Ordu Street.

Rumeli Hisar. A.D. 1452. Turkish fortress. Recently very well restored.

Galata Tower. A.D. 1349. Intact, though twice burnt in the 18th and 19th centuries.

Aqueduct of Valens. A.D. 378. Part still standing between Third and Fourth Hills.

(This list is not exhaustive, but gives the principal survivals.)

Note on Place-names and names of Buildings

As the civilizations passed, so the place-names have changed, which can be confusing in the extreme. Greek, Byzantine, Ottoman-Turkish, and Republican-Turkish; and in many cases, English. For the purposes of this book I have tried to keep to the Byzantine or English names, with their modern equivalents in brackets afterwards. There are a few exceptions: to refer to the Black Sea as the Euxine, or the Sea of Marmara as the Propontis would be confusing, not to say pedantic, in an area where the geography may not be over-familiar. For the same reason I have referred throughout to the Hellespont as the Dardanelles. For Turkish place-names I have used the spelling current in Istanbul today: which differs considerably from that in use only thirty-five years ago. In 1928 Kemal Atatürk abandoned Arabic for the Latin alphabet, with the result the old phonetic spelling of some Turkish words is quite different to that now in use. The more so as the Turkish alphabet consists of twenty-nine letters, some of which bear no resemblance to their English equivalents: C being pronounced as J, while Ç becomes tchay, and so on. For example: phonetically, the word for Mosque used to be spelt Djami, now it is Camii.

GREEK (*Byzantine*)	OTTOMAN TURKISH	REPUBLICAN TURKISH
Adrianople	Adrianople	Edirne
Ankyra	Angora	Ankara
Constantinople	Constantinople	Istanbul
Chalcedon	Kadiköy	Kadiköy
Chrysopolis	Scutari	Üsküdar
Cyzacus	Erdek	Erdek
Hebdomon	Bakirköy	Bakirköy
Nicaea	Iznik	Iznik
Papadanisia	Kizil Adalar	Kizil Adalar (Princes' Islands)
Sycae	Galata	Galata (Now almost merged with Beyoğlu)
Thessalonika	Salonika	Thessalonika
Trebizond	Trebizond	Trabzon

Bibliography

The number of books available about Christian Constantinople and Byzantium is considerable, and yet at the same time limited, at least as far as the general reader is concerned. To all who wish to write about Byzantium or some particular aspect of it, Edward Gibbon must surely remain the father-figure *par excellence*. There may be a tendency to laugh at his white marble prose and prolixity: yet he is the foundation on which nearly all modern scholarship about the East Roman Empire rests. And it is only in the last two hundred years that serious research has been done on the subject. After the mid-1460s the Byzantine Empire had quite vanished behind that earlier Iron Curtain, the Ottoman Empire: penetrated only by merchants and ambassadors who had little freedom of movement. In Constantinople itself the whole population of about 50,000 people was deported to such cities as Edirne, Philippolis, or Gelibolu after the conquest of 1453. As a result the living tradition of a great and ancient city died almost overnight, including the knowledge about buildings which had been handed down from one generation to the next.

Today few people have the time or the inclination to work their way right through Gibbon, following the involved religious controversies which make up so much of the story, or for that matter unravel the various campaigns and the rise and fall of neighbouring states. It must be admitted there is something very daunting about a history which includes well over ninety emperors and ruling empresses, but they form an integral part of the history not only of Byzantium but of the city of Constantinople itself. In a very real sense the history of Constantinople is the history of the Empire. The Imperial family seldom moved far from the palaces in or around the city, while the whole bureaucratic organization of the Empire was centred there. The provinces, though after the seventh century divided into military Themes, were not encouraged to think too much for themselves.

It is perhaps in the anecdotes with which the historians liked to enliven their histories that we can learn most about the details—possibly trivial—of every-day life in the capital. History is not all battles, coronations, assassinations, and earthquakes. To find much that may give flesh to very dry bones means a great deal of research in books long out of print and difficult to obtain. Possibly the most monumental piece of research in recent years on the subject is G. Ostrogorsky's *History of the Byzantine State*. It covers every aspect of the Empire, but is frankly specialist. A small but most excellent introduction to the subject is J. M. Hussey's *The Byzantine World*. Another similar book is *The Byzantine World* by N. Baines, which however does not give any detailed history after the overthrow of the Latin Empire in 1261. A more detailed work is *Byzantium* by Baines and Moss. But one of the most readable and also authoritative is Sir Stephen Runciman's *Byzantine Civilization*, recently republished as a paper-back.

Turning to the city of Constantinople itself the list of books is not extensive by any means. In *Constantinople, des origines à nos jours*, Georges Young surveys the whole history of the city up to the present century, with the result there are some large gaps, and only a few of the buildings can be mentioned. Then there is Liddell's very good *Byzantium and Istanbul*; the city as it stands today. Most valuable for a fully documented account of the Christian buildings, are *Byzantine Churches in Constantinople* and *Byzantine Constantinople, the walls and adjoining historical sites*, both by Professor Arnold van Millingen. They must surely still be the standard works on the subjects (though Santa Sophia is not dealt with). *Byzantium* by Talbot-Rice, and a book which goes very fully into one particular period is *The Age of Justinian and Theodora* by Holmes: *Byzantine Legacy* by Cecil Stewart has a chapter on Constantinople and its principal churches. Much restoration of monuments has been done in the years since the Second World War, and also rehousing. For a detailed account of Byzantine architecture—from Greece to Armenia—there is Arnott Hamilton's *Byzantine Architecture and Decoration*. Bannister Fletcher has a section on Byzantine architecture in his *History of Architecture*, while Jackson's *Byzantine and Romanesque Architecture* goes into the subject fully.

By its very scarcity and inaccessibility Byzantine art must remain comparatively unfamiliar, except through the pages of art books, and today the quality of colour reproduction really is astonishing. A most comprehensive volume with beautiful coloured plates is *Byzantine Painting* by Andre Grabar. Then there is *Byzantine Mosaic Decoration* by Otto Demus, while Pelican have published their *Byzantine Art*. A recent publication which is a mine of information and beautifully illustrated is *The Art of Constantinople* by John Beckwith, and of especial interest is Dr Gervase Mathew's *Byzantine Aesthetics*.

Books by Byzantine authors are few and far between; not many have been translated. Three to which I referred are *Psellus's History of his own time*, in 'Selected Essays', translated by J. Bury, dealing with events in the eleventh century: *Alexiad*, by Anna Komnena, translated by E. A. S. Dawes, which is a biography of Alexios I

(1081–1118) by his daughter; and *De Ceremoniis* by Constantine VII Porphyrogenitus, in the Greek and French edition in two volumes (French translation by A. Vogt). The last, a manual of Byzantine Court Ritual, is fascinating, but admittedly of very limited general interest. For anyone actually visiting Istanbul, Hachette's *Turkey* is indispensable. Published in 1960 it is the most up-to-date and accurate guide there is. Lastly, one book which, whilst not directly concerned with Constantinople, deals with what might be called the last leaf on the branch that was Byzantium: Mount Athos, where in the twenty monasteries on the peninsular the religious life as it was in the days when Constantinople was a Christian city still lives on almost unaffected by the passing centuries. It is *Athos, the Mountain of Silence* by Philip Sherrard, beautifully produced with colour photographs of the highest quality.

Index